Better Homes and Gardens®

Scrapcrafts
from A *to* Z

BETTER HOMES AND GARDENS® BOOKS
Des Moines, Iowa

BETTER HOMES AND GARDENS® BOOKS
An Imprint of Meredith® Books

SCRAPCRAFTS FROM A TO Z
Editor-in-Chief: Carol Field Dahlstrom
Managing Editor: Susan Banker
Art Director: Gayle Schadendorf
Copy Chief: Eve Mahr
Senior Writer: Barbara Hickey
Assistant Art Director: Becky Lau
Technical Editor: Colleen Johnson
Administrative Assistant: Peggy Daugherty
Contributing Technical Illustrator: Chris Neubauer
Production Manager: Douglas Johnston

Vice President, Publishing Director: John Loughlin
Vice President, Retail Marketing: Jamie L. Martin
Vice President, Direct Marketing: Timothy Jarrell

Meredith Corporation
Chairman of the Executive Committee: E.T. Meredith III
Chairman of the Board and Chief Executive Officer: Jack D. Rehm
President and Chief Operating Officer: William T. Kerr

All of us at Better Homes and Gardens® Books are dedicated to providing you with the information and ideas you need to create beautiful and useful projects. We guarantee your satisfaction with this book for as long as you own it. We welcome your questions, comments, or suggestions. Please write to us at: Cross Stitch & Country Crafts®, Better Homes and Gardens® Books, RW 235, 1716 Locust Street, Des Moines, IA 50309-3023.

If you would like to order additional copies of any of our books, call 1-800-678-2803 or check with your local bookstore.

Cover: Photograph by Scott Little
Poem by Carol Dahlstrom

Our "Mark of Excellence" craft seal assures you that every project in this publication has been constructed and checked under the direction of the crafts experts at Better Homes and Gardens® Cross Stitch & Country Crafts® magazine.

Your cupboards are bulging
They are filled to the brim,
With fabrics and zippers and
Buttons and trims.

Your drawers are exploding
With ribbons and lace,
There is felt, beads, and sequins
All over the place!

But don't part with a piece
Of that valuable lot,
Every tiny bright scrap has
Its own special spot.

We've created a book with ideas galore,
Projects and patterns and oh, so much more!

From angels to zebras
From quilts to warm mittens,
There are tote bags and dresses,
Fun frames and sweet kittens.

Lampshades and gift wraps
Striped afghans and hats,
Rugs and initials
Dolls and place mats.

It's all here to please you
So hurry come see,
These wonderful Scrapcrafts
from A to Z.

Table of Contents

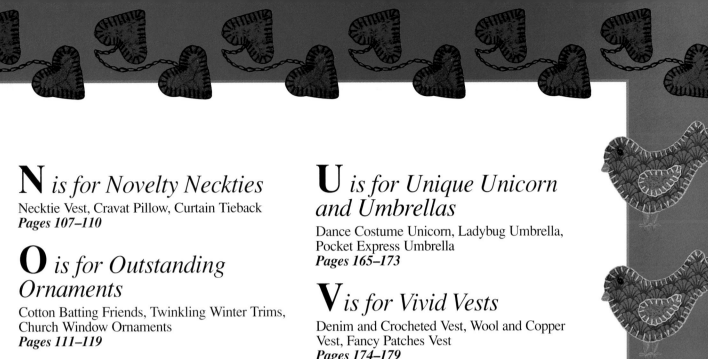

A is for *Adorable Angels and Afghans*

Clever Cookbook Angel

Everyone needs an angel in the kitchen and ours is sure to be your favorite! Whipped up from scraps of plaid, this angelic kitchen character has quilted wings, an adorable painted apron, and is topped with a shiny wire halo. Instructions and patterns begin on page 11.

DESIGNER: SUSAN CAGE-KNOCH ● PHOTOGRAPHER: SCOTT LITTLE

Tea Towel Cherub

With a halo of stars and a sweet smile, our golden-haired angel is as old-fashioned looking as the tea-towel gown she wears. Choose an embroidered tea towel or dresser scarf from a flea market (or your own kitchen drawer) to make a gown that's simply heavenly. Add chintz wings and rosy cheeks, and this personable angel will be ready to fly. Complete instructions and patterns begin on page 13.

DESIGNERS: JIM WILLIAMS AND BARB HICKEY ● PHOTOGRAPHER: SCOTT LITTLE

Whimsical Pipe Angel

As a Christmas tree-topper or year-round friend, this angel simply shines. Fashioned from a wooden tavern pipe, she features movable arms, a flowing gown, and gold ribbon wings that give her an extra glow. With her sweet painted face and a carrot-top mane of crepe wool, she makes an angelic gift for family or friends. Instructions and patterns begin on page 15.

DESIGNER: PHYLLIS DUNSTAN ● PHOTOGRAPHER: SCOTT LITTLE

Granny Square Doll Afghan

Doll lovers of all ages will adore this colorful afghan that brings cozy comfort to any miniature doll bed. Simply gather bits and pieces of bright sport yarn to crochet this afghan that is just 22½x29½ inches in size. These easy-to-make granny squares are worked in the traditional fashion from rounds of double crochet stitches. Complete instructions for this delightful project are on page 17.

DESIGNER: GARY BOLING ● PHOTOGRAPHER: HOPKINS ASSOCIATES

Sporty Plaid Afghan

With soft gray yarn as the background, this afghan, knitted in stockinette stitch, comes to life with bold horizontal bands of color. The vivid vertical stripes are woven in after knitting and a lovely crocheted border of scallops adds the perfect finishing touch. Complete instructions begin on page 17.

DESIGNER: MARGARET SINDELAR ● PHOTOGRAPHER: SCOTT LITTLE

CLEVER COOKBOOK ANGEL

As shown on page 6, angel measures 8 inches tall.

MATERIALS
6 tea bags
Tracing paper
6x12-inch piece of white cotton fabric
6x6-inch piece of white felt
10x6-inch piece of red and white checked cotton fabric
4x6½-inch rectangle of red and black plaid fabric
3x4-inch rectangle of muslin
Transfer paper
Sewing thread to match fabrics
Burnt sienna, mocha, cardinal red, black, and white acrylic paints
Small stencil brush
Artist's brushes
Fine-line permanent black marker
Medium-grit sandpaper
Polyester fiberfill
4x8-inch piece of interfacing
17-inch piece of gardener's twine
8-inch piece of copper wire

INSTRUCTIONS

To tea-dye fabrics, prepare a strong tea solution by steeping tea bags in 4 cups of *hot water.* Soak white cotton fabric and felt in tea until they are slightly darker than desired color. Squeeze out excess liquid and place on a flat surface to dry. Fleck remaining tea over red and white checked, red and black plaid, and muslin fabrics. Let pieces dry completely, then press on medium heat.

Trace pattern pieces, *page 12,* including the hair, facial features, and shoes; cut out. All pattern pieces and measurements include a ⅛-inch seam allowance. Stitch all seams with *wrong* sides together unless noted otherwise.

Cut body, leg/foot, and arms from white cotton fabric, bodice from red and white-checked fabric, and wings from felt.

Using a sharp pencil, trace hair, facial features, and shoes onto appropriate body pieces.

Sew arms together in pairs, *wrong* sides together, leaving end open for stuffing. Clip curves between thumb and hand.

For legs, sew pieces together in pairs, *wrong* sides together, leaving an opening at top for stuffing.

For body, sew body front to back, *wrong* sides together, along shoulders and around head. Clip seam at points where head and shoulders meet.

To paint head, first slip a small piece of paper into the head so paint won't bleed through. Paint hair with burnt sienna on both front and back. When dry, add swirls of mocha to hair, front and back. Apply rosy cheeks using a stencil brush and light dabs of cardinal red paint. Paint the mouth and a dot at the inside corners of the eyes with red paint. Paint the eyes and eyebrows with mocha. Dot the pupils black. When completely dry, sand painted areas lightly. Outline the eyebrows, edge of the hair, nose, eyes, and mouth with black permanent marker. Add highlights to eyes with dots of white paint.

Paint the shoes black, front and back. Let dry, then sand lightly.

Stuff the legs and arms firmly with polyester fiberfill, stopping ½ inch from tops. Pin arms to the wrong side of body back, with thumbs pointing down. Sew body front and back together at sides, wrong sides facing. Sew legs to bottom of body *front only,* with toes pointing outward. Stuff body and head firmly with fiberfill. Turn under raw edge along bottom of body; sew opening closed.

For apron, paint three red hearts along one long edge of the muslin rectangle, referring to the photograph for placement. Using a fine-tip permanent black marker, write "Love one another" between the hearts. Fringe the sides and bottom of apron.

For skirt, hem one long edge of the red and black plaid rectangle. Match the center of the top of the skirt rectangle to the center of the apron and pin raw edges together. Run a gathering thread together along the entire top edge of skirt.

Sew the bodice front and backs together at shoulders, right sides facing, then sew the underarm/side seams. Narrow-hem the neck and back opening. Pull up gathers on skirt and apron to fit the bottom of the bodice and stitch in place, right sides together. Press seams flat. Put dress on doll. Close dress at neck and waist with small stitches. Turn under the raw edges around the sleeves and gather to fit the doll's arms at wrists; secure thread.

Cut a piece of interfacing slightly smaller than the wings. Sandwich the interfacing between wings. Using a running stitch, sew around the outside of wings.

Cut length of twine in half; align the two pieces and tie them together with knot in center. Position felt wings on back of doll. Hold the knot of the twine to the center back of the wings, then bring two ends of the twine over the shoulders of the doll. Bring remaining two ends under arms of doll. Pull all ends firmly and tie in knots in center of doll's chest. Tie a double bow and cut off uneven ends of twine.

For halo, wrap the copper wire loosely around two fingers twice, then wrap remaining wire up and over the wire loop, securing it in place. Tuck in the ends. Secure the halo to the back of the doll's head using tiny stitches.

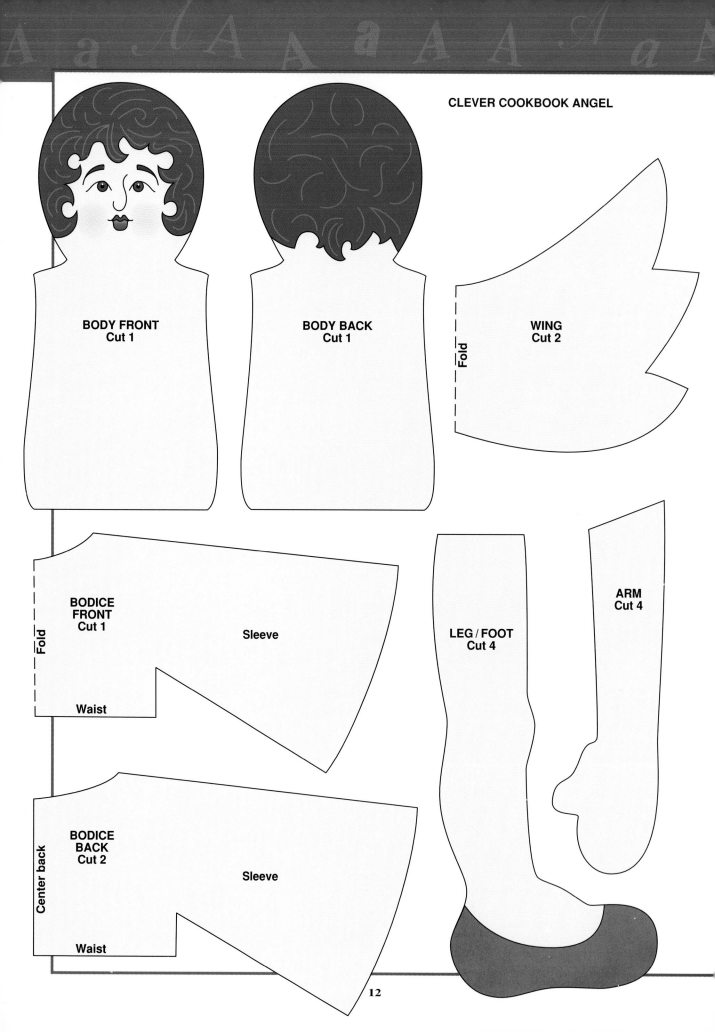

BODY FRONT
Cut 1

BODY BACK
Cut 1

CLEVER COOKBOOK ANGEL

WING
Cut 2

Fold

BODICE
FRONT
Cut 1

Fold

Sleeve

Waist

LEG / FOOT
Cut 4

ARM
Cut 4

BODICE
BACK
Cut 2

Center back

Sleeve

Waist

12

TEA TOWEL CHERUB

As shown on page 7, angel measures 16 inches tall.

MATERIALS
Tracing paper
9x28-inch of muslin
12x20-inch piece of blue and white chintz
Lace-edged and/or embroidered tea towel or dresser scarf measuring 10 to 12 inches wide and 38 to 40 inches long
Sewing thread to match fabrics
Erasable marker
Pink embroidery floss
Two blue or green beads for eyes
Powdered blush
One skein of yellow sport yarn
Polyester fiberfill
Two 12-inch-long pipe cleaners
12 to 14 inches of metallic gold star garland
Crafts glue

INSTRUCTIONS
Trace pattern pieces, *page 14.* Cut out. All pattern pieces and measurements include a ¼-inch seam allowance. Stitch all seams with right sides together unless noted otherwise.

Cut two 5x14-inch rectangles of muslin for body. Cut head, hands, and feet from muslin and transfer face and toe markings. Cut wings from chintz.

For dress, cut two rectangles from embroidered ends of tea towel or dresser scarf, each measuring width of towel and 14 inches long. From remaining scarf fabric, cut two 5¼x4-inch sleeves (arms), so one 4-inch end of each is trimmed with lace from edge of towel. If desired, remove 8 inches of lace from unused portion or sides of towel for neck trim.

Sew hands and feet together in pairs, leaving top open. Trim seam to ⅛ inch. Clip curves; turn

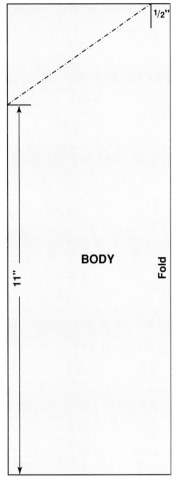

Diagram 1

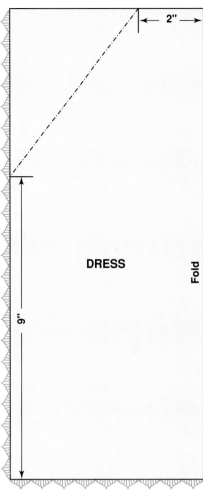

Diagram 2

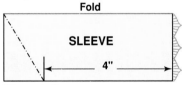

Diagram 3

and press. Stuff lightly with fiberfill. To define a toe in each foot, topstitch along the line indicated on pattern.

For shoulders, fold one body rectangle in half lengthwise, right sides together. Referring to diagram 1, *above,* measure 11 inches from one short end along cut edges and mark with erasable marker. Measure ½ inch from fold along adjacent short edge and mark. With a ruler, connect two marks. Turn folded rectangle over and repeat markings.

Pin feet to one short edge of remaining body rectangle, right sides together and raw edges even, positioning feet so they almost meet in center. Pin the two body rectangles together, right sides facing, with the feet

sandwiched between them. Stitch along short end first, catching raw ends of feet in stitching. Continue stitching around body rectangles, turning and stitching on shoulder marking lines and leaving an opening for turning. Trim shoulder seams to ¼ inch. Clip corners; turn and press. Stuff lightly with fiberfill and hand-stitch opening closed. Set aside.

For head, sew pieces together with right sides facing, leaving an opening for turning. Clip curves, turn, and press. Stuff with fiberfill and sew opening closed.

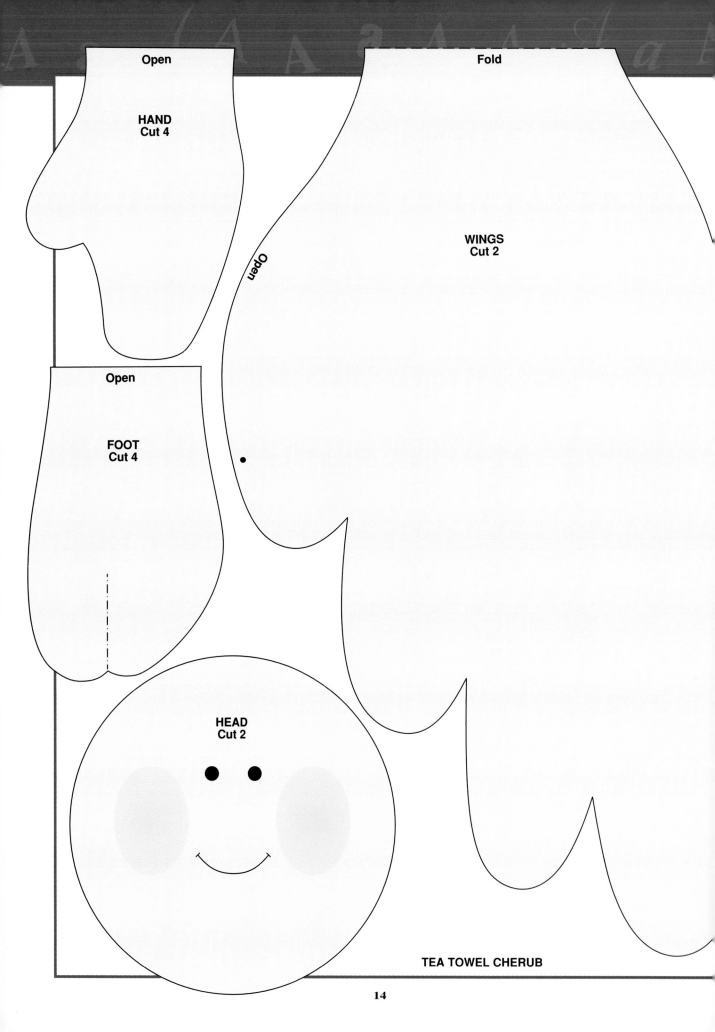

Open

HAND
Cut 4

Fold

Open

WINGS
Cut 2

Open

FOOT
Cut 4

HEAD
Cut 2

TEA TOWEL CHERUB

14

For features, embroider mouth with pink floss, using stem stitches. Sew beads for eyes, pulling stitches tightly through to back of head to create a slight indentation around each one. Brush powdered blush on cheeks.

For hair, cut skein of yarn in half to form 18-inch lengths. Arrange in a flat bundle about 4 inches wide. Machine-stitch through center three or four times to create a part and hold yarn together. Center part at top of head and glue or tack hair to back of head. Divide hair into sections of 10 to 12 strands. Twist each section until it begins to coil around itself. Tack each coil to head, tucking end under. Glue or hand-stitch head to top center of body. Set aside.

For dress, fold each rectangle in half lengthwise. Referring to diagram 2, *page 13,* measure and mark in same manner as for body. Trim ¼ inch beyond marker line.

Fold each sleeve in half lengthwise, right sides together, and stitch along long edge. Referring to diagram 3, *page 13,* measure along seam line and mark 4 inches from lace edge. Measure ¼ inch from cut edge on fold. With a ruler, connect marks. Trim ¼ inch beyond marker line. Turn and press. Insert stitched hands into lace ends of sleeves with thumbs pointing in same direction as fold. Topstitch sleeves closed, catching hands in stitching.

Pin each arm to one shoulder on right side of one dress rectangle, with raw edges even, so top edge of arm is about 2 inches from top edge of dress. Pin other dress rectangle to first, right sides together. Stitch along one side and shoulder edge of dress, catching arms in stitching. Sew remaining side and shoulder in same manner. Turn and press. Turn neck edge of

dress under ¼ inch and press. Sew reserved lace close to fold, if desired. Run a gathering thread around neck. Insert the doll's body into the dress, and adjust gathers around neck of angel; tack in place. Tack the front of dress to the body below neck with a length of embroidery floss; tie ends in a bow.

For wings, sew pieces together with right sides facing, leaving the entire bottom edge open. Clip curves, turn right side out, and press. To give wings support, twist pipe cleaners together to fit length of top edge of wings and insert into wings. Pin in place along top edge, then topstitch below pipe cleaners to hold them in place. Fold under raw edges of bottom opening; pin in place. Topstitch along bottom and sides of wings.

To finish, glue or hand-stitch wings in place at back of head and body. Coil star garland into a 3-inch-diameter halo and glue or stitch it in place.

WHIMSICAL PIPE ANGEL

As shown on page 8, angel measures 13 inches tall.

MATERIALS
13-inch-long tavern pipe (available at tobacco shops)
Sandpaper
Transfer paper
Brown, red, and white acrylic paints
Paintbrush
Fine-tip permanent black marker
Green eye shadow
Clear acrylic spray
Tracing paper
4x20-inch piece gold lamé fabric
11x16-inch piece of print fabric for skirt
5x5-inch piece of muslin
4½x5-inch piece of white knit fabric
Sewing thread to match fabrics
Polyester fiberfill
Crafts glue
¾ yard narrow lace trim
½-inch-diameter gold sequin
Gold seed bead
Two ¼-inch-diameter gold beads
8-inch piece of crepe wool yarn for hair
8-inch piece of gold baby rickrack
10-inch piece of 3-inch-wide wired gold foil ribbon
½ yard of ¾-inch-wide ribbon
Gold cord for hanging

INSTRUCTIONS
Lightly sand bowl of pipe until surface is smooth. Transfer facial features pattern, *page 16,* onto pipe bowl. Paint eyes brown and lips red. Outline features with black marker. Add a dot of white paint to each eye. Brush green eye shadow over eyes. Dilute red paint with water and paint cheeks. Allow all paint to dry, then spray pipe bowl with clear acrylic spray.

Trace arm and sleeve patterns, *page 16;* cut out. From one end of lamé, cut a 4x5-inch rectangle for bodice. Fold remaining fabric in half, right sides together, and draw around the sleeve pattern twice; set aside. From skirt fabric, cut a 10x16-inch rectangle for skirt and a 1x5-inch rectangle for waistband. Fold muslin in half and trace arm twice.

For body, sew short sides of knit rectangle together, right sides facing, using a ¼-inch seam. Turn right side out. Turn under raw edge at top and bottom and run a gathering thread along each. Slip body over doll's head. Pull gathering thread at top edge and gather body tightly around stem of pipe under head. Secure thread, then glue neckline to pipe stem. Stuff body firmly with fiberfill.

Pull the gathering thread at the bottom of the body and gather it tightly around the pipe stem. Secure thread. Run another gathering thread around middle of body; pull it tightly to create a waist, then secure thread.

For bodice, stitch the short sides of the lamé rectangle together, right sides facing, using a ¼-inch seam. Turn right side out. Turn under one raw edge and run a gathering thread along it. Slip the bodice over the body, with the gathering thread at the top. Gather tightly around the neck; secure thread. Tack the bottom edge of the bodice to the fabric body. Glue a strip of lace trim around the neck, securing neckline in place. Sew sequin and seed bead to center front of bodice.

For skirt, sew the short ends of the skirt rectangle together, right sides facing, using a ¼-inch seam.

Turn right side out. Narrow-hem the bottom of the skirt, sewing lace trim along the edge. Run a gathering thread around the remaining raw edge. Slip over the doll, pulling the gathering thread around doll's waist. Adjust the gathers, secure the thread, and tack to the body.

For waistband, press the raw edges of the long sides to the center of the waistband strip and press. Wrap the waistband around the waist of the skirt; overlap the ends in back and stitch in place.

For arms, pin the layers together to prevent shifting. Stitch along the marker line for each arm, leaving an opening at top of each. Trim the seam to ⅛ inch, clip the thumb, and turn right side out. Stuff with fiberfill and stitch the top closed.

For sleeves, pin the layers together to prevent shifting. Stitch

along the marker line for each sleeve, leaving an opening at bottom of each. Trim the seam to ⅛ inch, turn right side out, and insert an arm through the opening in each sleeve. On one side of each sleeve, tack the sleeve to the arm at the wrist. Glue lace trim around the wrist.

To attach arms to body, push a needle and thread through body from one side to other, through one arm and a bead. Push needle back through arm and body and through remaining arm and bead. Push needle back through second arm and body to first side. Pull thread tightly to secure arms snugly to body. Knot thread.

For hair, gently pull crepe wool yarn apart. Add glue to inside of pipe bowl; fold crepe wool in half and push it inside bowl, allowing 3 inches of crepe wool to extend over each side of pipe bowl. Tie

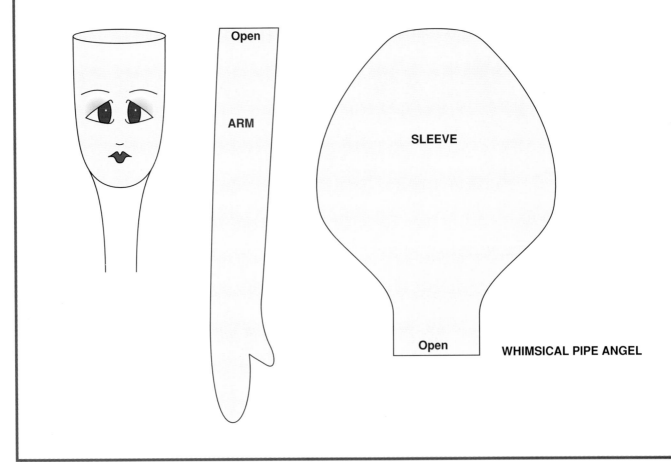

Open

ARM

SLEEVE

Open   **WHIMSICAL PIPE ANGEL**

baby rickrack along doll's fore-head and back of head.

For wings, cut ends of gold foil ribbon at an angle. Twist ribbon in center and fold it almost in half crosswise. Tack it to doll's center back at waist.

Tie ribbon in a bow around doll's waist. Stitch a loop of gold cord to back of angel for hanging.

GRANNY SQUARE DOLL AFGHAN

As shown on page 9, afghan measures 22½x29½ inches

MATERIALS
SUPPLIES
Three 1¾-ounce balls (125 yards each) black sport-weight yarn
Scraps of various colors of sport-weight yarn equal to about three balls (540 yards)
Size F aluminum crochet hook or size to obtain gauge
GAUGE
One square = 2½x2½ inches.

INSTRUCTIONS
For one granny square, with any color, ch 4, join with sl st to form a ring.

Rnd 1: Ch 3, 2 dc in ring, ch 1, (3 dc in ring, ch 1) 3 times; join to top of ch-3; fasten off.

Rnd 2: Join second color in any ch-1 sp; ch 3, 2 dc in same sp; ch 1, 3 dc—first corner made; (ch 1, 3 dc in next ch-1 sp, ch 1, 3 dc) 3 times; ch 1, join to top of ch-3; fasten off.

Rnd 3: Join black in any ch-1 corner sp and work first corner; (ch 1, 3 dc in next ch-1 sp; 3 dc, ch 1, 3 dc in next ch-1 corner sp) 3 times; ch 1, 3 dc in next ch-1 sp, ch 1, join to ch-3; fasten off.

Repeat to make a total of 63 granny squares.

Arrange squares in 7 rows of 9 squares each. Whipstitch squares together with black yarn.

For border, attach blue or desired yarn in any corner ch-1 sp, ch 3, in same sp work 2 dc, ch 1, 2 trc, ch 1, and 3 dc. *Ch 1, in next sp work 2 dc, ch 1, trc, ch 1, 2 dc. Rep from * to next corner sp; in corner sp work 3 dc, ch 1, 2 trc, ch 1, 3 dc. Work remaining 3 sides to correspond; end with ch 1, join to ch-3; fasten off.

SPORTY PLAID AFGHAN

As shown on page 10, afghan measures 68x56 inches.

MATERIALS
SUPPLIES
4-ounce skeins (125 yards each) of bulky-weight yarn: 13 skeins of main color (gray); one skein each of contrasting colors (violet, magenta, lavender, purple, turquoise, olive, hunter green, pink, and light blue); one additional skein each of two border colors (turquoise and hunter)
Size 10 knitting needles or size to knit gauge
Size K crochet hook
Yarn needle
GAUGE
4 stitches and 6 rows = 1 inch

INSTRUCTIONS
Work afghan in three separate panels, alternating bands of gray with bands of other colors chosen at random. For each panel, with gray, cast on 60 stitches.

Rows 1–12: Work in st st (k 1 row, p 1 row).

Rows 13–14: Change to any other color. Work in st st.

Rows 15–18: Change to gray. Work in st st.

Rows 19–22: Change to a third color. Work in st st.

Repeat these 22 rows 15 times, work rows 1–12. Bind off loosely.

Sew the panels together, matching stripes.

Thread yarn needle with three strands of any contrasting color. Beginning four st from one edge, weave through alternating stitches vertically from bottom to top. Rep with a different contrasting color every four st.

For border, Rnd 1: Beginning 1 inch from one corner, with crochet hook and gray, work shells of sc, hdc, dc, trc, dc, hdc, sc spacing stitches evenly across one side of afghan. For corner work a shell of sc, hdc, dc, 3 trc, dc, hdc, sc. Rep around.

Rnd 2: Join first border color. Sk first sc in prev rnd, (*2 sc, 3 sc in trc, 2 sc, sk sc in prev rd; rep from *across to corner shell. For corner, 3 sc, 3 sc in center trc, 3 sc, sk sc). Rep between ( ) three times.

Rnd 3: Join second border color. Sk first sc in prev rnd, (*2 sc, 3 sc next sc, 2 sc, sk 2 sc; repeat from * across to corner shell. For corner, 3 sc, 3 sc in next sc, 3 sc, sk 2 sc). Rep between ( ) three times. Weave in all ends.

Knit and Crochet Abbreviations

ch	chain
dc	double crochet
hdc	half double crochet
k	knit
prev	previous
p	purl
rep	repeat
rnd	round
sc	single crochet
sk	skip
sl st	slip stitch
sp	space
st	stitch
st st	stockinette stitch
trc	treble crochet

B is for *Beguiling Bears and Baby Things*

Lovable Snappy Bear

What could be sweeter than our tiny bear, Snappy? His name is fitting, because his head, arms, and legs all snap onto his chubby body, making it easy to pose him in clever ways. Fashion Snappy from pieces of a chenille robe, as we did, or from scraps of terry cloth. Soft, cuddly, and full of fun—you can create the perfect bear buddy for a child of any age. Instructions and full-size patterns begin on page 22.

DESIGNER: LINDA MEAD ● PHOTOGRAPHER: SCOTT LITTLE

Velveteen Twins

Tiny pieces of velveteen take on adorable personality when transformed into these sweet little bears. Our angel bear has cloth doily wings while her pastel-pink twin wears a miniature wreath of raspberries. Complete instructions and patterns begin on page 22.

DESIGNER: PAULA WALTON ● PHOTOGRAPHER: HOPKINS ASSOCIATES

Baby-Book Quilt and Album

Heart shapes, ruffles, and colorful embroidery stitches turn this personalized baby quilt and photo album into cherished keepsakes. The twelve blocks of the quilt chronicle the important "firsts" for Baby, while the embroidered album cover records a tiny handprint. Capturing memories to last a lifetime, they make unforgettable first birthday gifts. Instructions for both begin on page 24.

DESIGNER: MARGARET SINDELAR ● PHOTOGRAPHER: SCOTT LITTLE

Simple Funny Bunnies

These huggable bunnies will multiply quickly, because they're so simple to make! Crafted from scraps of terry cloth or floral fabrics to decorate Baby's room, they're soft to the touch, with funny wiggly ears and whiskers. These hoppy friends are perfect for shower gifts, so whip up a basketful, experimenting with fabrics and colors to make each one unique. Turn to page 27 for instructions.

DESIGNER: JIM WILLIAMS ● PHOTOGRAPHER: HOPKINS ASSOCIATES

LOVABLE SNAPPY BEAR

As shown on page 18, the bear measures 8 inches tall.

MATERIALS
Tracing paper
Lightweight cardboard
12x16-inch piece of chenille or terry cloth or three washcloths
Erasable fabric marker
Sewing and carpet thread to match fabric
Large-eye embroidery needle
Two 6-millimeter black animal safety eyes
Five ½-inch-diameter snaps
Polyester fiberfill
Dark brown #5 pearl cotton

INSTRUCTIONS

Trace pattern pieces, *opposite,* onto tracing paper. Trace head twice, once along head outline only and one with darts cut out and eye and ear placements marked. Cut out.

Draw around paper pieces on cardboard to create templates; cut out. Fold terry cloth in half, right sides facing. With marker, draw around templates on doubled fabric. Allow 1 inch or more between pieces. Trace one body, two arms, two legs, one head (using outline template), two ears, and one tail. Cut apart, leaving 1 inch between pieces, but *do not* cut out. Transfer dots and Xs onto pieces.

Baste fabric layers together at regular intervals to prevent shifting. Sew around tail pieces along outline, leaving straight edge open. Trim fabric close to stitching. Leave about ⅛ inch of fabric outside line along straight edge for seam allowance. Turn tail right side out; stuff lightly.

Sandwich tail between Xs on body pieces, matching tail and body outlines. Sew body along outline, leaving opening; set

aside. Stitch remaining pieces of each body part together along outlines, leaving openings. Trim seams as for tail, leaving ⅛-inch seam allowance along all openings *except* on ears. Cut straight edges of ears along outline.

Position second template on head and mark darts. Refold head, folding top dart in half lengthwise and matching marked edges of dart along center seam. Stitch dart. Repeat refolding and stitching in same manner for neck and nose darts; trim seams. Push large-eye needle through wrong side of head fabric at each eye mark to separate threads and create tiny holes. From inside, push stem of each eye through a hole; secure with lock washer following manufacturer's instructions.

Turn all pieces right side out. Determine a right arm, left arm, right leg, and left leg. Reposition templates atop parts and transfer markings. Mark *only* the inner side of limbs for snap placement.

Sew receiving halves of snaps (with hole in center) to body at marks. Sew remaining halves to marks on limbs and to head where neck dart and center seam meet.

Stuff all pieces except ears. Tuck in seam allowances; sew openings closed using carpet thread and ladder stitch (diagram, *opposite*). Whipstitch the straight edge of each ear closed; *do not* break thread. Use same thread to whipstitch the ear securely to head at markings.

Embroider paws, mouth, and nose, using one strand of dark brown pearl cotton. Work long stitches for paws and mouth.

Satin-stitch a triangle-shaped nose by inserting needle along the chin seam at the same place each time and exiting along nose dart seam. Snap head, arms, and legs in place.

VELVETEEN TWINS

As shown on page 19, each bear measures 5½ inches tall.

MATERIALS
For pink bear
9x18-inch piece of pale pink velveteen
Light brown embroidery floss
5-inch-long piece of artificial raspberry garland
Tiny white artificial flowers
For brown bear
9x18-inch piece of medium brown velveteen
Dark brown embroidery floss
6-inch-diameter Battenberg lace doily
9 inches of tiny gold star wire garland
¼ yard of ⅜-inch-wide aqua ribbon
For either bear
Tracing paper
Lightweight cardboard
Erasable fabric marker
Sewing thread to match fabric
Heavy-duty thread to match fabric
Polyester fiberfill
Tweezers; awl
Chopstick or other stuffing tool
Large-eye embroidery needle
Soft-sculpture needle
Two ¾-inch-diameter fiberboard joint discs with ⅛-inch-diameter center holes
⅛x1-inch bolt
⅛-inch nut
⅛-inch lock washer

INSTRUCTIONS

Trace the patterns, *page 24,* onto tracing paper and cut out. Draw around the paper pieces on lightweight cardboard to create templates; cut out.

Fold fabric in half, right sides facing, to make a 9x9-inch square. With the bottom edges of the ear pattern on the fold, trace the outline of the ear twice. Then trace body and head once and arm

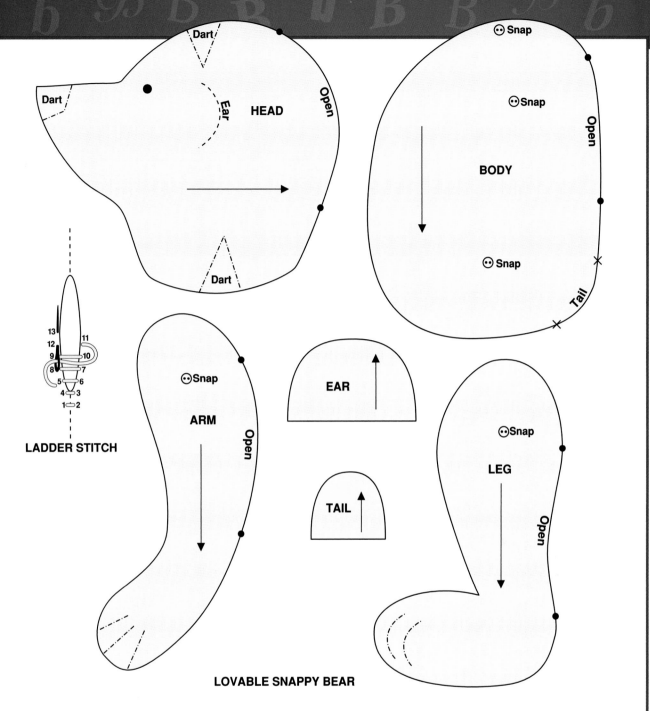

Dart

HEAD

Ear

Open

Dart

Dart

⊙⊙ **Snap**

⊙ **Snap**

BODY

Open

⊙ **Snap**

Tail

13 11
12
9 10
8 7
5 6
4 3
1 2

LADDER STITCH

⊙ **Snap**

ARM

Open

EAR

TAIL

⊙ **Snap**

LEG

Open

LOVABLE SNAPPY BEAR

and leg twice. Leave at least ½ inch of fabric between the pieces. Trace head gusset once on a single thickness of fabric.

Baste fabric layers together at regular intervals to prevent shifting. Sew around outlines of body, ears, arms, and legs, leaving marked openings unstitched. Sew chin seam from front bottom edge to nose. Cut out all pieces, including head gusset, a scant ¼ inch outside traced lines.

Baste the head gusset to the head, matching center mark on the gusset to the tip of the nose at the top of the chin seam; stitch. Turn head right side out. Stuff head firmly using chopstick to pack polyester fiberfill.

Work running stitches around the neck opening using a double strand of heavy-duty thread. Let the needle and thread hang from the last stitch while assembling the joint. Push one disc onto the

bolt. Press the head of the bolt and the disc into the neck opening. Tighten the thread to gather fabric firmly around the bolt, adding additional fiberfill as needed; knot thread.

Make a tiny slit in each ear along fold, taking care not to cut entire fold from seam to seam. Using tweezers, turn all pieces right side out through openings. Sew ears to head with upper edge of each ear on seam line.

Work French knot eyes using a six-ply strand of embroidery floss. Using a strand of heavy-duty thread, stitch back and forth several times between eyes, pulling the thread tight to shape the face. Then, stitch back and forth several times between the right eye and the back edge of the left ear. Repeat, stitching between the left eye and the right ear.

Work all remaining embroidery using two plies of floss and referring to nose/mouth diagram, *below right.* Satin-stitch nose.

For mouth, push the needle into the head from under the chin along the seam. Bring the needle out at A on the left side. Push the needle in at B, leaving thread slightly loose, and out at C. Slip the needle under the floss that runs from A to B and insert the needle at D. Bring the needle out at the top of nose and clip floss, hiding end under nose stitches.

Poke a hole in the top of the body at the dot using an awl. Push the bolt end that extends from head through the hole into the body. Entering the body from the back opening, push the second disc and then the lock washer onto the bolt. Push the nut onto bolt and tighten until the head will barely move. Stuff the body firmly; sew the opening closed.

Stuff arms and legs. Sew limb openings closed using ladder stitch (diagram, *page 23*) and heavy-duty thread. Use floss to embroider three straight stitch claws on each limb.

Thread soft-sculpture needle with four strands of heavy-duty thread; knot ends. Push needle through body from left to right, entering at one arm joint mark and exiting at other. Next, push needle all the way through right arm at mark and then back through arm and body, exiting at

starting point. Attach remaining arm. Continue stitching back and forth through arms and body several times. Knot thread under one arm. Attach legs as for arms.

For pink bear, twist flowers into berry garland. Wrap around neck, twisting wires together at back.

For brown bear, use running stitches to gather the doily along a vertical line through the center. Wrap thread around gathered area several times and knot. Tack doily wings to bear's back. Wrap the star garland into a small circle to resemble a halo and twist the ends together. Tack halo to head. Tie ribbon around neck and trim ends.

BABY-BOOK QUILT
As shown on page 20, quilt measures 32½x46½ inches, not including ruffle.

MATERIALS
3 yards of 45-inch-wide fabric for sashing and ruffle
1 yard of 45-inch-wide fabric for background
Twelve 7x10-inch pieces of assorted floral-print fabrics
Tracing paper
1¼ yards of 17-inch-wide paper-backed iron-on adhesive
1½ yards of 45-inch-wide fabric for back

VELVETEEN TWINS

Ear

HEAD

Open

Top

× Joint

Open

BODY

Front

× Joint

× Joint

NOSE/MOUTH DIAGRAM

A   B
C
D

EAR
Fold

Nose

HEAD GUSSET

Neck

× Joint

Open

ARM

× Joint

Open

LEG

Sewing thread to match fabrics
Polyester batting
Embroidery floss in assorted
 colors
10 yards of ¾-inch-wide flat lace

INSTRUCTIONS

From sashing fabric, cut fifteen 3x8-inch sashing strips, sixteen 3x9-inch sashing strips, and eight 7x45-inch ruffle strips. From background fabric, cut twelve 8x9-inch blocks. From floral-print fabrics, cut a total of twenty 3-inch squares, reserving a 6x7-inch piece of each fabric. Measurements include ¼-inch seam allowances.

Trace pattern, *below;* cut out. Draw around pattern on paper side of iron-on adhesive 12 times; cut out hearts. Fuse each to wrong side of a floral-print fabric piece, following manufacturer's directions. Trim fabric to match adhesive shapes. Remove paper backing from hearts; center each on a background block with 8-inch edge at top. Fuse as directed.

Machine-satin stitch around outside and inside edges of each heart using thread that matches floral fabric. By hand, print the following or other special events and dates in center of each heart: Name; First Little Smile; Slept All Night; First Rolled Over; Sat Up Alone; Began to Crawl; First Tooth; First Word Spoken; First Step; Wave Bye-Bye; Peek-a-Boo; and Pat-a-Cake.

Embroider the lettering in back-stitch or stem stitch. If desired,

BABY-BOOK QUILT

25

BABY ALBUM

embroider around the flowers of the floral print fabic using assorted stitches.

Arrange heart blocks in four rows of three blocks each. For each vertical row, sew a 3x9-inch sashing strip to each side of the left-hand block; sew left edge of center block to right edge of right-hand sashing. Sew a third sashing strip to remaining side of center block and right-hand block to third sashing. Complete row with a fourth sashing strip.

For horizontal sashing, sew a 3x3-inch floral block to each short end of an 8x3-inch strip, Sew another strip to the right of right-hand block. Continuing to work from left to right, sew on another block, another strip, and another block. Sew horizontal

sashing strips between rows of blocks and at top and bottom. Lay wrong side of quilt top on batting.

Sew short ends of ruffle strips together to form a continuous circle. Press in half lengthwise, wrong sides facing. Stitch lace to folded edge. Sew a gathering thread ¼ inch from raw edges. Pin ruffle to quilt top, raw edges even. Pull gathering thread to distribute gathers evenly. Sew around quilt top along gathering line.

Cut backing fabric same size as front. Stitch front to back, right sides together, with the ruffle tucked inside, leaving an opening for turning. Turn; slip-stitch the opening closed.

Machine-quilt around hearts. Tie corners of blocks with floss, stitching through all layers.

BABY ALBUM

Album shown on page 20 measures 7x6 inches. Additional fabric may be required for a larger album.

MATERIALS
Purchased 7x6-inch photo album

⅜ yard of 45-inch-wide background fabric

6x6-inch piece of calico fabric

6x6-inch piece of paper-backed iron-on adhesive

9x16-inch piece of polyester fleece

2 yards of ¾-inch-wide flat lace

2 yards of ½-inch-wide ribbon

Embroidery floss to match calico fabric

Assorted brass baby charms and glass or pearl beads (optional)

INSTRUCTIONS

For album pattern, open album flat on top of tracing paper. Draw around front, across top of spine, around back, and across bottom of spine. Mark points where front and back meet spine at top and bottom. Remove album and add ½ inch to all four outer edges. With a ruler, connect markings to indicate edges of the spine.

For flap pattern, measure half the distance from front edge seam allowance to front edge of spine; mark from top to bottom on album pattern.

From background fabric, cut album pattern twice (cover and lining) and two flaps. With erasable marker, mark front spine edge and seam allowances on cover piece. Trim 1½ inches from one end of lining.

Trace heart pattern, *opposite;* cut out. Trace around heart pattern on paper side of iron-on adhesive. Fuse to wrong side of calico, following manufacturer's directions. Cut out heart and remove paper. Center inside markings on front of cover.

Use a short machine zigzag stitch and thread to match the calico to satin stitch around the outside and inside edges of heart.

Trace around baby's hand; cut out tracing. Position tracing inside the calico heart and draw around it. By hand, write the baby's name and age inside the hand outline.

Embroider the hand outline and writing using two plies of floss and stem stitches. If desired, work assorted embroidery stitches on flowers of calico.

Pin the fleece to the wrong side of the background fabric. Machine-quilt through both layers, using matching thread, in diagonal rows spaced 1 inch apart, leaving the heart unquilted. Stitch charms and beads to the

heart, if desired, referring to photograph for placement.

Sew the straight edge of the lace on the seam line around the edge of the album cover, right sides together. On end flaps, narrow-hem one long edge, turning under ¼ inch. Stitch the end flaps to each end of the album cover, right sides together, using ¼-inch seams. Clip seam allowance.

Stitch the lining to the album along the top and bottom only. Trim the corners and turn right side out. Turn the end flaps right side out. Slip the cover over the album. Cut the ribbon into two 1-yard lengths. Tie the ribbons around the album spine.

SIMPLE FUNNY BUNNIES

As shown on page 21, bunnies are 6 inches long.

MATERIALS

For each bunny
Tracing paper
18x12-inch piece of terry cloth or floral print fabric
4x5-inch piece of coordinating print or solid fabric
Sewing thread to match fabrics
Polyester fiberfill
10 to 12 yards of yarn for tail
1 yard of pearl cotton or embroidery floss
1½-inch piece of cardboard
Tapestry needle

INSTRUCTIONS

Trace the patterns, *page 28,* and cut out. From the terry cloth, cut the body, bottom, and two (outer) ears. From the coordinating fabric, cut two more (inner) ears. Transfer markings.

Sew the body pieces together from the nose to the dot at the tail, right sides together. Starting at the tail, pin the bottom between

the body pieces. Sew, leaving an opening for turning along one edge. Clip the curves and turn. Stuff firmly with polyester fiberfill and sew the opening closed.

For ears, stitch the inner ears to the outer ears, right sides facing, leaving the straight edge open. Clip the curves, turn right side out, and press. Press the raw edges to the inside. Fold the ear in half, bringing the straight edges together and tack the corners together. Stitch the ears to the bunny's head at positions indicated by dotted line on pattern.

For the pom-pom tail, cut a 4-inch piece of yarn; set aside. Wrap the remaining yarn around the cardboard. Slip the 4-inch piece of yarn under the wrapped threads at one edge of the cardboard and tie securely. Clip the yarn at the opposite edge and remove the yarn from the cardboard. Trim the wrapped yarn into a round pom-pom. Thread the tie through a tapestry needle and tack in place on the bunny. Tie securely; trim ties.

For the eyes, thread pearl cotton or six plies of embroidery floss into the tapestry needle and knot one end. Thread it through the bunny at the point indicated on the pattern for the eyes, pulling firmly to create an indentation at knot. Work 4 to 6 satin stitches, then thread needle back to other side, pulling firmly. Work 4 to 6 more satin stitches; secure thread.

For the nose, with pearl cotton or floss, work 6 to 8 satin stitches in a triangle across the center seam just above the base.

For the whiskers, thread three strands of pearl cotton or floss through the bunny's face. Trim the threads, leaving 2-inch lengths on either side of the face. Knot the threads on each side of the face to secure in place.

SIMPLE FUNNY BUNNIES

BODY
Cut 2

EAR
Cut 4

BOTTOM
Cut 1

C is for *Clever* Curtains and Collars

Country Plaid Curtains

Strips of country plaid add color and warmth to any window of the house. The curtains are hung by tabs of fabric which are secured by a colorful assortment of buttons. This clever window treatment is so easy and versatile, you can personalize it to fit your own special tastes. Complete instructions are on page 32.

DESIGNER: KATHY MOENKHAUS ● PHOTOGRAPHER: HOPKINS ASSOCIATES

Pillowcase Curtains

Add a touch of romance with delicate curtains made from lace-trimmed
pillowcases. With minimal sewing, you can create this elegant designer look.
Whether your pillowcases are purchased or are handmade treasures from
Grandma, they will add loveliness to any room of your home.
Complete instructions are on page 32.

DESIGNER: MARGARET SINDELAR ● PHOTOGRAPHER: HOPKINS ASSOCIATES

Dresden Plate Collars

Pull out those favorite fabric scraps! Patterned after one of today's most widely recognized quilt patterns, this special occasion collar is eye-catching whether you choose elegant velvets and shimmering lamés as shown below, or quaint calicos as shown on page 33. Contrasting buttons and bits of lace add a festive finishing touch to the Dresden Plate design. Complete instructions and pattern begin on page 32.

DESIGNER: BARBARA BARTON SMITH ● PHOTOGRAPHER: HOPKINS ASSOCIATES

COUNTRY PLAID CURTAINS

As shown on page 29, a pair (two curtains) fits a window 60 to 75 inches wide. Each curtain measures 27¼x75 inches.

MATERIALS

FABRICS *for one curtain*
Fifteen 25½x6-inch rectangles of homespun or other cotton plaid fabrics
Sixteen 8½x4½-inch rectangles of homespun or other cotton plaid fabrics
32 assorted buttons
Sewing thread

INSTRUCTIONS

Join 25½-inch edges of larger rectangles to form a 75-inch strip using flat-fell seams. To make flat-fell seams, sew two rectangles together, wrong sides facing, using ½-inch seams. Press both seam allowances to one side of seam. Trim seam allowance on top to ¼ inch. Press raw edge of bottom seam allowance over cut edge of top, then press both seam allowances to opposite side of seam. Stitch through all layers, close to folded edge and seam.

For hems, turn raw edges under ¼ inch twice and stitch.

Sew long edges of each tab rectangle together, right sides facing, using ¼-inch seams. Turn right side out. Turn raw edges under ¼ inch. Stitch across each end ⅛ inch from edge.

Fold one tab in half. Position ends on each side (front and back) of far left top edge of curtain and pin tab so ends are 1¾ inches below top. Pin remaining tabs across curtain in same manner, placing one at each seam and one at far right side. To secure each tab to curtain, center a button on both sides, ¾ inch from bottom edge of tab. Hand-sew between the two buttons catching curtain fabric in stitches.

For wider windows, add one 25½x6-inch rectangle and one 8½x4½-inch rectangle to *each curtain* for every additional 6 inches of total window width.

For narrower windows, use one less of each size rectangle in each curtain for every 6 inches of total window width.

For longer curtains, increase 25½-inch length as needed.

PILLOWCASE CURTAINS

As shown on page 30, curtains fit a window 28 to 42 inches wide and up to 60 inches in length.

MATERIALS

Eight standard pillowcases with crocheted edging
Tension curtain rod
Double curtain rod
One 14x72-inch double bolster pillowcase or four additional standard pillowcases
2 yards of ribbon
1½ yards of coordinating crocheted edging
Thumbtacks or small nails

INSTRUCTIONS

For cafe curtains, create rod pockets in each of four pillowcases by stitching 1½ inches below seamed end. Stitch 1½ inches below first stitching. On each pillowcase, make a slit in each side fold between first and second rows of stitching. Gather pillowcases on tension rod; position in window, hiding seams in folds.

For top curtains, install double curtain rod at top of window. Create rod pockets by stitching 1½ inches below the seamed end of four pillowcases. On each pillowcase, make a slit at each side fold between between top of pillowcase and stitching. Gather pillowcases on inner rod of double curtain rod. Attach rod to window. Push two pillowcases to each end.

For valance, create a rod pocket in top of bolster pillowcase in same manner as cafe curtain. (If using standard size pillowcases, turn inside out. Sew straight seams 15 inches from open ends of pillowcases; turn right side out. Create rod pockets as for cafe curtain.) Gather pillowcase(s) onto outer rod of double curtain rod. Attach rod to window.

Cut ribbon and crocheted edging in half. Tie the ribbon into bows. Wrap one piece of edging around each upper curtain. Secure edging and bows to window with thumbtacks or small nails.

For wider or narrower windows, add or subtract one pair of pillowcases for every 20 inches of window width.

DRESDEN PLATE COLLARS

As shown on pages 31 and 33, collars fit children's sizes 5 to 10.

MATERIALS

Tracing paper
Pencil
Eight 5x9-inch pieces of desired plain or fancy fabrics
14x14-inch piece of fabric for lining
Sewing thread to blend with all fabrics
1¾ yards of 1¼-inch-wide pregathered lace
⅔ yard of ¼-inch-wide satin ribbon
25 assorted buttons, jingle bells, beads, charms, or ribbon roses

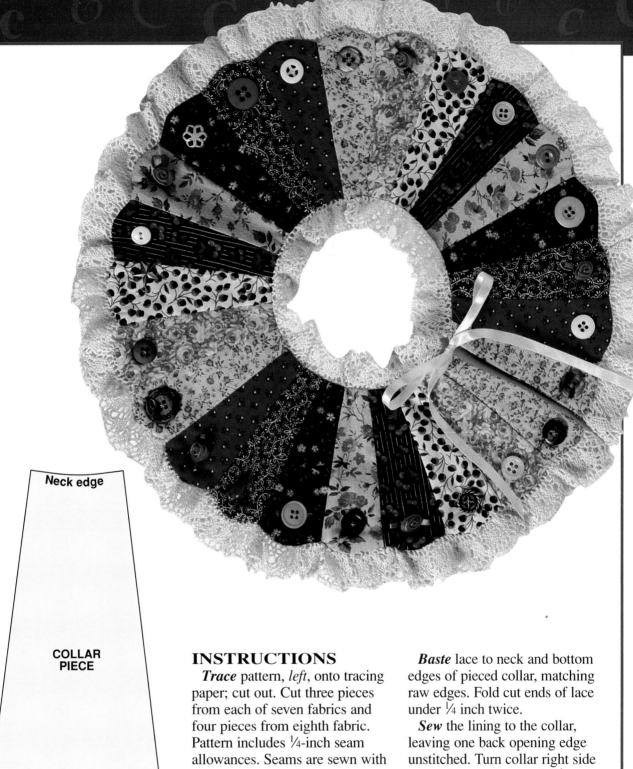

Neck edge

**COLLAR
PIECE**

DRESDEN PLATE COLLAR

INSTRUCTIONS

Trace pattern, *left*, onto tracing paper; cut out. Cut three pieces from each of seven fabrics and four pieces from eighth fabric. Pattern includes ¼-inch seam allowances. Seams are sewn with right sides of fabric facing.

Sew long edges of the twenty-five collar pieces together in desired order, making a scalloped circular collar with a back opening. Press collar, ironing all seams in same direction.

Trace around collar on tracing paper for lining pattern; cut out. Cut out lining and set aside.

Baste lace to neck and bottom edges of pieced collar, matching raw edges. Fold cut ends of lace under ¼ inch twice.

Sew the lining to the collar, leaving one back opening edge unstitched. Turn collar right side out and press. Turn under ¼ inch along opening edges and slip-stitch closed.

For ties, cut ribbon in half and tack each piece to one side of back opening near neck edge. Sew a button, bell, charm, bead, or ribbon rose to each scallop approximately ¾ inch from bottom edge.

D is for *Delightful Dolls and Dresses*

Happy Calico Dolls

Dolls can be just as individual as people—and this calico collection proves it. These five lassies are all made from the same basic pattern, but different hairstyles and clothing give them unique personalities. With their pleasant expressions and colorful finery, they'll be welcomed pals for friends and family. Instructions and patterns are on pages 38–39.

DESIGNER: PHYLLIS DUNSTAN ● PHOTOGRAPHER: HOPKINS ASSOCIATES

Tiny Friends

These little tag-alongs are only 5¼ inches tall, but they pack a lot of personality. Stitched to loops that fit over the ends of braids or on a favorite belt, they're constant companions. Made out of small bits of fabric and scraps, these pint-sized pals are ready to go anywhere. Instructions and patterns begin on page 38.

DESIGNER: SANDI HIXON ● PHOTOGRAPHER: SCOTT LITTLE

Lovely Pillowcase Dress

What young miss wouldn't love to wear our lovely-and-lacy dress adorned in fancywork? The handwork and fabric is really recycled pillowcases cleverly remade into a delightful dress. One pair of pretty pillowcases is all you need to create the graceful collar and gathered skirt. Instructions for making this adorable dress in any child's size begin on page 41.

DESIGNER: EVE MAHR ● PHOTOGRAPHER: SCOTT LITTLE

Cathedral Window Dress

Using calico scraps and lots of love, stitch this elegant party dress for a girl of any age.
The cathedral patchwork technique creates a stained-glass effect along the skirt hem
and sleeves, making this a special-occasion dress to be handed down for years to come.
To perfect the cathedral window technique, follow our step-by-step instructions
and photographs on pages 42–43.

DESIGNER: MARGARET SINDELAR ● PHOTOGRAPHER: HOPKINS ASSOCIATES

HAPPY CALICO DOLLS

As shown on page 34, doll measures 8¾ inches tall.

MATERIALS *for one doll*
Tracing paper
12x36-inch piece of calico
5x10-inch piece of off-white single-knit fabric
Sewing thread to match fabrics
Black #5 pearl cotton
Black and pink embroidery floss
Powdered blush
Polyester fiberfill
Two skeins #5 pearl cotton in desired hair color
Soft-sculpture needle
Carpet thread to match buttons
Two ¼- to ⅜-inch-wide buttons
Four ⅛-inch-diameter beads
Lace trims and accessories as desired
½ yard of ⅜-inch-wide ribbon
3¾x13- to 5¼x13-inch rectangle of fabric for apron (optional)

INSTRUCTIONS
Trace patterns, *opposite,* onto tracing paper; cut out. All patterns and measurements include ¼-inch seam allowances. Sew the seams with the right sides facing unless otherwise indicated.

From calico, cut bodies, base, one 10½x24-inch rectangle for skirt, and one 3½x10-inch rectangle for sleeves. From knit fabric, cut head and one 1½x10-inch rectangle for hands.

For arms, sew the 10-inch edges of the sleeve and hand rectangles together, right sides together. Press seam toward calico. Cut arms from pieced square, placing hand on knit fabric with seam at wrist.

For head, make black pearl cotton French-knot eyes on head front. Work straight stitches for eyelashes and to underline eyes with one ply of black floss.

Embroider mouth with two plies of pink floss using stem stitches. Work a French knot at each end of mouth. Brush cheeks with blush.

Sew head front to back, leaving marked opening unstitched. Turn right side out, stuff with fiberfill, and sew opening closed.

For hair, untwist two skeins of pearl cotton thread. Lay the skeins together lengthwise; spread them to a 2-inch width. Machine-sew through the center of skeins to form a stitched part. Center the part on doll's head; tack in place. Style hair as desired.

For body, sew body front to body back, leaving marked opening and bottom unstitched. Sew base to body bottom. Turn body right side out. Stuff with fiberfill, then slip-stitch opening closed. Hand-sew head to body.

Sew arms together in pairs, leaving marked openings unstitched. Clip curves and turn to right side. By hand, run a gathering thread along stitched seam between markings indicated on pattern. Pull gathering thread until space between markings is about ⅜ inch. Stuff arms, then sew openings closed.

Thread soft-sculpture needle with a doubled length of carpet thread. Push needle through body from left side to right side at dots indicated on pattern. Poke needle through right arm at dot indicated on pattern; thread a button onto needle. Push needle back through button, arm, and body to left side. Attach left arm as for right. Repeat this process until arms are securely held in place.

For skirt, sew short edges of skirt rectangle together, forming a tube. Fold tube in half lengthwise with wrong sides facing and seam matching (fold forms skirt hemline). Sew a gathering thread through both layers, ¼ inch from the raw edges. Pull up gathers to fit around the doll's waist; hand-sew skirt onto doll. (*Do not* turn under raw edges; these will be concealed with a ribbon sash or an apron.)

To finish, sew tiny bead buttons to bodice fronts, add ribbon bows to hair, and trim as desired with purchased miniature accessories. Tie ribbon or apron around waist to hide raw skirt edges.

For apron, hem one long and two short sides of apron rectangle folding ¼-inch under. Trim the bottom edge of apron with decorative ribbon or sew a ¼-inch-deep tuck ¼ inch above hem, if desired. Sew a gathering thread ¼ inch from raw edge. Pull up gathers to 4½ inches. With ribbon and fabric right side up, center gathers on ribbon and topstitch through both layers.

TINY FRIENDS

As shown on page 35, dolls measure 5¼ inches tall.

MATERIALS *for one doll*
4 tea bags (optional)
Tracing paper
Erasable fabric marker
5x20-inch-piece of muslin
6x4-inch piece of fabric for belt loops and shirt or dress
3x7-inch piece of fabric for pants
Sewing threads to match fabrics
Polyester fiberfill; graphite paper
Black and barn-red acrylic paints
Small stencil brush
#1 liner artist's brush
Black fine-tip permanent marker
1½x2½-inch piece of print fabric for hat
Tan, red, and blue embroidery floss
Light-weight cardboard
Crafts glue

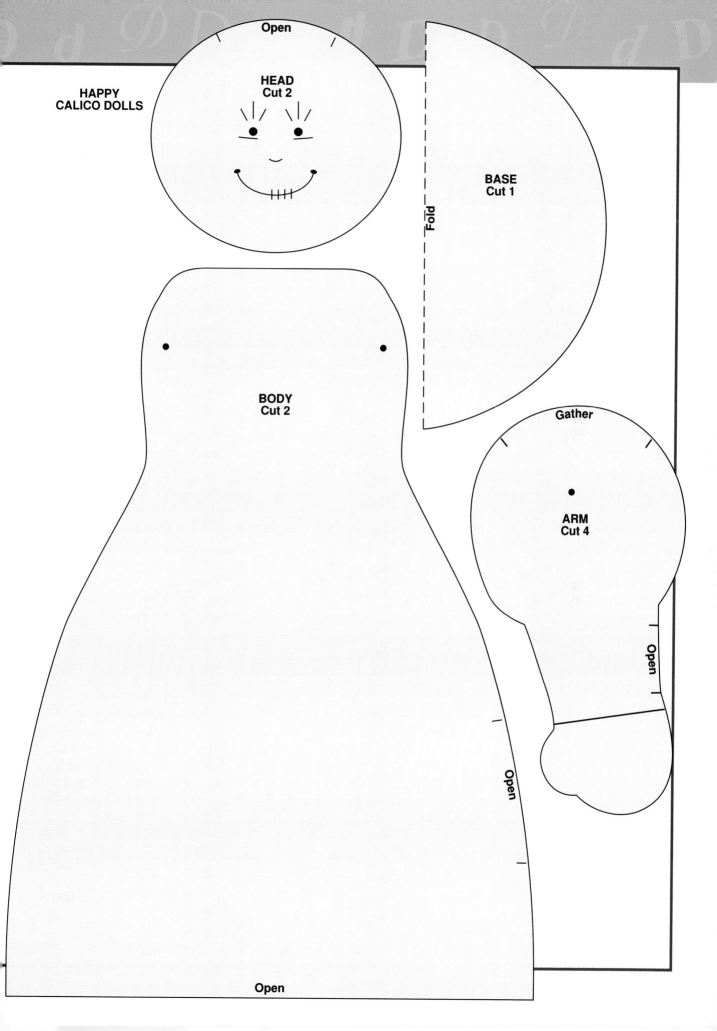

INSTRUCTIONS

To tea-dye fabrics, steep tea bags in 3 cups of *hot water*. Soak fabrics in tea until they are slightly darker than desired color. Squeeze out excess liquid and place on a flat surface to dry. Let pieces dry completely and press.

Trace head/body and shirt/dress patterns, *right,* on a folded piece of tracing paper, aligning folds; cut out and unfold. Trace remaining patterns on a single thickness of tracing paper and cut out.

From muslin, cut one 1¾x5-inch apron rectangle. Fold remaining muslin to make a double thickness. With erasable marker, draw around head/body piece once and around legs and arms twice each. *Do not* cut out.

From dress or shirt fabric, cut two 1x4-inch belt loop rectangles. Fold the remaining fabric to make a double thickness. Draw around the shirt/dress pattern. For boy only, on double thickness of pants fabric, trace around the pants pattern. *Do not* cut out.

Sew around head/body, arms, and legs leaving openings as indicated on patterns. Cut out ¼ inch beyond marker lines. Clip curves and turn right side out. Stuff body with polyester fiberfill, leaving lower 1 inch unstuffed. Turn under ¼ inch along bottom.

Stuff legs to dotted line. Matching front and back seams at leg top opening, insert leg tops into body bottom; topstitch across bottom of body. Stuff arms as for legs. Stitch arms to body between dots as indicated on pattern.

For face, transfer facial features to head using graphite paper. Using barn-red paint on stencil brush, lightly brush in rosy cheeks. Using artist's brush, paint eyes black and nose and lips red. Draw eyelashes, eyebrows, and smile lines with fine-tip marker.

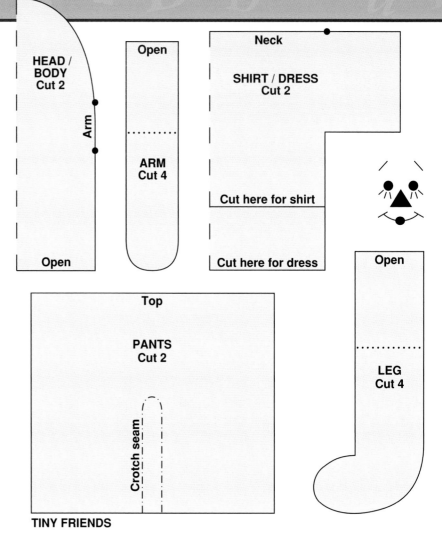

TINY FRIENDS

For girl's hair, run a line of glue along head seam from ear level to ear level. Loop one 6-ply strand of red floss back and forth across seam 4 to 6 times to make ½-inch loop bangs; press into glue at seam. Wrap floss around a 5-inch piece of cardboard ten times; cut strand, but *do not* cut loops. Slide loops off cardboard and set aside, keeping loops in a bundle. Wrap floss around a 2-inch piece of cardboard; cut strand and slide loops off. Layer shorter floss bundle atop larger one; tie together in center with floss. With shorter bundle on top, glue floss hair to seam line atop bangs. With a 6-ply, 4-inch-long strand of blue floss, take a small stitch through each side of head at ear level. Gather floss hair into a pony tail on each side of face and tie blue floss in a bow around each one.

For boy's hair, wrap a 6-ply strand of red floss around a 1½-inch piece of cardboard 5 times. Cut strand, but *do not* cut loops. Slide loops off cardboard. Cut four 1-inch floss strands; lay atop longer bundle. Tie center with floss scrap. Glue to top of head.

For dress, sew along marker lines from dot indicated on pattern to edge of sleeve. Sew underarm/side seams. Cut out ¼ inch beyond marker line. Press under ¼ inch along neck opening. Beginning at center front, use a 6-ply strand of tan floss to hand-sew a gathering thread around neck opening, ⅛ inch from fold. Leave 3 inch tails on each end. Put dress on doll. Pull ends firmly to gather neck; tie in bow.

For apron, use tan floss to hand sew a gathering thread ½ inch from one long edge of apron rectangle. Leave 5-inch floss tails on each end. Put apron on doll; tie floss ends in bow.

For shirt, sew shirt and gather neck edge as for dress. Tie floss in knot and trim ends.

For pants, sew side seams; cut out ¼ inch beyond marker line. Sew crotch seam along dotted line; slit between stitching and turn. Turn under ¼ inch along waist edge; gather waist with floss as for shirt neck. Put pants on doll; tuck in shirt. Tie floss to fit.

For hat, fold hat rectangle widthwise, wrong sides facing. With fold at top, fold each upper corner to midline, forming a point at center of folded edge. Fold and press each bottom edge up. Glue as necessary; glue to boy's head.

To make belt loops, fold each belt loop rectangle lengthwise; stitch using ⅛-inch seam; turn. Stitch ends together to form loop. Tack loop to back of each doll. Slide belt through loop.

PILLOWCASE DRESS

Dress shown on page 36 is a size 12 girl's pattern.

MATERIALS

Tracing paper; pencil
Purchased child's dress pattern with plain neckline, center back zipper, and gathered skirt
Two pillowcases with crocheted or embroidered edging
Coordinating fabric for bodice and sleeves as specified on pattern envelope
Zipper and/or other notions as directed on pattern
Sewing thread to match fabrics

INSTRUCTIONS

To make collar patterns, pin tracing paper on top of the front and back bodice pieces from the dress pattern. (Diagram 1 shows the front only; complete all steps on both front and back.) On bodice front and back, trace the

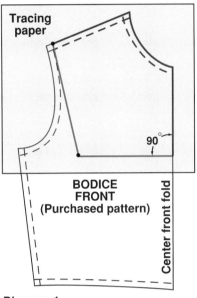

BODICE FRONT (Purchased pattern)

Center front fold

90°

Tracing paper

Diagram 1

— **Purchased pattern**
— **Traced lines**
— **Drawn lines**

shoulder and neckline cutting lines and seam lines. On the bodice front, trace center front fold. On the bodice back, trace center back seamline.

Determine the length of the collar by measuring the child and/or the pattern from the neckline seam to the desired length at center front and back. (The collar in the photo is 8 inches long.) Mark measured distance on the tracing paper along center front and back. Referring to diagram 1, *left,* draw a line, at a right (90°) angle to the center front fold (or the center back seam), that extends from the mark almost to the side seam of the pattern.

Determine the width at the bottom of the collar by measuring child and/or pattern from the center front to desired width. (Width of the collar in the photo is 5 inches.) Mark width on drawn line. Draw another line that extends from point where armhole and shoulder seams meet to the width mark on first line. Cut out collar patterns.

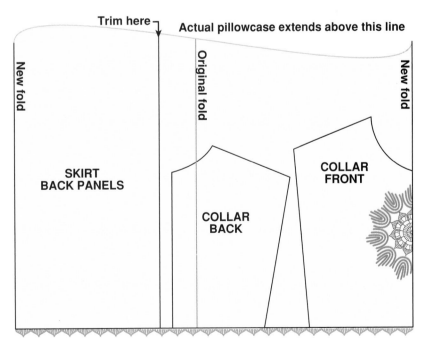

Trim here ⌐   Actual pillowcase extends above this line

New fold

Original fold

New fold

SKIRT BACK PANELS

COLLAR BACK

COLLAR FRONT

Diagram 2
PILLOWCASE DRESS

To cut out collar, remove the seams from the end (opposite crocheted motif) of each pillowcase. Refold one pillowcase so the center crocheted motif is on the fold. Referring to diagram 2, *page 41,* pin the front collar pattern to the pillowcase, matching folds. Pin the back collar pattern close to the front collar, reserving as much excess fabric of the pillowcase as possible. Cut out collar pieces.

For skirt, trim excess fabric from the first pillowcase evenly. Cut into two equal rectangles with crocheted edging on one short side; set aside. Refold second pillowcase with central crocheted motif on fold. Slit fabric from crocheted edging to top. Sew edges of fabric reserved from first pillow case to cut edges of second pillow case. Lay skirt pattern on second pillowcase with hem line fold on crocheted edge. Trim top of pillowcase to appropriate length.

Cut bodice pieces, sleeves, and any facings from coordinating fabric for dress.

Sew collar front to backs at shoulders. Press center back and outer edges of collar under ¼ inch; press under again ⅜ inch and hem.

Sew the shoulder seams of the dress bodice. Baste the collar to the bodice with the wrong side of collar facing the right side of bodice, matching neckline edges and markings. Assemble the bodice and sleeves according to pattern directions.

Sew short edges of skirt piece together, leaving an opening for zipper as indicated on pattern. Run a gathering thread around top edge of skirt. Pull up gathers to fit bodice, adjusting evenly. With right sides facing, stitch skirt to bodice. Apply zipper according to pattern directions.

CATHEDRAL WINDOW DRESS

As shown on page 37.

MATERIALS
Purchased child's dress pattern with set-in sleeves and gathered skirt
45-inch-wide ecru or white cotton fabric in amount specified on pattern envelope
2¼ additional yards of same fabric for cathedral windows
Ecru or white thread
Assorted scraps of calico
85 buttons (optional)
Eight yards of ¾-inch-wide flat lace
½ yard of ¼-inch-wide ribbon

INSTRUCTIONS
For cathedral windows, cut forty-four 8½x8½-inch squares of ecru and forty 2¾x2¾-inch squares of calico.

Fold one ecru square in half, right sides together and stitch both ends (step 1, opposite). Refold fabric, bring raw edges together, and match seams. Starting at one end, stitch a seam about 4½ inches long. Starting from other end, stitch a seam about 1 inch long (step 2).

Turn and press into a square with seams forming an X through center. Fold corners to center of X and press (step 3). Repeat to make forty-four squares.

For block, unfold one square and sew one flap to a flap on another square (step 4). Sew two more squares together in the same manner. Lay the strips side by side and sew the adjoining flaps together to form a square.

Refold the flaps of each square so they meet in center; tack securely (step 5). Center and pin a calico square to each of the four

central squares in the block, *below.* Fold bias edges of the ecru fabric over the raw edges of the calico and blindstitch in place (step 6).

Stitch nine cathedral window blocks together in a row with right sides facing, using a slight zigzag stitch, catching just folded edge of each side.

Cut dress according to pattern. Adjust length and width of skirt to accommodate border. Clean-finish hem edge of skirt. Topstitch border to hem edge, using a narrow zigzag stitch and transparent nylon thread, catching lace between skirt and border. Zigzag lace to bottom edge of border.

Assemble bodice and attach skirt according to pattern directions, adding lace to neck edge.

For sleeves, make two blocks, adding just two calico squares to each. Machine-stitch several times diagonally across the center of each block. Trim diagonally through each block, close to stitching, discarding unfinished side. Run a gathering stitch close to cut edge. Center the half block at shoulder seam, right sides together; pull up gathers to fit baste. Make sleeve according to pattern, adding lace to bottom edge. Stitch sleeve to dress.

Stitch buttons at corners of calico squares, if desired. Add bow and button to neck edge.

Cathedral Windows

Cathedral windows are a unique quilt form, because they contain no batting. For convenience, you can work steps 1–4 on a sewing machine.

Fold the large solid-colored square half and stitch across both short ends ng ¼-inch seam allowances. When ching by hand, try to make stitches inch long.

2. Refold the square, bring unstitched edges together, and match seams. Sew a short seam from one end and a longer seam from the other so stitching crosses the first seams, but leaves an opening.

3. Turn the square right side out through the opening and press so seams form an X from corner to corner. Fold each corner to the center of the X, forming flaps, and press again.

Unfold the corner flaps of one uare. Align one flap to a flap on a second square; pin the two squares together. Stitch the flaps together along the d line. To create a block, join another ir of squares to one side of the first.

5. Fold the corner flaps back to the center of each one's original square. By hand, tack the four points of each square together securely. Notice that a diagonal square has formed where the two squares meet.

6. Center and pin a calico square in the center of the diagonal square formed between two squares. Fold the bias edges of the diagonal square over the raw edges of the calico square and blind stitch in place.

E is for *Easy* *E*lephants and *E*ggs

Eliza the Elephant

Eliza, our very feminine elephant, is "tutu" cute! Cleverly designed using scraps of flannel, satin, and tulle, Eliza stretches to a demure 9 inches tall. Her sweet face and ballerina slippers are created with paint and her costume is trimmed with pearls and a satin rose. Instructions begin on page 48.

DESIGNER: SUSAN CAGE-KNOCH ● PHOTOGRAPHER: SCOTT LITTLE

Mama and Baby Elephants

Scraps of felt or pieces of a favorite old coat, embroidery floss, and imagination are all you need to create this family of petite pachyderms. Filled with stuffing pellets for realistic heft, they can be made in two sizes with tiny tufts of floss at the ends of their tails and on the tops of their heads. Simple button eyes add special charm to this trio of big-eared characters. Complete instructions and patterns begin on page 49.

DESIGNER: JIM WILLIAMS ● PHOTOGRAPHER: SCOTT LITTLE

Needlepoint Eggs

Our elegant yet easy needlepoint eggs are wonderful additions to any egg collection. Trimmed with satin edging, these pastel beauties feature specialty stitches, iridescent beads, and metallic gold thread. Used as ornaments or among spring flowers, these eggs add color and richness to any vignette. Instructions are on page 52.

DESIGNER: MARGARET SINDELAR ● PHOTOGRAPHER: SCOTT LITTLE

Felt and Tatted Eggs

*Bits of felt are all you need to fashion the three pretty Easter eggs in our basket.
Start with pastel-colored eggs, then get the kids involved in gluing the felt shapes in place.
In no time at all, you'll make a basketful of butterflies, bows, and hearts to brighten the
spring holiday. To make the Easter Bunny proud, create our gorgeous tatted eggs in
a variety of spring colors using soft pearl cotton. Complete instructions for all of
these Easter basket brighteners are on pages 52–53.*

DESIGNERS: FELT EGGS, KAREN TAYLOR; TATTED EGGS, JANE MOODY ● PHOTOGRAPHER: HOPKINS ASSOCIATES

ELIZA THE ELEPHANT

As shown on page 44, elephant is 8 inches tall.

MATERIALS
Tracing paper
10x20-inch piece of light gray or other light-colored cotton flannel
3x6-inch piece of pink satin
Erasable fabric marker
Sewing threads to match fabrics
Polyester fiberfill
Black embroidery floss
Embroidery needle
Fine-line pink shiny paint pen
Paper plate
Artists' brushes
Tiny stencil brush
White stretchable, flexible fabric paint
Fine-line white glitter paint pen
Pink glitter paint
27-inch-long strand of iridescent pearl beads by the yard
⅓ yard of 108-inch-wide tulle
½ yard of ½-inch-wide pink satin ribbon
Pink satin ribbon rose

INSTRUCTIONS

Trace patterns, *right,* onto tracing paper and cut out. Patterns include ¼-inch seam allowances. Sew all seams with right sides of the fabrics facing unless otherwise indicated.

From flannel, cut elephant body, trunk, and two (outer) ears. From satin, cut two more (inner) ears. Transfer markings to right side of fabrics with marker.

Use three plies of black floss to work French knot eyes and straight stitch eyebrows on one body piece.

Sew inner and outer ears together in pairs leaving openings. Turn ears right side out and press. Fold satin side of each ear together along fold line. With felt sides up

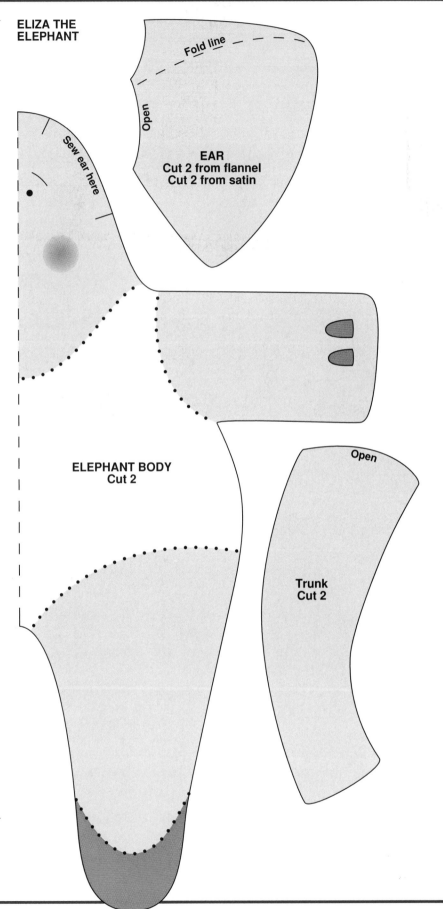

ELIZA THE ELEPHANT

EAR
Cut 2 from flannel
Cut 2 from satin

ELEPHANT BODY
Cut 2

Trunk
Cut 2

and raw edges even, baste each to body front between marks.

Sew body front to back, leaving an opening at the inside edge of one leg for turning. Turn right side out and stuff firmly with polyester fiberfill. Turn under ¼ inch along opening edges and slip-stitch closed.

Sew trunk pieces together, leaving the end open as indicated on pattern. Turn right side out and stuff with fiberfill. Turn under ¼ inch along the trunk opening edges. With trunk curving downward, whipstitch it firmly to center of face.

Squeeze a little pink shiny paint onto a paper plate. Use a small brush to paint shoes and nails. Blush cheeks pink using stencil brush. Outline shoes using tip of pink shiny paint pen.

Paint leotard with white flexible paint. Cut bead strands to fit around neck, legs, and arms of leotard. Working one area at a time, outline neck, leg holes, and arm holes with white glitter paint pen. While paint is still wet, press beads into paint lines and allow paint to set, securing beads. Brush pink glitter paint over shoes.

Unfold tulle to its full width. Refold into sixths to make a 12x18-inch rectangle with six layers. Next, fold piece lengthwise into fourths for a 3x18-inch piece with twenty-four layers. Run a gathering thread ¼ inch from one long edge. Trim that edge to ⅛ inch beyond gathering thread. Trim opposite long edge even, cutting down total width to 1½ inches. Set scraps aside. Pull gathering thread until edge of tulle measures 8 inches. Center gathered strip on one edge of ribbon; stitch. Fold ribbon over raw edge of tulle and hand stitch in place. Tie tulle tutu around elephant's waist.

Crisscross and tie a tulle scrap around each leg above shoe; trim ends. Tie a tulle scrap in a bow and tack to head. Glue rose to bodice of leotard.

MAMA AND BABY ELEPHANTS

As shown on page 45, mama measures 7¾x9 inches; babies each measure 6x7¼ inches.

MATERIALS
For mama
Three 8½x11-inch pieces of dark gray felt or firmly woven wool fabric
For each baby
Three 7x9-inch pieces of gray or violet felt or firmly woven wool fabric
For each elephant
Tracing paper
Erasable fabric marker
Straight pins
Ruler
Black cotton embroidery floss or black string and sewing thread
Sewing thread to match fabrics
Polyester stuffing pellets, rice, or beans
Two ⅜-inch-diameter buttons

INSTRUCTIONS
Trace pattern pieces, *pages 50–51,* and cut out. Fold one piece of felt in half; cut ears and two 3x¾-inch tail strips. On each remaining felt piece (or the wrong side of woven fabric), draw around the body pattern reversing pattern on second piece and marking opening; cut out ¼ inch beyond outline.

To transfer ear position markings, with tracing paper pattern and outline on felt aligned, insert a straight pin at each end of the placement line. Turn felt over and use the erasable marker to make a small dot at each pin. Remove pins and use marker and ruler to connect the dots. Mark the tail and placement eye position using the same method.

Machine-zigzag stitch around each ear, if using woven fabric. Position each ear, right side up, on the right side of one body piece, matching straight edge of ear to line indicated on pattern. Topstitch ears to bodies, stitching close to straight edge. Set the bodies aside.

Place felt tail strips one atop other. Cut twelve 6-inch strands of floss or string. Align the strands, fold in half, and place folded end between layers at one end of tail strips. Sew tail ends together ⅛ inch from edge, securing floss. Sew long sides together ⅛ inch from edge. For woven fabric, zigzag stitch around tail once after straight stitching.

Pin tail to the right side of one body piece with base of tail extending ¼ inch beyond body outline. Position body pieces right sides facing, enclosing tail and aligning ears and outlines carefully. Sew bodies together along drawn outlines, leaving marked opening unstitched. Clip curves and turn right side out. Fill with polyester pellets, rice, or beans. Sew opening closed.

Sew a button eye to each side of head at marking, using one thread to sew between both buttons.

For hair, thread needle with two plies of black floss or a double strand of black sewing thread. Knot 1 inch from end. Push needle into top of head and then out where hair is desired; pull needle until knot is against fabric. Knot thread at the exit point and trim ends 1 inch from knot. Repeat until several tufts of thin hair have been created.

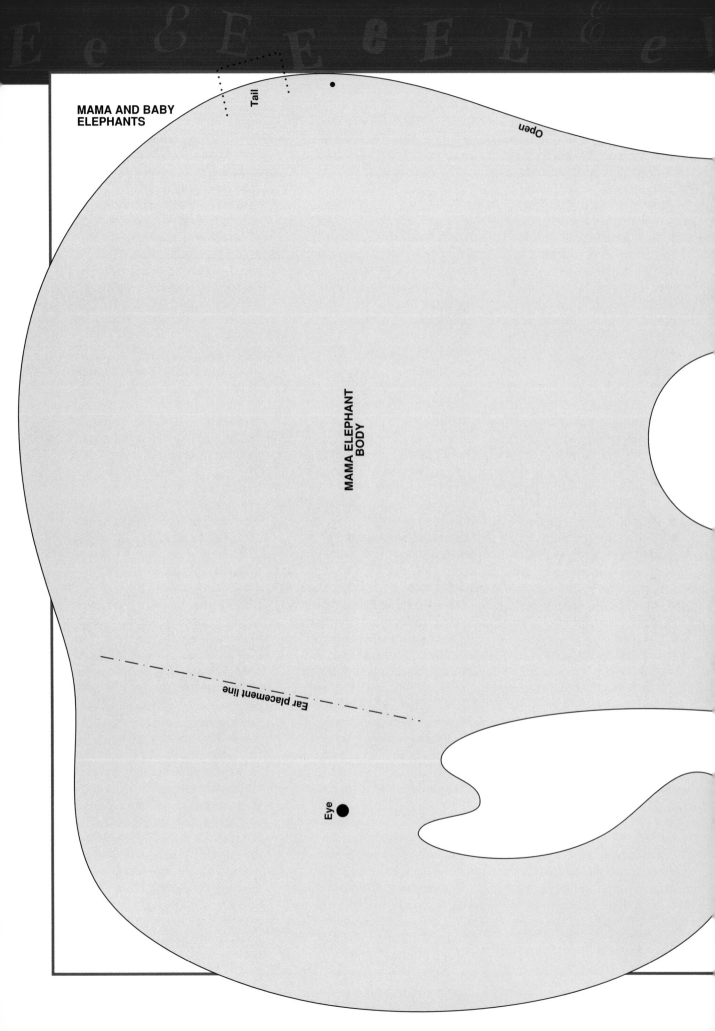

**MAMA AND BABY
ELEPHANTS**

Tail

Open

MAMA ELEPHANT
BODY

Ear placement line

Eye ●

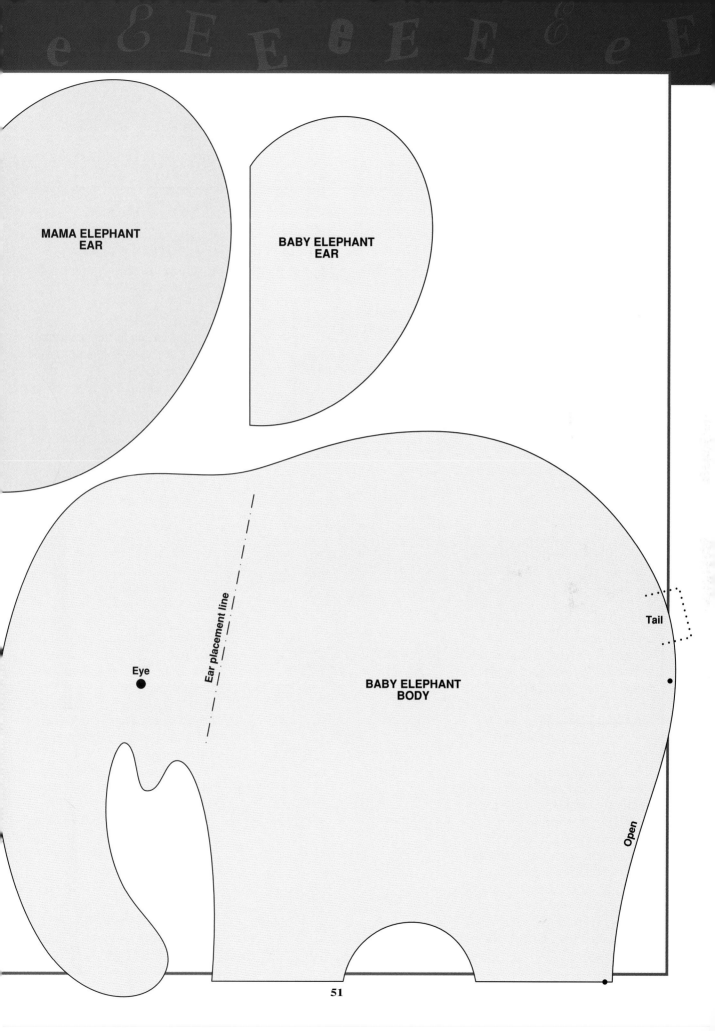

MAMA ELEPHANT
EAR

BABY ELEPHANT
EAR

Ear placement line

Eye

BABY ELEPHANT
BODY

Tail

Open

NEEDLEPOINT EGGS

As shown on page 46, eggs measure 5½ inches tall.

MATERIALS *for each egg*

FABRICS
8x7-inch piece of 12-count needlepoint canvas
7x6-inch piece of white felt

THREADS
#5 pearl cotton in three different colors
16 yards of 3-ply needlepoint yarn for background
#8 metallic gold braid

SUPPLIES
Erasable fabric marker; needle
Seed beads; sewing thread
8x6-inch piece of foam-covered mounting board
Crafts glue; crafts knife
15-inch piece of ⅝-inch-wide flat pleated ribbon

INSTRUCTIONS

Tape edges of canvas to prevent fraying. Use erasable marker to draw an oval, 5 inches tall and 3⅝ inches wide, in center of canvas; *do not* cut out. Find center of oval; begin stitching center of cross there. Work eleven rice, Scotch, or Smyrna cross stitches to form cross using two strands of pearl cotton. Work outline of cross using tent stitches and two strands of pearl cotton. Work remainder of oval using tent stitches and two plies of yarn. Work straight stitches using one strand of braid. Attach seed beads randomly using sewing thread.

Use tracing paper to trace egg outline; cut out. Cut one oval shape from mounting board and one from felt. Peel paper from mounting board. Center foam side on the back of stitchery and press to stick. Trim canvas ½ inch beyond mounting board. Fold excess canvas to back and glue.

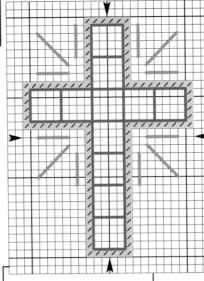

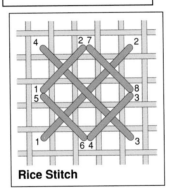

NEEDLEPOINT EGGS
SMYRNA CROSS, SCOTCH, OR RICE STITCH
⟋ Color A # 5 pearl cotton
⟋ Color B # 5 pearl cotton
TENT STITCH
▨ Color C # 5 pearl cotton
STRAIGHT STITCH
⟋ Gold braid

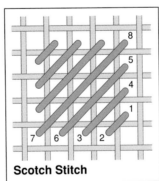
Rice Stitch

Scotch Stitch

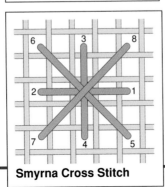
Smyrna Cross Stitch

Position and glue ribbon around front edges of egg, overlapping ends at bottom. Glue raw edges to back. Glue felt to back of egg.

CENTER BAND TATTED EGG

As shown worked with blue pearl cotton on page 47.

MATERIALS

#8 pearl cotton in desired color
Tatting shuttle; #9 crochet hook
Tapestry needle
Plastic or blown-and-dyed real eggs

INSTRUCTIONS

Work all p ¼-inch long unless otherwise indicated.

For first motif in band, r of 5 ds, p, 5 ds, p, 1 ds, ½-inch p, 1 ds, p, 5 ds, p, 5 ds; cr. (R of 5 ds, join to last p of previous r, 5 ds, p, 1 ds, ½-inch p, 1 ds, p, 5 ds, p, 5 ds; cr.) Repeat between ( ) twice, joining last p of last r to first p of first r. Cut and tie ends.

For second motif in band, r of 5 ds, p, 5 ds, p, 1 ds, join to ½-inch p of third r of previous motif, 1 ds, p, 5 ds, p, 5 ds; cr. Repeat between ( ) three times. Repeat second motif three times.

For sixth motif in band, repeat second motif, except, at ½-inch p of third r, join to ½-inch p of first r of first motif.

For end motifs, repeat first motif in band motif, except make six r. Make two end motifs.

Slide band around center of egg. Position one end motif over one end of egg. Thread needle with 18 inches of thread and weave between pieces around the egg. Cut thread, but *do not* tie. Repeat with remaining end motif. Adjust tension on lacing threads so band is centered. Knot ends securely.

TATTING ABBREVIATIONS	
r	ring
ch	chain
cr	close ring
ds	double stitch
p	picot
rw	reverse work
rnd	round

BOW MEDALLION TATTED EGG

As shown worked with lavender pearl cotton on page 47.

MATERIALS
#8 pearl cotton in desired color
Tatting shuttle
#9 crochet hook; tapestry needle
Plastic or blown-and-dyed real eggs

INSTRUCTIONS
Work all p ¼-inch long unless otherwise indicated.

For medallions, Rnd 1: (R of 4 ds, p, 4 ds, p, 4 ds; cr. Rw; ch of 4 ds, p 4 ds, rw) six times. Cut and tie, joining last ch to base of first r.

Rnd 2: R of 4 ds, p, 4 ds, ½-inch p, 4 ds, join to left-hand p of any r in Rnd 1, 4 ds, cr. *R of 4 ds, join to remaining free p, of same r, 4 ds, ½-inch p, 4 ds, p, 4

ds; cr. Rw; ch of 4 ds, p, 4 ds, p, 4 ds, p, 1 ds, ½-inch p, 1 ds, p, 4 ds, p, 4 ds, p, 4 ds. Rw; r of 4 ds, p, 4 ds, join to ½-inch p of previous r, 4 ds, join to left p of next r in Rnd 1, 4 ds; cr. Repeat from * around joining at ½-inch p of last r to ½-inch p of first r and last ch to base of first r. Cut and tie. Repeat to make a total of two medallions.

Position medallion over ends of egg. Thread needle with 18 inches of thread and join medallions together, weaving though ½-inch p of each ch. Knot ends securely.

FELT-DECORATED EGGS

As shown on page 47.

MATERIALS
Tracing paper
Scraps of felt in medium pink, blue, yellow, light pink, lavender, and light green
9x12-inch piece of cardstock
Hard-boiled eggs dyed in pastel shades
Crafts glue; hole punch
Erasable fabric marker

INSTRUCTIONS
Trace patterns, *below,* onto tracing paper; cut out. Draw around patterns on cardstock; cut out.

For butterfly, draw around two A's on blue felt, two B's on light green felt, two C's and two D's on lavender felt; two E's on yellow felt, and one F on medium pink felt; cut out. Referring to butterfly diagram below patterns, stack upper and lower wing pieces on a 2½x1¾-inch piece of light pink felt; glue. Glue butterfly body (F) between wings. Trim light pink felt, leaving a ⅛-inch border. Glue to egg.

For bow, draw around one A, two B's, and one C on blue felt; cut out. Referring to bow diagram below patterns, stack pieces on a 1¾x1¼-inch piece of light pink felt. Trim pink felt around bow, leaving a ⅛-inch border. Glue to a 2x2-inch piece of yellow felt. Trim to make a second ⅛-inch border. Glue to egg.

For heart, cut four hearts from medium pink felt. Using hole punch, cut four circles from blue felt. Glue each heart to a 1x1-inch piece of lavender felt. Trim lavender felt around each heart, leaving a ⅛-inch border. Referring to heart diagram below pattern, arrange hearts and circles on a 2½x2½-inch piece of yellow felt. Trim yellow felt, leaving a ⅛-inch border around heart and circle pattern. Glue to egg.

FELT-DECORATED EGGS

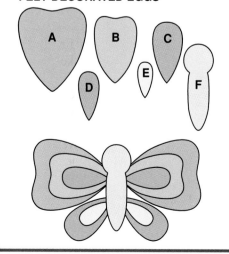
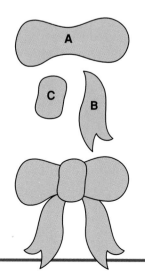

F is for *Fabulous Frames*

Ribbon Frames

Simple frames are all dressed up with ribbons, buckles, and buttons creating the loveliest of accents for treasured poses. The trims are simply glued to the frames in clever combinations to add special sparkle to already special people. Instructions are on page 57.

DESIGNERS: SUSAN BANKER AND MARGARET SINDELAR ● PHOTOGRAPHER: HOPKINS ASSOCIATES

Painted Frames

Color and imagination and a little paint can bring a tired frame back to life.
These two frames were base-coat painted first, and then accented with festive stripes
and dots. A coat of clear varnish finishes these graphic frames that can be used at home
or given away as personalized gifts. Instructions are on page 57.

DESIGNER: DIANE SHANNON ● PHOTOGRAPHER: HOPKINS ASSOCIATES

Fabric Frames

Show off your family's best photographs with these elegant, easy-to-make frames. Plaid linen fabric creates a sharp finish for the larger frame, while vintage floral and natural linen fabrics contrast on the versatile double frame. Padded with fleece and decorated with buttons, they create a soft backdrop for heirloom photos or your favorite family snapshots. Instructions are on page 58.

DESIGNER: JIM WILLIAMS ● PHOTOGRAPHER: HOPKINS ASSOCIATES

NAUTICAL FRAME

Frame shown on page 54 measures 9½x7¼ inches with a 6½x4½-inch opening.

MATERIALS
Purchased 9½x7¼-inch frame
½ yard of 1-inch-wide royal blue grosgrain ribbon
¾ yard of 1-inch-wide red with white polka dots grosgrain ribbon
Six 1-inch-diameter gold nautical buttons
Two gold 1½-inch-wide interlocking belt buckles
Hot glue gun and glue sticks

INSTRUCTIONS
Cut the blue ribbon in half. Center one piece across the top and one piece across the bottom of the frame. Glue in place, folding the raw edges of the ribbon to the back.

Cut the polka-dot ribbon into quarters. Thread ½ inch of each piece into a buckle opening. Fold the ½-inch end to the back and glue. Latch buckles together and center on vertical sides of frame. Glue ribbon to frame, folding raw edges to the back.

Space buttons equally on blue ribbon. Glue buttons in place.

LACE AND HEART FRAME

Frame shown on page 54 measures 6½x5½ inches.

MATERIALS
Purchased 6½x5½-inch frame with heart-shaped opening and Battenberg lace trim
1½ yards of ⅜-inch wide picot-edged pink satin ribbon
Satin carnation rosettes in desired colors
Crafts glue

INSTRUCTIONS
Cut enough ribbon to fit the outer edge of the frame and glue in place.

Tie the remaining ribbon in a bow about 3 inches wide. Glue the bow to the upper left-hand corner of the frame about ¾ inch from the heart-shaped opening. Twist each end of the bow two or three times and fasten to the top and left side of the frame with dots of glue.

Arrange rosettes as desired on frame. Glue in place.

RIBBONS AND ROSES FRAME

Frame shown on page 54 measures 9¼x11 inches with a 4½x6½-inch opening.

MATERIALS
Purchased 9¼x11-inch frame with a 1½-inch-wide mat
4-inch piece of 1-inch-wide pink satin ribbon
15-inch piece of 1-inch-wide mint green satin ribbon
15-inch piece of 1-inch-wide lavender satin ribbon
Three 1-inch D-rings
6-inch piece of ¼-inch-wide light blue satin ribbon
6-inch piece of ¼-inch-wide lavender satin ribbon
6-inch piece of ¼-inch-wide mauve satin ribbon
Two burgundy satin roses
Two purple satin roses
One mauve satin rose
One lavender satin rose
Hot glue gun and glue sticks

INSTRUCTIONS
Remove the mat from the frame. Insert pink ribbon through one D-ring; bring ends of the ribbon together and glue. Glue ribbon to the top of the mat at center. Insert mint green and lavender ribbon through D-rings in the same manner. Bring edges of each together. Glue green ribbon to the left edge of the mat and lavender to the right side of the mat.

Tie one piece of ¼-inch ribbon around each D-ring and tie into a bow at the bottom of the ring. Group satin roses into sets of three and glue to the ribbons at the left and right side of the mat. Reassemble mat and frame.

PAINTED FRAMES

Frames shown on page 55 measure 9¾x7¾ inches and 10½x12½ inches.

MATERIALS
Old wood frames
Light gray spray primer
Acrylic paints in desired colors
Artists' brushes
½- and 1-inch flat paintbrushes
Fine-tip metallic silver or gold marker
Clear gloss interior wood finish

INSTRUCTIONS
Remove the glass and backing from each frame; set aside. Spray the frame with primer. Allow to dry one hour.

Paint each groove and ridge as desired, referring to photograph, *page 55,* for ideas. Begin with the inner edge of the frame opening, paint solid colors first and allow to dry. Then, add stripes and dots to desired areas next; allow to dry. Paint fine details last, using the metallic marker; allow to dry.

When paint is dry, apply two coats of gloss wood finish, allowing it to dry one hour between coats. After the final coat of finish, let dry two hours before reassembling the frame.

LINEN AND BUTTON FRAME

Frame shown on page 56 measures 10x8 inches, with a 5½x3½-inch opening.

MATERIALS

Two 10x8-inch pieces of fusible fleece
Two 10x8-inch pieces of sturdy cardboard
Metal ruler
Crafts knife
14x12-inch piece of plaid linen or other textured plaid fabric
14 buttons to coordinate with fabric or enough to cover each exposed intersection of the plaid
Off white embroidery floss
Hot glue gun and glue sticks

INSTRUCTIONS

For frame front, following manufacturer's directions, fuse two layers of fleece to one piece of cardboard, one layer at a time. On other side, draw a 5½x3½-inch rectangle in center of interfaced cardboard; cut out.

Use remaining piece of cardboard (back) as a pattern to cut two pieces of linen, centering plaid and cutting 1 inch beyond edge of cardboard. Center cardboard back on wrong side of one piece of fabric. Spread hot glue along one edge of cardboard back; fold fabric over edge and allow glue to set. Repeat for opposite edge of frame back, stretching fabric evenly taut. Repeat for other two edges, trimming corners to minimize bulk.

Cover frame front as for back, stretching fabric evenly across fleece. For front opening, cut a slit in center of fabric. Carefully clip fabric to corners of opening. Pull resulting flaps to back of frame and glue. Place a dot of glue in each corner and, using fingers or edge of a pencil, press clipped fabric against glue.

Place frame front on top of back and hot glue along top and sides, leaving bottom open to insert photograph.

To finish, thread embroidery floss through holes in buttons. Clip floss close to button backs and glue ends to backs of buttons. Glue buttons to frame front at intersections of woven plaid.

FLORAL AND LINEN DOUBLE FRAME

As shown on page 56, each half of the double frame measures 8x6 inches with a 3x2-inch opening.

MATERIALS

8x24-inch piece of fusible fleece
Four 8x6-inch pieces of sturdy cardboard
Metal ruler
Crafts knife
12x16-inch piece of floral drapery or other fabric
10x16-inch piece of solid-colored linen or other textured fabric
Two 1-inch-diameter buttons
Coordinating embroidery floss
Hot glue gun and glue sticks

INSTRUCTIONS

For frame fronts, cut four 8x6-inch pieces of fusible fleece. Following manufacturer's directions, fuse two layers of fleece to two cardboard pieces, one layer at a time. On other side, draw a 3x2-inch rectangle in center of each interfaced piece; cut out.

Use one remaining piece of cardboard (back) as a pattern to cut two pieces each of floral fabric and linen, cutting 1 inch beyond edge of cardboard. Center each plain piece of cardboard on the wrong side of one piece of each fabric. Spread hot glue along one edge of cardboard back; fold fabric over edge and allow glue to set. Repeat for opposite edge of frame back, stretching fabric evenly taut. Repeat for other two edges, trimming corners to minimize bulk.

Cover frame fronts as for backs, stretching fabric evenly across fleece. For front openings, cut a slit in center of fabric. Carefully clip fabric to corners of opening. Pull resulting flaps to back of frame and glue. To ensure neat corners, place a small amount of glue in each corner and, using fingers or edge of a pencil, press clipped fabric into corner.

Cut a 1½x12-inch strip of floral fabric. Fold edges in and fold in half lengthwise to make a ½-inch-wide strip; topstitch ⅛ inch from both edges. Cut strip in half to make two 6-inch pieces. To shape loop, hold one strip vertically and mark crosswise center. Fold ends of strip diagonally so top edges meet at center, forming a point at the top; press. Refer to photograph, *page 56,* if needed.

Glue ends of loops to wrong side of linen-covered back one inch from top and bottom edges. Place floral front on top of linen back, wrong sides facing. Place remaining front and back together in same manner. Hot-glue along top and sides of each frame, leaving bottom open to insert photograph. Lay finished frames side by side, ¼ inch apart, with linen-front frame on right. Glue loops to front of linen frame.

To finish, thread embroidery floss through holes in buttons. Clip floss close to button backs and glue ends to backs of buttons. Glue buttons to frame fronts on top of loops.

G is for *Glorious Gift Wraps*

Colorful Balloon Flowers

Brightly colored party balloons are stretched over floral wire to create this festive package trim and the clever floral centerpiece. After creating a few of these regal irises, perky pansies, and dainty impatiens, experiment with different shapes to make your own favorite flowers. Instructions and step-by-step photos are on pages 61–62.

DESIGNER: AMY KOEPKE ● PHOTOGRAPHER: HOPKINS ASSOCIATES

Tinsel Trims

Clever and quick, these easy-twist trims add magic to any gift. Created using bright tinsel pipe cleaners, the shapes are formed using a simple cookie cutter. We've shown stars tucked into the curly ribbon—hearts and flowers would be fun, too! Complete instructions are on page 62.

DESIGNER: KAREN TAYLOR ● PHOTOGRAPHER: SCOTT LITTLE

Pastel Toppers

Turn an ordinary package into something spectacular by trimming it with pastel sponges cut into simple shapes! Just a few unused sponges in a variety of colors, pieces of pipe cleaner, and curling ribbon is all it takes. Complete instructions for these delightful package trims and the heart patterns are on page 62.

DESIGNER: KAREN TAYLOR
PHOTOGRAPHER: SCOTT LITTLE

BALLOON FLOWER GIFT TRIM

As shown on page 59.

MATERIALS

18-inch-long pieces of 20-gauge floral wire
White floral corsage tape
Very small pink latex rubber balloons
Small yellow and green latex rubber balloons
Green floral corsage tape
Wire cutters
Red permanent fine-line marker
Pen or pencil
3 to 4 yards of 1- to 1½-inch-wide ribbon

INSTRUCTIONS

Wrap 20 to 30 wires with white floral tape (step 1, right).

For each petal or leaf, cut the rolled end (open end) off the desired color balloon. Bend one piece of white-taped wire in half and insert it into the balloon. Stretch the balloon against the loop while securing it in place using the green floral tape (step 2). Cut off one end of the wire and continue taping to the end of the other wire. Bend the flower petal into desired shape (step 3).

For pink impatiens, using pink balloons, shape five oval petals for each flower. Make each petal ¾-inch long and ¼- to ½-inch wide. For stamen, snip through the rolled end of a yellow balloon, forming a fringe and tape to a wire. Tape one petal and the stamen together using green floral tape. Tape remaining petals to flower, one at a time.

For yellow pansies, use yellow balloons to shape five petals for each flower. Make each petal diamond shaped, ¾-inch long and ¾-inch wide, with rounded

Step-by-Step Balloon Flowers

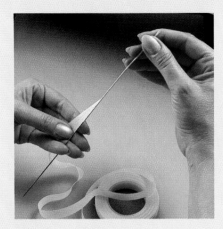

1. To wrap wires, hold wire and floral tape together at one end. Stretch the tape slightly and rotate the wire with the other hand. Bend each taped wire in half.

2. Snip the open end off each balloon and insert a wire into it. Stretch balloon while securing it to doubled wire with green tape. Snip off one end of wire; continue taping.

3. Use fingers to shape each petal. For a stamen, snip rolled end of balloon to form a fringe and attach to a wire with floral tape.

4. Add detail to petals using a permanent marker. Tape petals together to form each flower and shape as desired.

corners. With red marker, draw short straight lines across the center of each petal (step 4). Tape two petals together using green floral tape. Tape remaining petals to flower, one at a time.

For leaves, use green balloons and shape each leaf into an oval that is slightly pointed on the end and 1¼- to 1½-inches long and 1- to 1¼-inches wide. Attach to flowers, if desired.

For green spirals, wrap wires with green floral tape. Wind wire around a pen or pencil several times to create spirals. Pull spirals apart and bend as desired.

Wrap the package as desired. Tie a ribbon around the wrapped package, leaving a looped bow on the top. Secure flowers, leaves, and spirals to package by twisting the stem wires around the ribbon bow as desired.

BALLOON FLOWER CENTERPIECE

As shown on page 59.

MATERIALS

18-inch-long pieces of 22-gauge floral wire
White floral corsage tape
Medium lavender latex rubber balloons
Small yellow, coral, and green latex rubber balloons
Green floral corsage tape
Wire cutters
Black permanent fine-line marker
Red permanent fine-line marker
Pen or pencil
2 yards white 4-inch-wide tulle ribbon
5-inch-wide piece of cardboard
5-inch-tall metal watering can
3x6-inch piece of floral foam
Spanish moss

INSTRUCTIONS

Wrap 40 to 50 wires with white floral tape (step 1 on page 61).

For each petal or leaf, cut rolled ends (open end) off balloon. Bend one piece of taped wire in half and insert into balloon. Stretch balloon against loop while securing it in place using green floral tape (step 2). Cut off one end of wire, leaving a stem. Continue taping to end of other wire. Bend flower petal into desired shape (step 3).

For irises, using lavender balloons, shape six petals for each flower. Make three circular petals approximately 1¾ inches in diameter and three oval petals 1¼-inches long by ¾-inch wide. Tape two smaller petals together with green floral tape, then tape remaining small petal to first two. Shape them to arch upward toward each other. Tape the

remaining petals around these, shaping them with a slight downward curve. Secure with green tape, covering stems.

For coral pansies, follow directions for yellow pansies, *page 61, except* make each petal 1- to 1½-inches long and 1- to 1½-inches wide. Use black marker to draw short straight lines close to stem and red marker to make longer lines radiating from black ones.

Make yellow pansies, leaves, and green spirals as directed on page 61.

For tulle bow, wind tulle around a 5-inch-wide piece of cardboard. Remove from cardboard. Twist a wire around center of tulle bundle and gently separate loops.

To assemble centerpiece, place floral foam inside watering can; cover with moss. Insert flowers, spirals, and bow into foam.

TINSEL TRIMS

As shown on page 60.

MATERIALS

Tinsel pipe cleaners in assorted colors
Star-shaped cookie cutter
Shiny curling ribbon in assorted colors

INSTRUCTIONS

Bend each pipe cleaner in half to find center. Starting at center, press pipe cleaner around outer edges of cookie cutter. Remove cookie cutter. Twist ends together to hold star shape. Set stars aside.

Wrap package as desired. Tie curling ribbon around package, leaving a mass of ribbon curls on top of wrapped package. Use additional lengths of pipe cleaners to attach each star to curling ribbon bow. Bend pipe cleaners to make stars stand up, if desired.

PASTEL TOPPERS LARGE HEART

PASTEL TOPPERS SMALL HEART

PASTEL TOPPERS

As shown on page 60.

MATERIALS

Tracing paper
Sponges in assorted colors
Scissors; glue
Pipe cleaners
Curling ribbon in assorted colors

INSTRUCTIONS

Trace heart patterns, *above;* cut out. Draw around patterns on sponges. Cut out shapes. Insert a pipe cleaner in bottom of each heart and secure with glue.

Wrap package as desired. Tie curling ribbon around package, leaving a mass of curls on top. Attach to bows, varying lengths as desired.

H is for *Happy* *Hats and Hot Pads*

Sweet Floral Hat

Circles of satin stitches, lovely lazy daisy stitches, and colorful French knots turn a plain black felt hat into a little girl's favorite. Use short lengths of bright tapestry yarn to create the beautiful blooms that adorn this hat's crown and brim. Complete instructions and helpful stitching diagrams are on page 68.

DESIGNER: KAREN TAYLOR ● PHOTOGRAPHER: SCOTT LITTLE

Beribboned Hat

A few quick stitches and drops of glue is all it takes to transform a plain-Jane topper into a charming brimmed hat. Adorned with bits and pieces of iridescent ribbon, brightly colored beads from old jewelry, and carnation rosettes, this hat becomes a fashionable chapeau. Complete instructions are on page 68.

DESIGNER: MARGARET SINDELAR ● PHOTOGRAPHER: HOPKINS ASSOCIATES

Ticket Cap

Take me out to the ball game and don't forget my hat! This fun-to-make, fun-to-wear cap makes great use of old ticket stubs by laminating them and trimming them with felt pieces. Add favorite sports pins to personalize the cap for that dedicated sports fan. For a matching key ring he'll never lose, laminate a special ticket stub. Instructions for both projects are on page 69.

DESIGNER: MARGARET SINDELAR
PHOTOGRAPHER: HOPKINS ASSOCIATES

Fishing Hat

Here's a whimsical cap an avid fisherman will love to wear while baiting hooks. This catch-of-the-day hat features a patchwork fish trimmed in colorful blanket stitches. Real lures and a backstitched name worked in pearl cotton add the perfect finishing touches. Complete instructions and pattern are on page 69.

DESIGNER: MARGARET SINDELAR
PHOTOGRAPHER: HOPKINS ASSOCIATES

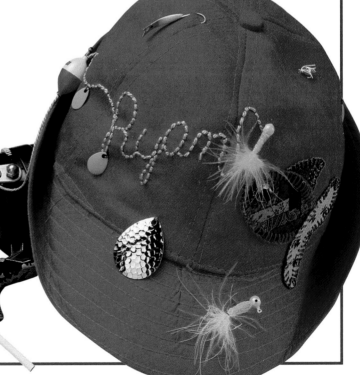

Wintry Hot Pads

Here's a set of homespun hot pads that truly spells crafting fun! This frosty set incorporates a touch of quilting, sponge-painting, and hand embroidery. The cabin and trees are appliquéd on the "let it snow" hot pad while the primitive snowmen and trees on the companion project are sponged on using paint. Complete instructions and patterns for this wintry set begin on page 70.

DESIGNER: SUSAN CAGE-KNOCH ● PHOTOGRAPHER: SCOTT LITTLE

Chicken Hot Pads

Country charm comes to the kitchen with these clever hot pads sewn into lovable chicken shapes. For just chicken feed, you can duplicate these feathered friends using a variety of colors and fabrics. And since the sewing can be done on the machine, a dozen kitchen helpers can be made in an evening. Instructions and patterns begin on page 72.

DESIGNER: JIM WILLIAMS ● PHOTOGRAPHER: SCOTT LITTLE

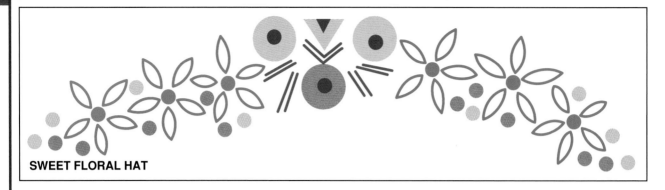

SWEET FLORAL HAT

SWEET FLORAL HAT

As shown on page 63.

MATERIALS

Tracing paper
White dressmaker's carbon
  paper
Purchased soft black felt hat
  with large brim
Deep pink, medium pink, light
  pink, bright green, yellow
  green, and light blue tapestry
  yarn scraps
Large crewel needle
Tailor's chalk; black thread

INSTRUCTIONS

Trace the pattern, *above,* onto
tracing paper. Use dressmaker's
carbon paper to transfer pattern
onto underside of brim of hat at
center front. Referring to the
diagrams, *right,* stitch the three
round flowers and the one triangular flower in center motif using
three plies of yarn. Use dark pink
yarn and satin stitches for center
(step 1) of every flower. Use
medium pink yarn and straight
stitches for four petals (steps 2
and 3) of center flower and light
pink for the petals of the outer
two flowers. Work triangular
flower using red yarn and satin
stitches for center and medium
pink yarn for the outer petals.
Work the leaves using bright
green yarn and straight stitches.

Work the blue petaled flowers
on each side of the center motif

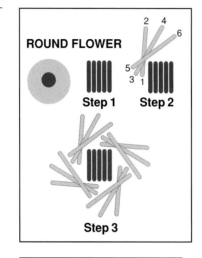

ROUND FLOWER

Step 1 Step 2

Step 3

TRIANGULAR FLOWER
Step 1 Step 2

using lazy daisy stitches and three
plies of blue yarn. Work a yellow
green French knot in the center of
each flower. Work the remaining
circles indicated on the pattern
using light or medium pink yarn
and French knots.

Use tailor's chalk to randomly
mark the positions for nine or ten
round flowers on the crown of the
hat, spacing flowers about 2 inches apart. Work one round flower
and four leaves at each mark,
using dark pink yarn for the centers, light or medium pink yarn
for the petals, and bright green
yarn for the leaves.

Turn the hat brim up and tack it
to the crown of the hat using
black thread.

BERIBBONED HAT

As shown on page 64.

MATERIALS

Felt hat with plain or
  whipstitched brim
2 yards of ⅛-inch-wide leather
  lacing or ribbon (optional)
Gold metallic thread; needle
Small pink beads from old
  necklace or other jewelry
2 yards of 2-inch-wide burgundy
  organdy ribbon
2 yards of 2-inch-wide fuchsia
  organdy ribbon
One heavily beaded drop or hoop
  earring
Three carnation rosettes in
  desired colors
Crafts glue

INSTRUCTIONS

For hat with plain brim, work
whipstitches around the brim,
spacing stitches ½ inch from edge
and ¾ inch apart. Use gold thread
to sew the pink beads at the top
of each stitch.

Measure circumference of hat
just above brim; add 12 inches.
Cut a piece of each ribbon that
length. Layer ribbons, one on top
of the other. Wrap around hat and
criss-cross at one side, leaving
6-inch tails. Tack ribbons to hat at
point where they cross. Layer
remaining ribbons; tie a double-
looped bow. Tack bow to side of
hat; stitch earring to center. Glue
rosettes to center of bow.

FISHING HAT

As shown on page 65, finished fish appliqué measures 3x3½ inches.

MATERIALS
Tracing paper
6x6-inch piece of muslin
6x6-inch piece of paper-backed iron-on adhesive
Erasable fabric marker
2x4-inch piece *each* of blue and yellow cotton fabric
Red sportsman's cap
Ten ¾x2-inch strips of six different red, green, brown, and blue cotton prints
Red #5 pearl cotton
Green #5 pearl cotton
#3 pearl cotton in desired color for name
Crewel needle
10-millimeter blue glass animal eye with shank
Old fishing flies, lures, and small bobber

INSTRUCTIONS
Trace fish body, fin, tail, and mouth patterns, *above right*, onto tracing paper and cut out. Cut fish body from muslin.

Draw around mouth, fin, and tail patterns, wrong side up, on paper side of iron-on adhesive; cut out. Following manufacturer's directions, fuse the fin and mouth pieces to blue fabric and the tail piece to yellow fabric. Cut out pieces. Following manufacturer's instructions, fuse mouth in place on muslin fish body. Fuse the fin and tail to small pieces of muslin, cut out, and set aside.

To strip piece fish body, use fabric marker to transfer diagonal stitching lines to muslin. Press under ¼ inch on one long edge of each ¾x2-inch strip of fabric. Lay the first strip on the fish, right sides together, with fold of strip on line 1 of muslin and larger portion of strip facing mouth. Stitch along fold. Press strip back over muslin so strip is right side up. Lay second strip on line 2 (across first strip) and stitch along fold. Press second strip back over muslin. Continue until all strips are used. Turn muslin over and trim all strips even with cut edge of muslin.

Pin fin, body, and tail to hat, referring to photograph, *page 65*. Overlap the body ¼ inch over the fin and tail ¼ inch over body. Work buttonhole stitches around body, fin, and tail, using red and green #5 pearl cotton as desired.

Make a tiny slit for eye. Push animal eye shank through hat to inside. Knot pearl cotton around shank to secure.

Write desired name freehand on hat as shown in photograph using fabric marking pen. Extend last letter to within 1 inch of fish's mouth. Backstitch name using #3 pearl cotton. Attach a fly close to fish's mouth at end of name. Attach the additional lures, hooks, and the bobber to the hat randomly using pearl cotton.

FIN

TAIL

Top front MOUTH

Mouth area

BODY

5 7 9
3
1
2
4
6 8 10

FISHING HAT

TICKET CAP AND KEY RING

As shown on page 65.

MATERIALS
Ticket stubs from sports events
Scraps of felted imitation suede or felt slightly larger than tickets in assorted colors
Scissors; fabric glue
Pinking shears
Purchased baseball cap
Assorted sports pins
Round metal key ring

INSTRUCTIONS
Laminate tickets at a photo copy store. (Color-copy and reduce large tickets before laminating, if desired.)

Trim laminate to ½ inch from ticket edges. Glue each ticket to a scrap of imitation suede, spreading glue under ticket area only. Cut around ticket a scant ¼ inch from edge using pinking shears. Glue finished pieces to hat. Add sports pins, if desired.

For key ring, laminate a full-size ticket with heavy-weight plastic. Trim to desired shape. Punch hole in one end; insert key ring.

SNOWMAN AND TREE HOT PAD

As shown on page 66, hot pad measures 6½x6½ inches.

MATERIALS
Tracing paper
Synthetic sponge
Black fine-line marker
Scissors
7½x5-inch piece of black cotton fabric
5x5-inch piece of white cotton fabric
8x26-inch piece of green print cotton fabric
Green and white acrylic paints
Paintbrush
Sewing thread to match fabrics
6½x6½-inch piece of batting
Embroidery needle
White, spruce green, and orange cotton embroidery floss
25 white seed pearls
Five ⁷⁄₁₆-inch-diameter pearl shirt buttons
One ½-inch-diameter button
4-inch piece of ⅜-inch-wide green ribbon

INSTRUCTIONS
Trace the snowman and tree patterns, *opposite*. Cut out. Draw around each pattern on the sponge using marker. Cut out with scissors.

Cut five 2½x2½-inch squares from black fabric and four 2½x2½-inch squares from white fabric. From the green fabric, cut a 6½x6½-inch square back and a 1x26-inch binding. All of the measurements include ¼-inch seam allowances.

To sponge-paint, wet both sponges and squeeze out all excess water. Brush green paint on top of the tree sponge and test the thickness of the paint by sponging on paper first. Sponge

paint a tree in the center of each white block. Repeat the process for the snowmen, sponging white paint on the black fabric squares. When paint is completely dry, heat-set it by ironing on the wrong side of the fabric.

Sew blocks together in rows of three. For top and bottom row, sew a white square between two black squares. For middle row, sew a black square between two white squares. Stitch rows together, referring to photograph, *page 66*. Place batting under hot pad top and quilt (using short running stitches) around trees, snowmen, and perimeter of each block using one ply of green floss on the white blocks and one ply of white floss on the black blocks.

For snowmen's noses, use two plies of orange embroidery floss to work four ¼-inch-long straight stitches in a narrow V shape at the center of face; loop thread around straight stitches two or three times and secure to fabric near the bottom of the straight stitches. Sew seed pearls to the snowmen for eyes and buttons, using one ply of white floss and referring to photograph, *page 66*, for the placement. Sew the shirt buttons to four corners of the center block.

Pin back to batting, wrong sides together, and stitch around edges. Trim batting and backing even with top. Sew the binding strip to front of hot pad with raw edges together; trim the excess length. Fold the binding over back of hot pad; turn remaining raw edge under ¼ inch. Hand-sew in place, mitering the corners.

Fold the 4-inch piece of ribbon into a loop. Secure the ends to the corner of hot pad by sewing remaining buttons on top of the loop, stitching through all of the layers and eyes of both buttons.

LET IT SNOW HOT PAD

As shown on page 66, hot pad measures 8x9⅜ inches.

MATERIALS
Tracing paper
12½x5-inch piece of sky blue cotton fabric
3x7½-inch piece of white cotton fabric
10x35-inch piece of pine green cotton print fabric
3x7½-inch piece of brown print cotton fabric
8 inches of ¼-inch-wide rust satin ribbon
8x9½-inch piece of batting
Light blue sewing thread
Rust, white, and pine green embroidery floss
Embroidery needle
Dressmaker's carbon paper

INSTRUCTIONS
Trace the patterns and lettering, *opposite,* onto tracing paper. Cut out the patterns. The snow and block patterns include a ⅛-inch seam allowance.

Cut the following: nine sky blue blocks and nine white strips for snow. Cut satin ribbon into nine ¾-inch-long pieces. From green fabric, cut an 8x9½-inch backing and a 1¼x35-inch binding, leaving a rectangle at least 7x14 inches. Fold rectangle in half, right sides together, to make a 7x7-inch square. Draw around tree pattern on doubled fabric eight times, leaving ¼ inch between each tree. Machine stitch all the way around each tree. Cut out trees, leaving ⅛-inch seam allowance around each tree. Cut a slit in center of one side of each tree; turn right side out and press. Set trees aside.

Fold brown fabric in half; draw around house pattern. Sew around house leaving bottom open. Trim sides and roof, leaving ⅛-inch

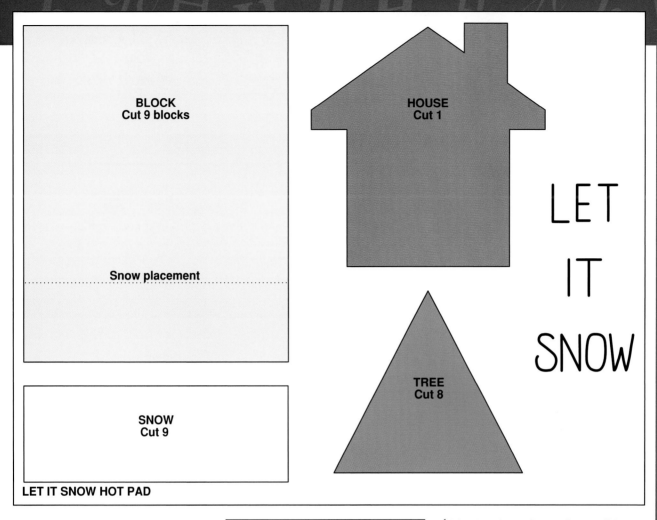

BLOCK
Cut 9 blocks

Snow placement

SNOW
Cut 9

HOUSE
Cut 1

TREE
Cut 8

LET

IT

SNOW

LET IT SNOW HOT PAD

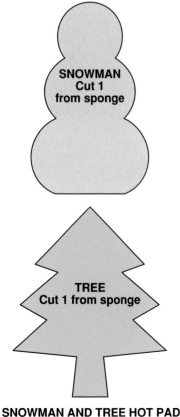

SNOWMAN
Cut 1
from sponge

TREE
Cut 1 from sponge

SNOWMAN AND TREE HOT PAD

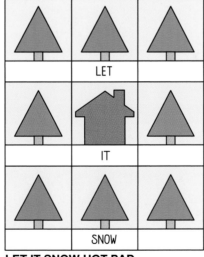

LET

IT

SNOW

**LET IT SNOW HOT PAD
ASSEMBLY DIAGRAM**

seam allowance. Trim bottom on marked line. Turn and press. Pin house to one blue block with bottom extending ⅛-inch below placement line.

For each block, fold one long edge of each white strip under ⅛ inch. Pin a piece of rust ribbon to center of eight strips, right sides together, with one raw edge of ribbon is aligned with raw edge on folded side. Lay the ninth white strip on house block, right sides together, with fold on placement line. Lay strips with ribbon on remaining blue blocks, aligning fold and placement line in same manner. Sew along the fold of each white strip. Press snow towards the bottom of each block and ribbon or house toward top. Pin one tree, slit side down, to the unstitched end of each ribbon.

Appliqué house and trees to blocks. Sew blocks together in rows of three. For top and bottom row, sew three trees together. For middle row, sew the house square between two tree squares. Stitch rows together, referring to photograph, *page 66*. Place batting under hot pad top and quilt (using

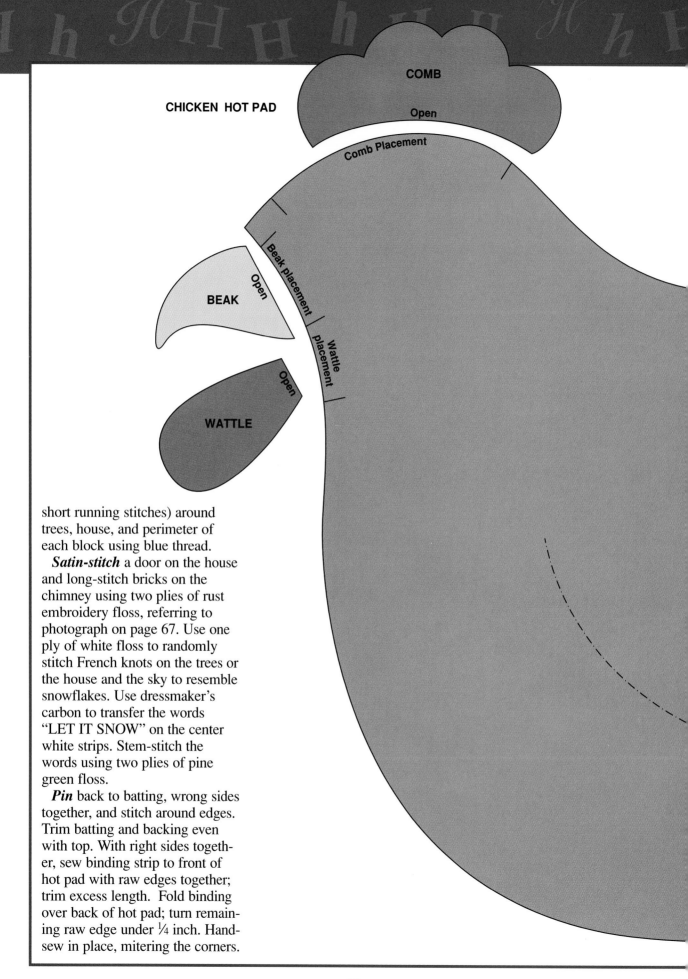

CHICKEN HOT PAD

COMB

Open

Comb Placement

BEAK

Open

Beak placement

Open

WATTLE

Wattle placement

short running stitches) around trees, house, and perimeter of each block using blue thread.

Satin-stitch a door on the house and long-stitch bricks on the chimney using two plies of rust embroidery floss, referring to photograph on page 67. Use one ply of white floss to randomly stitch French knots on the trees or the house and the sky to resemble snowflakes. Use dressmaker's carbon to transfer the words "LET IT SNOW" on the center white strips. Stem-stitch the words using two plies of pine green floss.

Pin back to batting, wrong sides together, and stitch around edges. Trim batting and backing even with top. With right sides together, sew binding strip to front of hot pad with raw edges together; trim excess length. Fold binding over back of hot pad; turn remaining raw edge under ¼ inch. Hand-sew in place, mitering the corners.

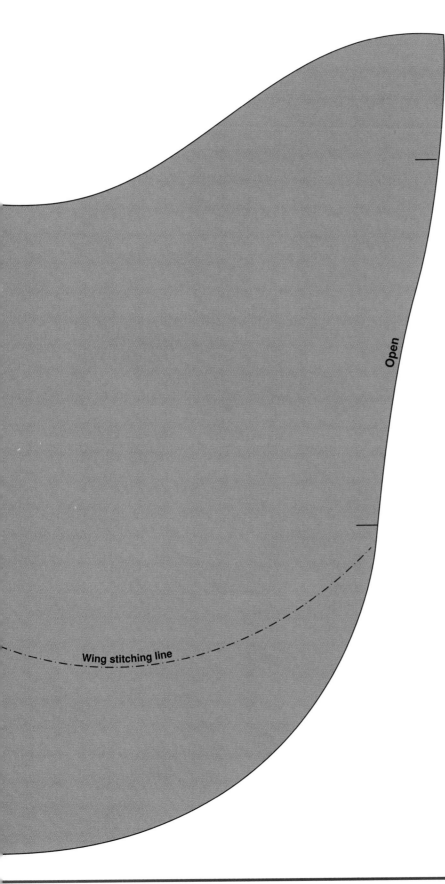

Open

Wing stitching line

CHICKEN HOT PADS

As shown on page 67, hot pads measure 8½x10 inches.

MATERIALS
Tracing paper
10x10-inch piece of batting
10x20-inch piece of fabric for body
Erasable fabric marker
8x3-inch piece of red print fabric
2x2½-inch piece of yellow or gold fabric
Sewing threads to match fabrics
⅜-inch-diameter yellow button

INSTRUCTIONS
Trace patterns, *left;* cut out. Body pattern includes ¼-inch seam allowances. Sew seams with right sides facing.

Cut one body from the batting and trim ⅜ inch from the edges. Fold the body fabric in half, right sides facing, to form a square. Cut two bodies and transfer the markings from pattern.

Fold red fabric in half, right sides facing; draw around comb pattern once and wattle pattern twice, but *do not* cut. Fold gold fabric in half; draw around beak pattern once, but *do not* cut. Stitch around wattle, comb, and beak outlines, leaving openings. Trim fabric around each, leaving ¼-inch seam allowances. Clip curves, turn, and press.

Baste comb and beak to right side of one body piece, matching raw edges. Position wattles together and baste to body in same manner.

Sew body together, leaving opening as indicated. Clip curves, turn, and press. Insert batting into body; adjust as necessary to fit. Sew opening closed.

Topstitch ¼ inch from edge of body and along wing line. Stitch button eye to one side.

I is for *Incredible Initials*

Elegant Ribbon Initials

Old-fashioned stitchery shimmers with the soft sheen of silk, embroidered into a classic floral alphabet. Use our full-size alphabet on pages 78–79 to make this handkerchief, box, or brooch, or use your imagination to add a touch of silk ribbon embroidery to all the items on your gift-giving list. Complete instructions begin on page 77.

DESIGNER: MARGARET SINDELAR ● PHOTOGRAPHER: HOPKINS ASSOCIATES

Playful Stenciled Alphabet

Decorative craft projects are as easy as ABC when you stencil our letters on books, blocks, linens—or an unadorned chambray jumper as shown above. Add a cat and mouse for a whimsical homespun touch. Instructions are on page 77. The alphabet and cat-and-mouse patterns appear on pages 80–81.

DESIGNER: SUSAN CAGE-KNOCH ● PHOTOGRAPHER: SCOTT LITTLE

Versatile Needlepoint Alphabet

With our needlepoint alphabet, you can add a personal touch to dozens of hand-stitched gifts, starting with our striking luggage tag and colorful bargello eyeglass case. Simply follow our complete instructions beginning on page 79 to create any monogram in your favorite color combinations. The chart for the alphabet appears on page 82.

DESIGNER: MARGARET SINDELAR ● PHOTOGRAPHER: SCOTT LITTLE

ELEGANT RIBBON INITIALS

As shown on page 74.

MATERIALS *for each letter*
Tracing paper; crewel needle
Dressmaker's carbon paper
4 mm silk ribbon in four different
  colors
For handkerchief
Purchased linen handkerchief
  with hemstitched edge
For brooch
6x6-inch piece of velveteen
1⅞-inch-diameter button form
6 inches of ½-inch-wide flat lace
Crafts glue; wire cutters
Pin back; all-purpose cement
For box
3x3-inch papier-mâché box with
  lid
4x4-inch piece of felted
  imitation suede
3x13-inch piece of striped
  cotton fabric
Two 3x3-inch squares of
  polyester fleece
13-inch piece *each* of two
  different ½-inch-wide flat
  braids
Paper-backed iron-on adhesive
Crafts glue

INSTRUCTIONS

Trace desired initial, *pages 78–79.* Transfer initial to specified fabric. Begin at one end of initial with first ribbon color and work a lazy daisy stitch. Outline initial with a long-and-short backstitch and end each letter with a lazy daisy stitch. With a second ribbon color, work a lazy daisy flower in center of initial. Use a third ribbon color for the French knots in center of flower. Add lazy daisy leaves in a fourth ribbon color.

For handkerchief, position initial diagonally in corner, 2 inches above point. When stitching is complete, thread a length of ribbon through hemstitched edge.

For brooch, center and stitch initial on velveteen. Center initial on button form; trim fabric ½ inch beyond edge. Run a gathering thread ¼ inch beyond cut edge. Tighten gathers. Assemble button following manufacturer's instructions. Remove shank. Attach pin back with cement.

For box, transfer initial to center of imitation suede. Complete embroidery, adding French knots and lazy daisy leaves to corners. Glue two layers of fleece to top of box lid. Center initial over fleece. Glue edges to sides of lid, mitering corners. Trim extra fabric. Glue flat braid around sides. Fuse iron-on adhesive to wrong side of striped fabric following manufacturer's instructions; fuse to outside of box. Glue flat braid around bottom edge of box.

PLAYFUL STENCILED ALPHABET

As shown on jumper on page 75.

MATERIALS
Two 9x12-inch pieces of stencil
  acetate
Permanent fine-line black marker
Crafts knife and cutting mat
Masking tape
Purchased chambray or denim
  jumper
Red, green, blue, gray, and
  antique gold acrylic paints
Four medium stencil brushes
One large stencil brush
White vinegar; spray bottle
Cotton towel; black seed beads
Scraps of ribbon; two small bells

INSTRUCTIONS

Trace alphabet, *pages 80–81,* onto one sheet of stencil acetate using fine-line marker (step 1, page 81). Trace cat and mouse onto second sheet. Cut out and remove inside of each shape using crafts knife and mat (step 2).

Tear off long strips of masking tape to use on hem of jumper. Lay tape on hem of jumper as a guide for stenciling, if necessary. Lay stencil on jumper, aligning bottom of letters with upper edge of tape. Use additional masking tape to keep stencil in position.

Stencil letters with red, green, and blue paints, alternating colors until hem of jumper is completely stenciled and using a separate medium stencil brush for each paint color (step 3).

Use a medium stencil brush and gray paint to stencil the mouse five times, positioning mice as if they are running diagonally across the front of the bodice. Randomly stencil additional letters on the bodice of the jumper with red, green, and blue paint.

Lay tape on the skirt from the right front waist, diagonally toward the hem at left front. Stencil the phrases, "cat & mouse" and "run, mouse, run" on skirt as for alphabet, using the top of the tape as a guide. Stencil the cat chasing the mouse twice, once above each phrase. Use the large stencil brush and antique gold for the cat and gray for the mouse. Remove all of the tape and allow the paint to dry completely.

Pour white vinegar into spray bottle and spritz onto a cotton towel. Lay dampened towel over stenciled areas and press with a medium to hot iron to set paint, leaving iron on each painted area for approximately 3 seconds.

Sew a seed bead to each mouse for an eye. Tie ribbons into bows and stitch them to the necks of the stenciled cats. Secure small bells to the ribbons.

**ELEGANT RIBBON
INITIALS**

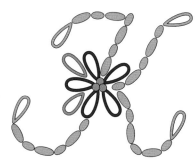

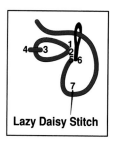

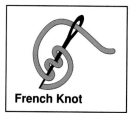

Lazy Daisy Stitch

French Knot

NEEDLEPOINT EYEGLASS CASE

As shown on page 76, finished size is 3½x 6½ inches.

MATERIALS
10x10-inch piece of 10-count needlepoint canvas
3 yards *each* of 12 different colors of 3-ply needlepoint wool yarn
Tapestry needle
15 yards of metallic yarn
7x7½-inch piece of cotton lining fabric

INSTRUCTIONS
Tape or zigzag edges of canvas to prevent fraying.

Measure 3½ inches from top and 4 inches from right edge of canvas. Work the top left-hand stitch of first initial (from chart *page 82*) there using continental stitches, *page 82,* and three plies of yarn. Leave one row of mesh and work second initial to the right of the first. Use metallic yarn and continental stitches to fill in around the letters and to work two rows on each side of the pair of initials. Work one row border of continental stitches around the metallic yarn stitches.

Measure 2½ inches from top and 1½ inches from right edge of canvas. Work first set of bargello stitches as shown in diagram, *page 82,* using three plies of darkest color yarn. Repeat eight times across top row.

Work second row immediately under first using a slightly lighter shade of yarn. Work third row in a shade of yarn lighter than the second, working compensating stitches around initial block. Work fourth row using metallic yarn.

Continue working bargello pattern around initials, stitching three rows in different shades of wool yarn and one row of metallic yarn. Work a total of four patterns of wool yarn, filling in stitches at top and bottom.

To finish, block needlepoint. Trim canvas ½ inch beyond stitching. Fold unstitched canvas at top to back. Work binding stitch, *page 82,* over two canvas threads along the fold. Turn remaining edges of canvas to back and fold case in half. Work binding stitch along bottom and sides, stitching over one thread from each side.

For lining, fold fabric rectangle in half, right sides together to form a 7x3¾-inch rectangle. Stitch sides and bottom edge, using a ¼-inch seam. Turn under ¼ inch along top edge. Slip lining into case, matching side seam. Slip stitch to case at top edge.

NEEDLEPOINT LUGGAGE TAG

As shown on page 76, finished size is 3x5 inches.

MATERIALS
4x6-inch piece of 10-count needlepoint canvas
Four yards *each* of four different colors of 3-ply needlepoint wool yarn
Four yards of metallic yarn
6x12-inch piece of felted imitation suede
Tapestry needle; pinking shears
Two ¾-inch D-rings

INSTRUCTIONS
Tape or zigzag edges of canvas to prevent fraying.

Select initials from chart, *page 82.* Find center of canvas and begin stitching center of middle
Continued on page 82

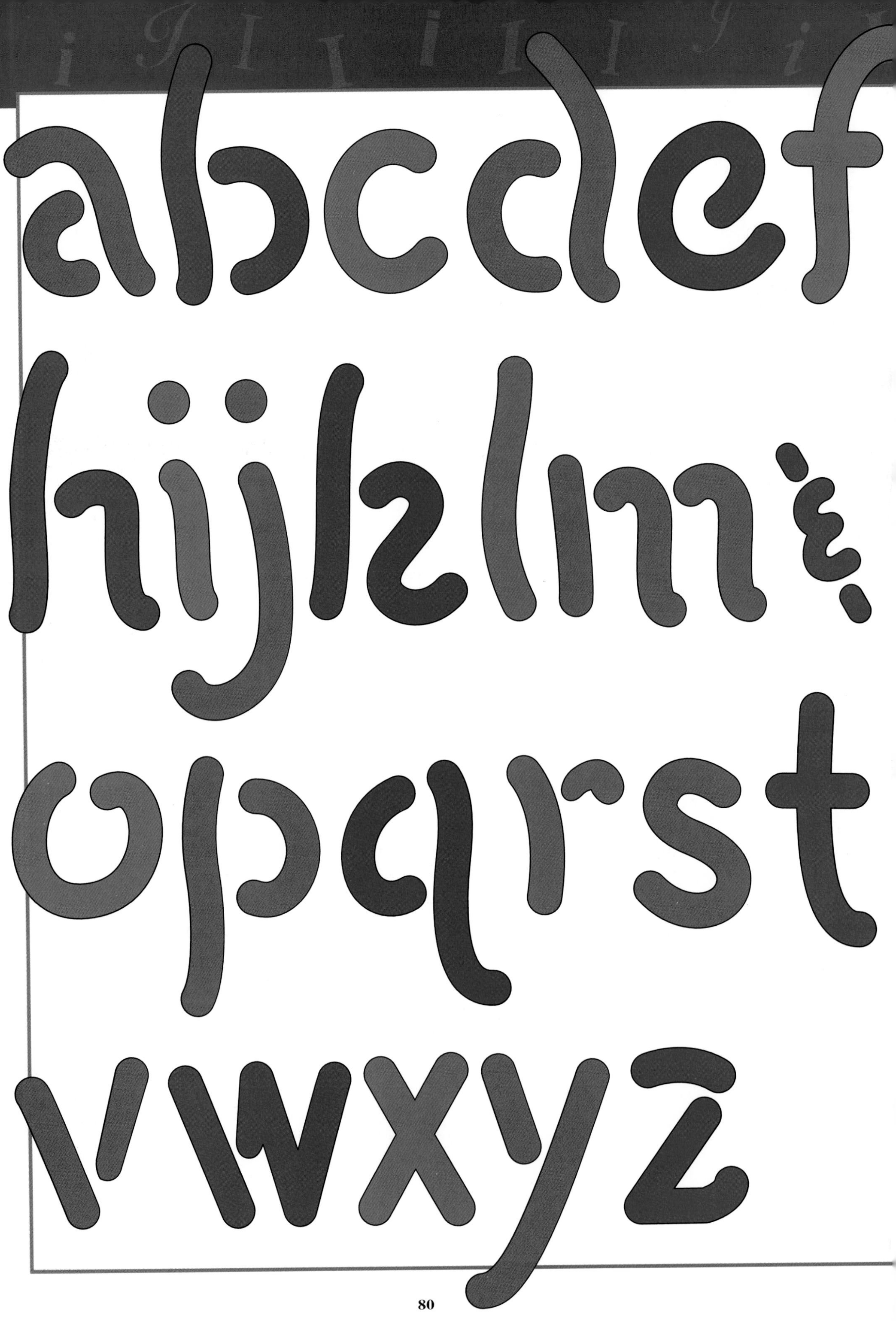

abcdef

hijklmn

opqrst

vwxyz

PLAYFUL STENCILED ALPHABET

1. *Place a sheet of stencil acetate over the letters, left. Use a fine-tip permanent marker to outline each letter or design.*

2. *Place stencil acetate on a cutting mat or old magazine. Carefully cut around the marker outlines with a crafts knife. Remove the acetate center of each letter or design.*

3. *Tape the stencil to the fabric. Dip just the tip of the brush into paint. Set the tip down lightly in the opening of the stencil, then lift. Repeat this up and down motion until the opening is filled with paint.*

NEEDLEPOINT EYEGLASS CASE

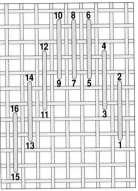

Bargello Stitch

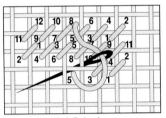

Continental Stitch

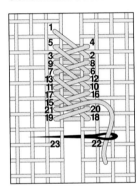

Binding Stitch

initial there using three plies of yarn and continental stitches. Leave one row of mesh on each side of middle initial and work first and last initials.

Use contrasting color yarn and continental stitches to fill in around the initials and to work two rows on each side of the initial block. Work first border row of continental stitches using a second contrasting color, a second border row of metallic yarn, a

third border row in a third contrasting color, fourth row of metallic yarn, and two rows of second contrasting yarn color. Block needlepoint.

Trim canvas to measure $2\frac{3}{4}$x$4\frac{1}{2}$ inches. From imitation suede, cut two $3\frac{1}{2}$x$5\frac{1}{2}$-inch rectangles and two 1x10-inch strips for strap. With pinking shears, cut a 2x4-inch opening in center of one rectangle, leaving a $\frac{3}{4}$-inch margin at top, bottom, and right

side. Center design under opening and topstitch through both layers close to pinked edge. Place second suede rectangle under needlepoint, matching edges. Topstitch through all layers $\frac{1}{4}$ inch beyond first stitching. On left side, topstitch again, forming a point between the two corners about $\frac{3}{8}$ inch beyond second topstitching. Trim $\frac{1}{8}$ inch beyond topstitching with pinking shears.

For strap, topstitch strips together $\frac{3}{8}$ inch in from edge all around, tapering to a point at one end. Trim $\frac{1}{8}$ inch beyond topstitching with pinking shears. Fold straight end over D rings; topstitch in place. Cut slit in pointed end of tag; insert strap.

J is for *Jingle-Jangle Jewelry*

Button Heart Necklaces

You'll fall in love with these romantic heart necklaces—especially because they are so simple to make! Soft-sculpted from muslin and batting, they're covered with buttons for an old-fashioned look. Add charms, roses, or a soft oil-paint blush to give each necklace a personality of its own. Complete instructions and pattern are on page 85.

DESIGNER: MARGARET SINDELAR ● PHOTOGRAPHER: SCOTT LITTLE

Hooked Rug Jewelry

*Using a simple rug-hooking technique, create your own unique wearable art.
These folk art pins and necklace take shape in soft colors, using narrow strips
of wool to make traditional designs. Instructions and patterns begin opposite.*

DESIGNER: MARGARET SINDELAR ● PHOTOGRAPHER: SCOTT LITTLE

Simple Fabric Jewelry

*Accessorize your wardrobe with
our lovely fabric jewelry, using
fabric scraps to match or contrast
with your favorite outfits. Add
charms or beads to add an
elegant touch and create a
different fashion statement with
every one you make. Complete
instructions and pattern
are on page 86.*

DESIGNER: JIM WILLIAMS
PHOTOGRAPHER: HOPKINS ASSOCIATES

BUTTON HEART NECKLACES

As shown on page 83.

MATERIALS
For each necklace
Tracing paper
Erasable fabric marker
3x7-inch piece of muslin
6x7-inch piece of batting
50 to 75 small pearl buttons
**Ivory embroidery floss or gold
    metallic thread**
**Satin ribbon rose or brass bow
    charm**
Crafts glue
**1 yard of narrow satin cord or
    metallic trim**
**⅓ yard of ¾-inch-wide flat lace
    (optional)**
**Fine-tip gold metallic ink pen
    (optional)**
Oil stick stencil paint (optional)

INSTRUCTIONS
Trace pattern, *below;* cut out. Fold muslin in half with the right sides together, to form a 3x3½-inch rectangle. Draw around heart pattern on doubled muslin. Stitch along heart shape. Cut out, leaving a ⅛-inch seam allowance. Clip curves. Make a small slit in back. Turn right side out.

Cut several heart shapes from batting. Insert layers through slit in muslin. Whipstitch closed.

For heart with rose, stitch buttons onto the heart at random,

using ivory floss. Sew through all layers, pulling the floss tight to curve heart. Glue the lace to the back around the outside edge, gathering slightly. Stitch the ends of the satin cord to the center of the heart, adjusting the length as desired. Apply glue to ends of cord to prevent fraying. Glue ribbon rose to center of heart.

For heart with bow charm, use gold pen to draw around edges of each button. Stitch buttons onto heart with gold metallic thread, pulling tightly to curve heart. Stitch ends of metallic trim to center of heart, adjusting length as desired. Apply glue to ends of trim to prevent fraying. Buff buttons with oil stick stencil paint. Add brass bow charm to center.

HOOKED RUG JEWELRY

As shown opposite.

MATERIALS
Tracing paper; transfer pen
**12-inch scraps of wool fabric in
    the following colors: light
    green, dark green, light yellow,
    medium yellow, pink, purple,
    light rust, and dark rust**
**5x9-inch scrap of 30- to
    40-count even-weave fabric**
Hoop or frame; hook
Crafts glue
For pins:
Scraps of felt
  Pin backs; all-purpose cement
  For heart necklace:
    **2-inch heart-shaped jewelry
       form**
    **¼ yard of ¼-inch-wide flat
       braid**
    1 yard of gold cord

INSTRUCTIONS
Trace patterns, *right.* Transfer to even-weave fabric, leaving at least 1 inch between designs. Cut wool

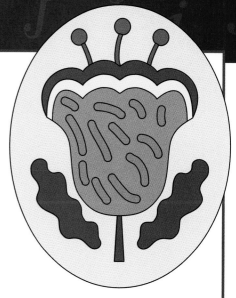

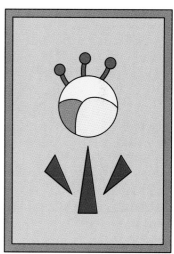

HOOKED RUG JEWELRY

into ¼-inch-wide strips following lengthwise grain of fabric.

To hook designs, mount even-weave fabric in hoop or frame. Hold one end of a wool strip under even-weave fabric. Push hook between threads from top and pull end of wool through to right side. Move two threads and repeat, pulling a loop to right side.

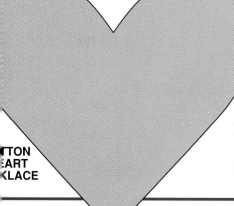

Keeping loop on hook, pull on wool from underside until loop is ⅛-inch tall. Referring to patterns on page 85 for colors, continue pulling up loops until entire area is covered. Trim ends even with loops.

For pins, coat back of hooked area with glue; let dry. Trim close to outer loops. Glue felt to back. Trim excess felt ⅛ inch beyond even-weave fabric. Repeat with contrasting felt. Attach pin back with cement.

For necklace, attach heart design to jewelry form according to manufacturer's directions. Glue flat braid around outside edge. Add gold cord for chain.

FABRIC NECK COLLAR

As shown on page 84.

MATERIALS
12x14-inch piece of tracing paper
Erasable fabric marker
Two 12x14-inch pieces of floral drapery, printed silk, or damask fabric
Sewing thread
2-inch piece of Velcro
24-inch length of ¾-inch-wide lace or other trims (optional)
Beads and/or charms

INSTRUCTIONS
Fold tracing paper in half; trace pattern, *right,* aligning folds. Cut

out and unfold. Layer fabrics, right sides together, and draw around pattern with fold on straight grain of fabric.

Stitch two layers together, right sides facing, leaving a 4-inch opening along curve for turning. Cut out ¼ inch beyond stitching; clip curves, turn, and press. Sew opening closed. Sew Velcro to strap ends.

If desired, stitch lace to outside edge of collar. Glue or stitch beads or charms to collar.

FABRIC CORD NECKLACE

As shown on page 84.

MATERIALS
2½x24-inch strip of floral chintz fabric
Sewing thread to match fabric
20-inch piece of ¾-inch-diameter upholstery cording
String; safety pin or paper clip
⅔ yard of pearls by the yard
Two ¼-inch-diameter metal end caps
Hot glue gun and glue stick
One gold metal necklace clasp
Two split rings
Needle nose pliers

INSTRUCTIONS
Fold fabric strip in half lengthwise, right sides together. Stitch long edge, using ¼-inch seam allowance and leaving ends open. Turn right side out.

Tie string to one end of cording and wrap tightly to prevent raveling; secure string leaving a loose tail. Tie loose end of string to safety pin or paper clip. Insert pin or clip into fabric tube and pull cording into tube. Gather fabric evenly along cording.

Trim cording to 18 inches leaving ½ inch of fabric tube extending beyond cording ends. Sew a gathering thread around each end of fabric tube and pull as tight as possible, but *do not* cut thread. Wrap pearls around fabric tube in a spiral pattern. Wrap gathering threads tightly around ends of fabric tube and pearls; secure. Hot-glue fabric ends into metal end caps.

To finish, attach clasp to end caps with split rings.

Fold

FABRIC NECK COLLAR

K is for *Kindly Kittens*

Calico Kitten

*What could be more fun than to craft and cuddle our adorable painted kitten?
Dress her in a three-tier calico dress with lacy bloomers, then add painted features
and paws to give her real "purr-sonality." The complete instructions and patterns for
this frolicking feline can be found on pages 89–92.*

DESIGNER: SUSAN CAGE-KNOCH ● PHOTOGRAPHER: SCOTT LITTLE

Playful Beanbag Kittens

Cats love to stretch—and that's just what these soft-knit kittens are doing. Made from imitation suede, sleepwear fleece, or other fuzzy fabrics, these playful friends are quick and easy to make and give. Create their winsome expressions with button-thread whiskers and bead eyes, then give them ribbon collars for a final touch. Instructions are on page 92 and patterns are on page 93.

DESIGNER: PHYLLIS DUNSTAN
PHOTOGRAPHER: SCOTT LITTLE

Rosie the Kitten

Colorful details make this wooden kitten the cat's meow. Crafted from a scrap of pine, she's painted to perfection, with a rose-trimmed pinafore and polka-dot pantaloons. Simple to paint, she makes an ideal friend in a kitchen window or in a child's room. Complete instructions and the pattern for Rosie are on page 94.

DESIGNER: SUSAN CAGE-KNOCH
PHOTOGRAPHER: HOPKINS ASSOCIATES

CALICO KITTEN

As shown on page 87, kitten is 13 inches tall.

MATERIALS

Tracing paper
⅛ yard of 45-inch-wide black chintz fabric
2x4-inch piece of pink cotton fabric
6x8-inch piece of muslin
6x7-inch piece of calico
2½x11-inch piece of calico
1½x14-inch piece of calico
1½x16-inch piece of calico
White dressmaker's carbon paper; pencil
Fine-line red paint marker
Sewing thread to match fabrics
Polyester fiberfill
White, antique rose, sea green, and black acrylic paints
Artist's brushes
Black and white button thread
¼ yard of ⅞-inch-wide ivory lace
5 inches of ¼-inch-wide ivory satin ribbon
16 inches of 2½-inch-wide ivory lace
Scrap of red cotton fabric

INSTRUCTIONS

Trace patterns, *pages 90–91*; cut out. All patterns and measurements include a ¼-inch seam allowance. Sew all seams with right sides facing unless otherwise specified.

Cut body pieces, head pieces arms, legs, tail, and *two* ears from from chintz fabric. Cut two ears from pink cotton fabric. Cut bloomers from muslin.

Cut bodice pieces and sleeves from 6x7-inch piece of calico. Cut cuffs and a 1½x11-inch piece from 2½x11-inch piece of calico.

Transfer face and paws onto appropriate pieces, using a sharp pencil and dressmaker's carbon paper. Draw over lines of mouth, nose, and paws with red paint marker. (Paint marker lines will fade through white paint after white paint has dried.)

Sew each pink ear piece to a chintz ear piece, leaving open along bottom. Clip corners and turn right side out. Press.

Stitch darts in head as indicated on pattern, *page 90*. Pin ears to head front as indicated on pattern, raw edges together. Sew head backs together along center back, from top to mark indicated on pattern. Pin head front to backs, with ears inside, and stitch around head, leaving neck edge open.

Sew tail pieces together, leaving straight edge open. Turn right side out. Stuff firmly with polyester fiberfill and baste to one body back as indicated on pattern. Stitch body backs together along center back seam from just above tail to bottom.

Stitch dart in body front as indicated on pattern. Sew body front and backs together at *shoulders only.* Sew head to body, stitching around neck several times to reinforce it.

For arms, sew pieces together in pairs, leaving tops open for stuffing. Clip curves and turn. Stuff arms firmly with fiberfill, stopping about ½ inch from top. Pin arms to body front as indicated on pattern. Sew side seams of body. *Do not* turn.

For legs, sew pieces together in pairs, leaving tops open. Clip curves and turn right side out. Stuff legs firmly with fiberfill, stopping about ½ inch from top. Bring seams together and pin. Slip legs between body front and back, heels facing the back, positioning open edge of legs between marks indicated on pattern. Sew across bottom of body, with arms and legs inside, being careful not to catch limbs in stitching. (Allow hands and feet to stick out center back opening, if necessary.) Clip curves and turn.

Turn under raw edges of center back edges. Hand-stitch head opening closed, but leave thread hanging. Stuff head firmly with fiberfill. Continue stuffing body, alternately stitching to close opening and adding stuffing.

To paint kitten, follow painting lines indicated on pattern. Allow each color to dry to the touch before painting a second color on top of it. Use a flat brush and white paint for tail and four paws. Dip tip of brush in paint and apply to tip of each limb feathering to a dry brush technique while working toward body. Paint muzzle white. Use a very fine brush and light strokes to paint white eyelashes under eyes.

Fill in marker outlines on paws and nose with rose paint. Use rose around outside of eye. Add water to make a wash to dab on cheeks and center of ear fronts. Paint irises of eyes green. Outline mouth with black paint and add small black dots to cheeks. Paint pupils black. Add white highlights to eyes and nose. Allow all paint to dry completely.

For whiskers, thread a needle with two strands of black or white button thread. Make a knot in one end, leaving a 1½-inch tail. Insert needle on one side of nose. Bring needle out on other side. Knot thread, securing it close to fabric. Cut thread, leaving a 1½-inch tail. Make two sets of whiskers with each color thread.

For bloomers, sew pieces together at center front and center back, leaving an opening in the center back seam as indicated on pattern. Cut ⅞-inch-wide lace into two 4½-inch lengths. Sew one length of lace to bottom of each bloomer leg. Press the seam

Continued on page 92

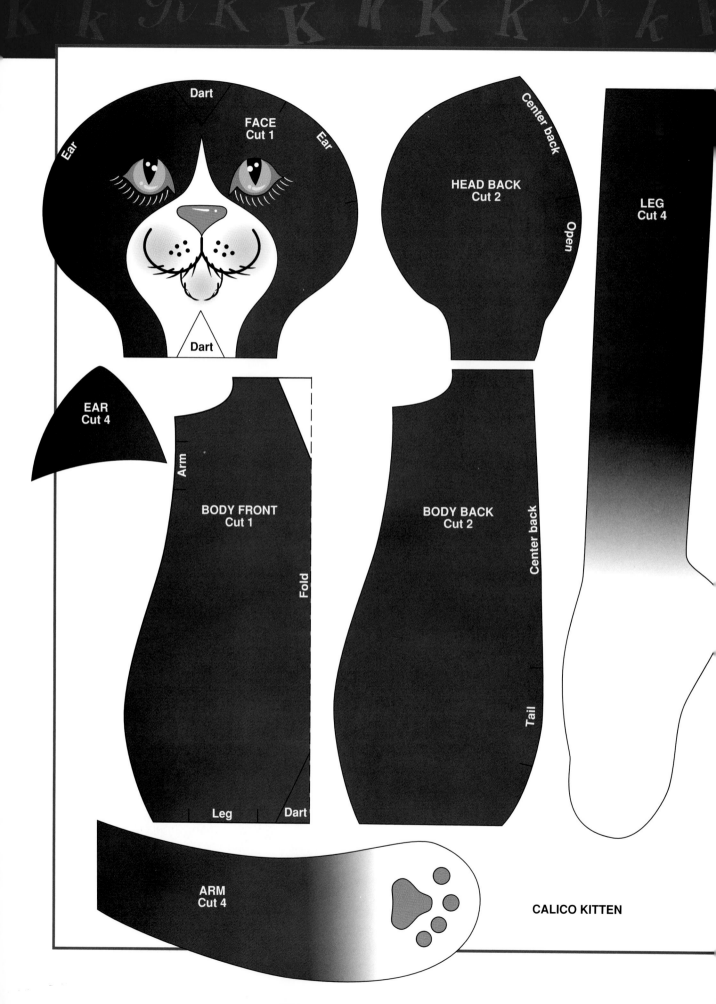

CALICO KITTEN

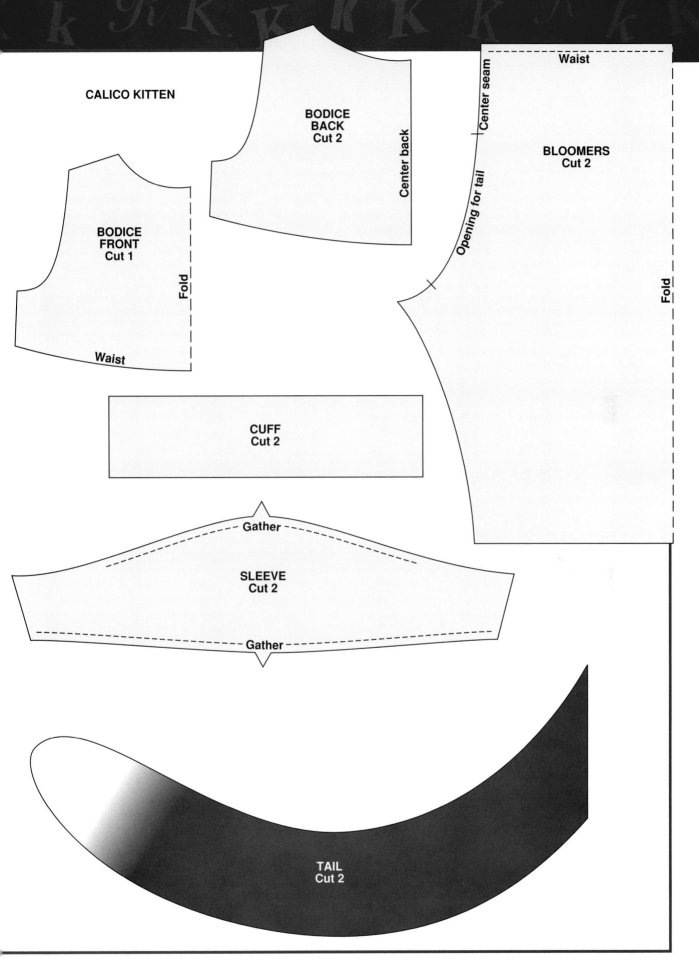

CALICO KITTEN

BODICE
BACK
Cut 2

Center back

BODICE
FRONT
Cut 1

Fold

Waist

Waist

Center seam

Opening for tail

BLOOMERS
Cut 2

Fold

CUFF
Cut 2

Gather

SLEEVE
Cut 2

Gather

TAIL
Cut 2

toward bloomers. Topstitch across bottom of each leg.

Sew inside leg seams. Turn under raw edges of tail opening in back and topstitch. Turn bloomers right side out. Turn under raw edges of waist and sew gathering stitches around. Pull up gathers to fit cat and secure.

For dress, sew bodice front to backs at shoulders. Press seam open. Sew satin ribbon to neck opening of bodice. Clip curve and turn ribbon to wrong side. Secure with small running stitches.

Sew gathering stitches at top and bottom edges of sleeve pieces as indicated on pattern. Pull top gathers to fit armhole and sew sleeve to bodice. Fold cuffs in half lengthwise with *wrong sides* facing and press. Gather bottom of sleeve to fit cuff. Pin sleeve to cuff, raw edges even, and sew pieces together. Repeat with other cuff. Sew underarm/side seams.

Turn under one long edge of 1½x16-inch calico strip and topstitch. Pin 2½-inch-wide lace under strip, top edge of lace aligned with raw edge of fabric. Sew a gathering thread close to raw edge. Sew a gathering thread along one long edge of each remaining 1½-inch-wide strip of calico. Pull up gathers on 11-inch strip to fit bottom of bodice and sew two pieces together. Pull up gathers on 14-inch strip to fit bottom of 11-inch strip and sew the two pieces together. Pull up gathers on 16-inch calico/lace strip to fit bottom of 14-inch strip and sew the two pieces together.

Sew short ends of lace and two bottom strips together. Turn under edges of back opening and hem.

Cut out a small heart shape from red fabric. Using a small running stitch, sew to front of bodice. Place dress on kitten and tack opening closed.

PLAYFUL BEANBAG KITTENS

As shown on page 88, each kitten is 9 inches long.

MATERIALS
For each kitten
Tracing paper
10x16-inch piece of children's sleepwear fleece or knitted suedecloth
Sewing thread to match fabric
Black button thread
Polyester fiberfill
Polyester stuffing pellets
Two 4-millimeter black beads
Scrap of black felt
⅓ yard of ¼- or ⅛-inch-wide ribbon
Small bell

INSTRUCTIONS
Trace patterns, *opposite,* onto tracing paper. Cut out the patterns. From the sleepwear fleece, cut two bodies, two tails, four ears, and two heads. All patterns include a ¼-inch seam allowance.

For body, sew body pieces together, right sides facing, leaving an opening between dots as indicated on pattern. Clip curves and turn body right side out. Lightly stuff paws with fiberfill and fill body with stuffing pellets. Hand-sew the opening closed. Use a double strand of the black button thread to stitch through the feet at the toe markings.

For head, sew head pieces together, leaving an opening between dots. Clip the curves and turn head right side out. Lightly stuff the head with fiberfill and hand-sew the opening closed.

For eyes, thread a needle with a double strand of black button thread. Insert needle at one of the Xs indicated on the pattern and bring it out at the other X,

catching the fiberfill inside of head. Thread a bead on the needle and take the needle back through the head to the first X, pulling gently to shape the nose. Thread the other bead on the needle. Repeat the stitch and secure the thread. Use a single strand of black button thread to work straight stitches for eyebrows and backstitches for the mouth.

For nose, cut a triangular nose from the black scrap of felt, using the nose on the face pattern, *opposite,* as a guide. Glue the nose to the face as indicated on the pattern.

For whiskers, thread a needle with one strand of black button thread. Make a knot in one end, leaving a 1½-inch tail. Insert the needle at one of the dots near the nose. Bring the needle out at a dot on the other side of the nose, pulling slightly to shape the face. Knot the thread, securing it close to the fabric. Cut the thread, leaving a 1½-inch tail. Make two more sets of whiskers at dots indicated on kitten face pattern.

Sew ear pieces together in pairs, leaving openings as marked on the pattern. Trim the seams to ⅛ inch and turn the ears right side out. Turn raw edges of the ears under ⅛ inch and hand-stitch the ears to the head. Tack back of the head to the body at the X.

For tail, sew tail pieces together, leaving an opening on straight edge. Trim seam to ⅛ inch and turn tail right side out. *Do not* stuff the tail. Turn the unfinished edges of tail under ⅛ inch and hand-stitch it to the underside of kitten's body at placement line as indicated on the pattern.

Slip the ribbon through the loop at the top of the small bell and tie the ribbon around the kitten's neck creating a bow. Trim ribbon ends if desired.

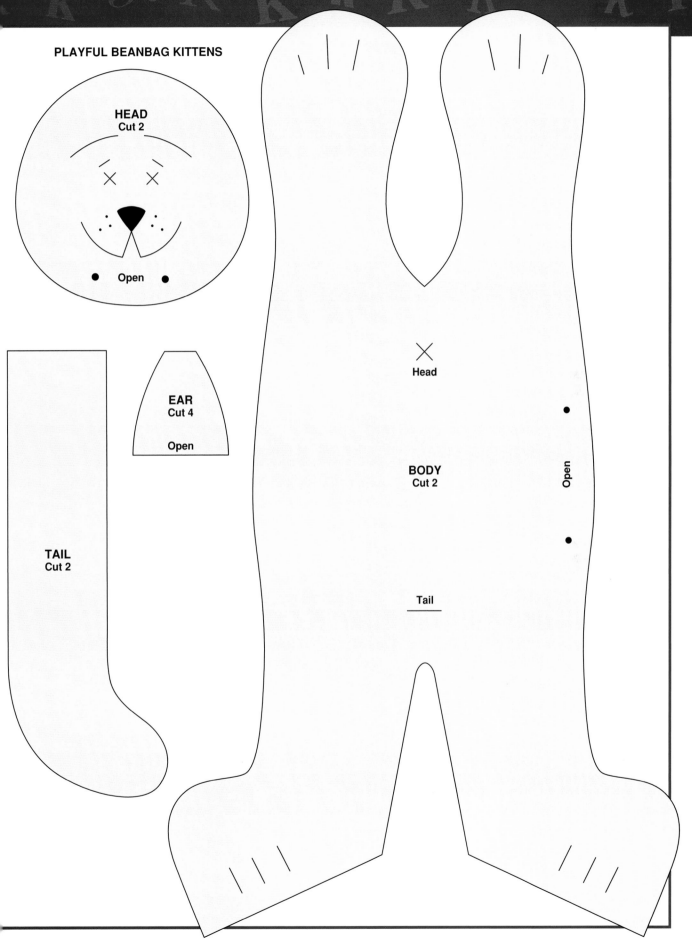

PLAYFUL BEANBAG KITTENS

HEAD
Cut 2

Open

EAR
Cut 4

Open

TAIL
Cut 2

Head

BODY
Cut 2

Open

Tail

ROSIE THE KITTEN

As shown on page 88, kitten measures 8½ inches tall.

MATERIALS

Tracing paper
Graphite paper; pencil
6x10-inch piece of 1-inch pine
Scroll saw
Medium and very-fine sandpaper
Clear semigloss polyurethane spray
Antique white, light brown, burgundy, white, pink, purple, holiday green, sky blue, and black acrylic paints
#1, #6, and #8 round artist's brushes

INSTRUCTIONS

Trace pattern, *right*. Transfer the outline to pine. Cut out with scroll saw.

Sand lightly using medium sandpaper. Spray front and edges with polyurethane. When dry, sand front again using fine sandpaper. Transfer details to wood.

Allow to dry before adding a second color on top or adjacent to it. Paint cat's body antique white. Use a thin wash of brown on muzzle, ears, hands, and feet. Paint dress burgundy; add water to make a light wash for cheeks and inside of ears. Paint bloomers and apron white.

Paint roses on dress and apron pink, with purple centers and green leaves. Add green polka dots to bloomers. Paint eyes blue.

Add shading with a thin wash of black paint, referring to pattern, *opposite*, and photograph, *page 88*. Outline shapes and face with black, using a small brush. Add black whiskers on cheeks and ears. Highlight eyes and nose with tiny dots of white.

Spray kitten with polyurethane and allow it to dry completely.

ROSIE THE KITTEN

L is for *Lively Lights and Lampshades*

Lace-Trimmed Candles

Decorated with lace trims, these candles are aglow with easy elegance. Simply use short pins to secure the lace in place. In no time, you'll transform plain candles into gracious gifts or beautiful holiday decorations. Instructions are on page 98.

DESIGNER: KAREN TAYLOR ● PHOTOGRAPHER: HOPKINS ASSOCIATES

Best-Friends Lampshade

Dress up a tired lampshade with calico, rickrack, and our simple best-friends shapes and you've created a bright spot in that special little girl's room. The paper-doll shapes are cut from favorite fabric scraps and fused to the covered lampshade. Complete instructions and patterns begin on page 98.

DESIGNER: MARGARET SINDELAR ● PHOTOGRAPHER: HOPKINS ASSOCIATES

Rice Paper Lampshades

Created with purchased rice paper, lacy trims, and bits of satin or metallic ribbons, these elegant shades will bring a touch of beauty to any room. An art supply store is a good source for fancy-patterned rice paper to give an old shade a new glow. Instructions are on page 99.

DESIGNER: MARGARET SINDELAR
PHOTOGRAPHER: HOPKINS ASSOCIATES

Pleated Lampshade

Add rich color to a den or study using plaid fabrics and a bit of imagination. By pleating the fabric in an accordion-like style, the look becomes strikingly traditional. Complete instructions for this handsome lampshade are on page 99.

DESIGNER: MARGARET SINDELAR ● PHOTOGRAPHER: HOPKINS ASSOCIATES

LACE-TRIMMED CANDLES

As shown on page 95.

MATERIALS

6-inch-tall pillar candles
Scraps of wide lace
Lace medallions
½-inch-long flat-head pins

INSTRUCTIONS

Wrap strips of lace around candles, referring to the photograph, *page 95,* for placement. Secure in place by inserting pins into candle. Or, position lace medallions as desired and pin in place.

BEST-FRIENDS LAMPSHADE

Lampshade shown on page 96 is 9 inches high and 14 inches in diameter.

MATERIALS

Lampshade
Large sheet of paper; pencil
1 yard of 45-inch-wide yellow gingham
Spray adhesive; waxed paper
⅝ yard of yellow jumbo rickrack
1¼ yards white jumbo rickrack
Crafts glue; tracing paper
6x18-inch piece *each* of three colors felt
6x6-inch piece *each* of nine different calico fabrics

INSTRUCTIONS

Draw a vertical line on lampshade from top to bottom. On large sheet of paper, draw a line the same length. Matching lines on shade and paper; rotate shade on paper while drawing top and bottom outlines. Add ¾ inch to top, bottom, and one vertical edge; cut out. Use paper pattern to cut one from yellow gingham.

Place shade on waxed paper and spray lightly with spray adhesive. Matching vertical lines, lay fabric on shade and press to stick.

Turn under extra fabric on vertical edge to cover joint and glue. Turn extra fabric at top and bottom to inside, clipping curves; glue.

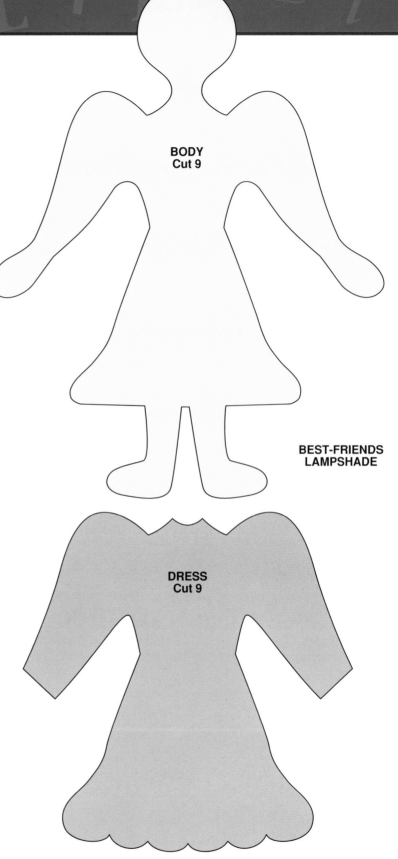

BODY
Cut 9

BEST-FRIENDS
LAMPSHADE

DRESS
Cut 9

Glue yellow rickrack around top edge of shade, turning under ends. Glue white rickrack around the bottom edge.

Trace doll body and dress patterns, *opposite;* cut out. Draw around dress pattern on each piece of calico; cut out. Draw around body pattern three times on each piece of felt. Place dresses, right side down, on waxed paper and lightly spray each with spray adhesive. Lay dresses on body outlines and press to stick. Cut out bodies and spray wrong sides lightly with spray adhesive. Arrange dolls evenly around bottom of shade, overlapping hands slightly to fit around bottom.

PINK RICE-PAPER LAMPSHADE

Lampshade shown on page 97 is 8 inches high and 10 inches in diameter.

MATERIALS
Lampshade
Large sheet of paper; pencil
24x36-inch sheet of pink rice paper
24x36-inch sheet of white lace rice paper
Spray adhesive; waxed paper
Crafts glue
1 yard of 2-inch-wide white flat braid trim
1¾ yards of ¼-inch-wide pink ribbon
1¾ yards of ¾-inch-wide white eyelet lace

INSTRUCTIONS
Draw a vertical line on lampshade from top to bottom. On large sheet of paper, draw a line the same length. Matching lines on shade and paper, rotate shade on paper while drawing top and

bottom outlines. Add ¾ inch to top, bottom, and one vertical edge; cut out. Use pattern to cut one from lace paper and rice paper.

Place shade on waxed paper; spray lightly with spray adhesive. Matching vertical lines, lay pink rice paper on shade and press to stick. Spray shade again and apply lace paper on top. Overlap extra paper on vertical edge to cover joint and glue. Turn extra paper along top and bottom to inside, clipping curves; glue.

Glue flat braid around bottom of shade. Thread eyelet lace with ribbon; glue over top edge of braid and around top of shade.

GOLD-TRIMMED RICE-PAPER LAMPSHADE

Lampshade shown on page 97 is 8 inches high and 13 inches in diameter.

MATERIALS
Lampshade
Large sheet of paper; pencil
24x36-inch sheet of white lace rice paper
Gold metallic spray paint
Spray adhesive; waxed paper
Crafts glue; crafts knife; awl
3 yards of ¼-inch-wide flat gold braid

INSTRUCTIONS
Draw a vertical line on lampshade from top to bottom. On large sheet of paper, draw a line the same length. Matching lines on shade and paper, rotate shade on paper while drawing top and bottom outlines. Add ¼ inch to top, bottom, and one vertical edge; cut out. Use paper pattern to cut one from lace paper.

Place shade on waxed paper and spray-paint gold. When paint

is dry, spray with spray adhesive. Matching vertical lines, lay lace paper on shade and press to stick. Overlap extra paper on vertical edge to cover joint and glue. Trim paper even with top and bottom of shade.

Use awl to pierce holes ½ inch from top and bottom edges, ¾ inch apart. Whipstitch gold braid through holes, tying ends to secure. Pierce shade around lace paper designs as desired.

PLEATED LAMPSHADE

Lampshade shown on page 97 is 5¼ inches high and 8 inches in diameter.

MATERIALS
6x31-inch piece of plaid fabric
5x31-inch piece of paper-backed iron-on adhesive
5x31-inch piece of card stock or construction paper
Purchased metal lampshade frame with 2¾-inch top and 4½-inch bottom diameter
Awl; scissors; crafts glue

INSTRUCTIONS
Press under ½ inch along both long edges of plaid fabric. Fuse iron-on adhesive to wrong side of plaid fabric. Remove paper backing; fuse to card stock.

Accordion-pleat shade, spacing pleats ½ inch apart and pressing with an iron.

With awl, pierce a hole in each pleat ½ inch from one long edge (top of shade). With scissors and working from paper side, make a slit joining every two holes.

Turn under raw edge along one short end of shade. Glue ends of shade together. Slip shade onto wire base, fitting slits over top wire of base. Adjust pleats so they are evenly spaced.

M is for *Merry Mittens and Mice*

Crazy Quilt Mittens

Favorite flannel shirts have a new life when assembled into our crazy quilted mittens. Made with polar fleece backing and lining, they're decorated with colorful embroidery stitches, buttons, and beads, and are oversized just for fun.
The complete instructions and pattern are on pages 103–104.

DESIGNER: MARGARET SINDELAR ● PHOTOGRAPHER: HOPKINS ASSOCIATES

Knitted Santa Mittens

Leftover pieces of red, white, and black yarn combine to make these jolly St. Nicholas mittens that kids will adore. Separate pinkie finger and thumb arms make each hand a tiny puppet. These mittens knit up quickly on four needles so every good boy and girl on your gift-giving list can enjoy a pair. Instructions begin on page 103.

DESIGNER: EVE MAHR
PHOTOGRAPHER: HOPKINS ASSOCIATES

Funny Finger Puppets

Scraps of felt and pieces of thread make our hickory-dickory mice come alive. Cut from just two simple pattern pieces, our trio of happy friends are stitched together by machine. Sewing thread for whiskers and tiny beads for eyes make these little puppets loads of fun. Complete instructions and patterns can be found on page 105.

DESIGNER: JIM WILLIAMS
PHOTOGRAPHER: HOPKINS ASSOCIATES

y, Dickory, Dock
y, dickory, dock.
mouse ran up the clock.
The clock struck one.
The mouse ran down,
ickory, dickory, dock.

Three Blind Mice

Playful Mice Sweatshirt

Calico prints and colorful paint pens combine to create our fun-to-wear sweatshirt. The chubby mice shapes are fused onto the fabric and embellished with floppy fabric ears and paint pen. Complete instructions and patterns begin on page 105.

DESIGNER: BARBARA BARTON SMITH ● PHOTOGRAPHER: SCOTT LITTLE

CRAZY QUILT MITTENS

As shown on page 100.

MATERIALS
Graph paper or tracing paper
Scrap of muslin (optional)
14x16-inch piece of white
    cotton fabric
Erasable fabric marker
Sewing thread
Scraps of nine different plaid or
    checked flannels
Pearl cotton and embroidery
    floss in assorted colors
Buttons and heart-shaped
    beads in assorted sizes
½ yard of 60-inch-wide rust
    ribbed polar fleece

INSTRUCTIONS
Enlarge pattern, *page 104,* using graph paper; cut out. Or, to make your own pattern, place your hand flat on tracing paper and draw a mitten shape around your fingers and thumb, adding approximately 1¼ inches all around to make mittens oversized as shown. Draw cuff pattern to extend 6 inches beyond wrist. (To test pattern for fit, make a sample mitten by cutting two pattern shapes from muslin. Stitch two pieces together using a ¼-inch seam allowance and leaving cuff edge open. Try sample mitten on to see how it fits and adjust pattern as necessary.)

For fronts, draw around pattern on white fabric with marker. Turn pattern over and draw around it again, leaving at least 2 inches between pieces. Using thread in a contrasting color, machine-baste on marker lines.

Cut two five-sided base pieces, each about 2½ inches across, from one piece of plaid flannel. Cut the remaining plaid flannel pieces into 2½-inch-wide strips. Baste one base piece to center of

one white mitten shape. Stitch a contrasting plaid strip to any side of the base piece, with right sides together and using a ¼-inch seam allowance. Press plaid strip right side up and away from the base piece, covering the seam.

Stitch a second plaid strip onto one adjacent side of base piece making sure it completely covers edges of base and first plaid strip. Trim excess fabric from seam allowance. Working clockwise, continue adding plaid strips in this manner, working outward from center until basted mitten shape is completely covered. Repeat for remaining mitten front.

Machine-baste again over contrast basting so mitten shape will be marked on pieced side. Cut out mitten shape just beyond basting stitches. Using assorted colors of pearl cotton and embroidery floss, add decorative stitches to mitten fronts, referring to photograph for ideas. Add beads and buttons.

For backs and lining, fold polar fleece in half. Use pattern to cut three pairs of mitten shapes from folded fleece.

Stitch each pieced mitten front to one polar fleece mitten shape, right sides together, using ¼-inch seam allowance and leaving top edge open. Double-stitch the curves between thumb and palm of hand to reinforce it. Clip curves and turn right side out.

Stitch remaining polar fleece pieces together in same manner, except leave an opening near finger tips and *do not* turn. Slip each pieced mitten into an all-fleece one. Stitch the lining to the mitten along top edge. Turn both pieces right side out through fingertip opening. Sew lining opening closed. Tuck lining into mitten; press. Topstitch through all layers of fabric ¼ inch from cuff edge. Turn down cuff.

KNITTED SANTA MITTENS

As shown on page 101.

MATERIALS
Four-ply 3½-ounce skein *each of*
    red and white yarn
Small amount of black yarn
Scraps of pink and blue yarn
Two ½-inch-diameter white
    pom-poms
Size 9 double-pointed knitting
    needles
Yarn needle
Two small stitch holders

INSTRUCTIONS
For size 3–4, follow directions as written. Directions for size 5–6 are in parentheses. *Note: Knitting abbreviations are on page 17.*

Cast on 28 (32) sts. Divide in following manner: 8 sts on first needle, 12 (16) sts on second needle, 8 sts on third needle. Join, placing a marker at beg of rnd and carrying it up as you work. Work in k 2, p 2 ribbing for 12 (14) rows.

Rnd 1: Join black. K in front and back of next 2 sts. K around—30 (34) sts.

Rnds 2–4: Knit.

Rnd 5: Join red. K in front and back of first st, k 2, k in front and back of next st, k around—32 (36) sts.

Rnds 6 and 7: Knit.

Rnd 8: K in front and back of first st, k 4, k in front and back of next st, k around—34 (38) sts.

Rnds 9 and 10: Knit.

Large size only: K in front and back of first st, k 6, k in front and back of next st, k around. K 2 rows—40 sts.

Rnd 11: Sl 7 (9) sts to holder for thumb. Cast on 3 sts. K around—30 (34) sts.

Rnds 12 and 13: Knit.

Rnd 14: K 13 (15). Sl 7 sts to holder for finger. Cast on 3 sts. K around—26 (30) sts.

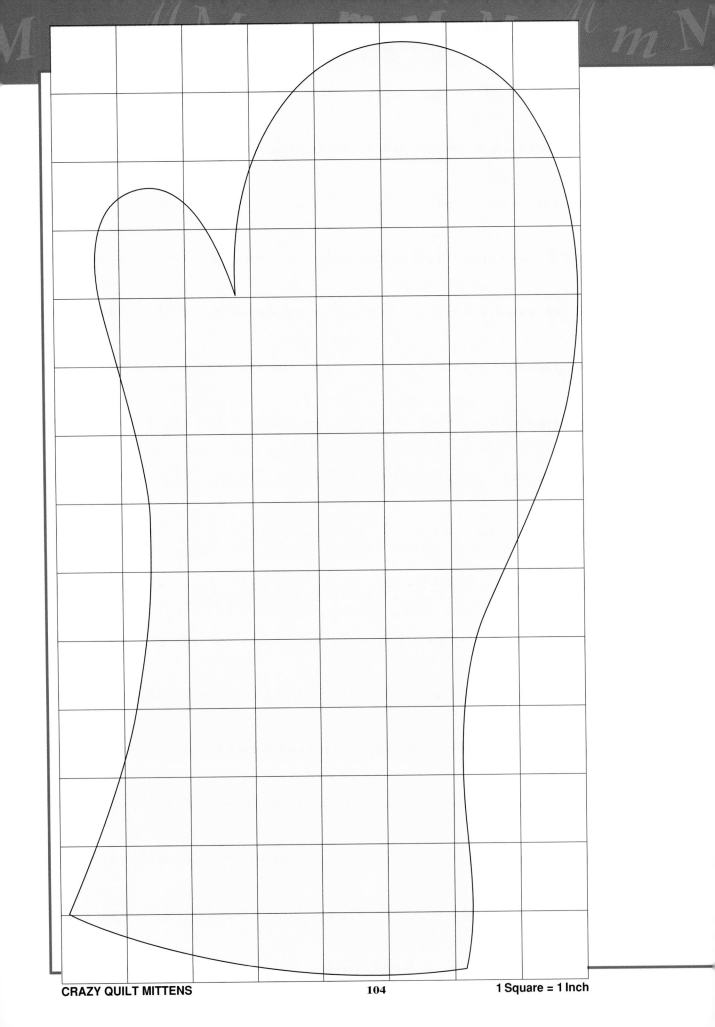

CRAZY QUILT MITTENS

104

1 Square = 1 Inch

Rnds 15–23: Join white. Knit.

Rnds 24–29: Join red. Knit.

Rnd 30: * K 3, k 2 tog. Rep from * around, ending k 1 (0).

Rnds 31, 33, 35, 37, and 39: Knit.

Rnd 32: K 2, k 2 tog. Rep around, * k 2, k 2 tog around, ending k 1 (0).

Rnd 34: K 1, k 2 tog. Rep around, * k 1, k 2 tog around, ending k 1 (0).

Rnd 36: K 2 tog. Rep around, ending with k 1 (0).

Rnd 38: K 2 tog around.

Rnd 40: K 2 tog, k 1.

Rnd 41: K last 2 sts tog.

Cut yarn, leaving a 6-inch tail. Run through rem st, keeping tail on outside of mitten.

For thumb, transfer 7 (9) sts on holder to two needles. With red yarn and third needle, pick up and k 5 sts. K 6 rows. Join white; k 3 rows. K 2 tog around. Cut yarn and thread into a yarn needle. Thread yarn through rem sts, pulling tail to inside.

For finger, work in same manner as for thumb.

To finish, use tail at top of mitten to secure point to front of mitten for Santa's cap. Thread a

pom-pom onto tail. Run tail to inside and secure.

With pink yarn, work two straight stitches for mouth. With blue yarn, work a duplicate stitch for each eye.

FUNNY FINGER PUPPETS

As shown on page 101, finished puppets measure 1³⁄₄x3³⁄₄ inches.

MATERIALS

For one puppet
Tracing paper
4x6-inch piece of white or gray felt
Fabric marking pencil or pen
Two black seed beads
Gray sewing thread
Black sewing thread
Sewing thread to match felt
Large-eyed needle
Hot glue gun

INSTRUCTIONS

Trace the patterns, *below*, onto tracing paper and cut out. Fold the felt in half lengthwise. Trace the body, placing the pattern on the fold as indicated; cut out. Cut two ears and one ¹⁄₄x4-inch tail from

remaining felt. Taper the end of the tail to a point.

Sew body along stitching line marked on pattern. Trim seam allowance to ¹⁄₈ inch, clip curves, and turn right side out.

Glue ears in place. Center wide end of tail inside body along top fold; glue. Use black thread to attach bead eyes at dots.

For whiskers, thread a needle with six strands of gray thread. Knot the threads together ³⁄₄ inch from ends. Push the needle through nose and pull until knot hits fabric. Knot thread on opposite side of nose, trim threads ³⁄₄ inch from knot.

MICE SWEATSHIRT

As shown on page 102.

MATERIALS

Purchased bright pink long-sleeved sweatshirt
Tracing paper
Paper-backed iron-on adhesive
4x6-inch piece of three different gray cotton print fabrics
4x6-inch piece of yellow cotton print fabric
4x12-inch piece of pink cotton print fabric
Erasable fabric marker
Gray sewing thread
Dressmaker's carbon paper
Black shiny paint pen
Twelve 4-millimeter black faceted beads
Six or seven 5-inch-long scraps of narrow ribbon in desired colors
6 small dark gray, blue, or brown trouser buttons

INSTRUCTIONS

Wash and dry shirt. Trace the cheese and ear patterns, *page 106;* cut out. Trace *just* the mouse outline; cut out. Trace the mouse

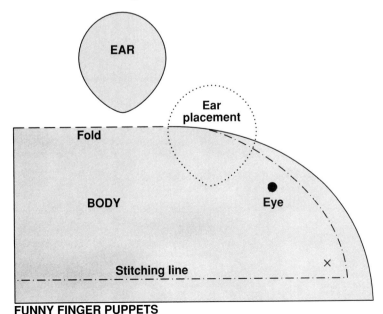

FUNNY FINGER PUPPETS

again with whiskers and features; set aside.

Draw around the cheese pattern once and the mouse six times on paper side of iron-on adhesive. Following the instructions, fuse cheese shape to the back of the yellow fabric and two mouse shapes to each of the gray fabrics. Cut out.

Cut four outer ears from the remainder of each gray piece of fabric. Cut twelve inner ears from the pink fabric.

Remove the paper backing from cheese and fuse it to the lower right front of the shirt approximately 4 inches above the ribbing. Arrange four mice on the shirt front so they appear to make a trail toward the cheese; fuse as directed. Position one mouse facing upward on the left sleeve and the remaining mouse at the top of the left shoulder; fuse as directed.

Transfer the markings from second mouse tracing to each fused mouse.

Sew one inner ear to each outer ear, right sides together using ¼-inch seam allowances and leaving the bottoms open. Turn right side out and press. Turn under ¼ inch along the opening edges, and press. Slip stitch the opening edges closed, pulling the thread to gather the ear bottoms slightly; knot thread.

Whipstitch ears in place following placement lines on pattern; tack ears to stand up. Sew a bead at each eye dot.

Use black paint pen to outline each mouse and draw a curvy tail. Use the whiskers on pattern as a guide or paint freehand whiskers. Fill in the point of the nose. Allow paint to dry for 24 hours.

Tie the ribbons into bows and tack one or two bows to the tail of each mouse as desired. Sew a button over the top of each bow.

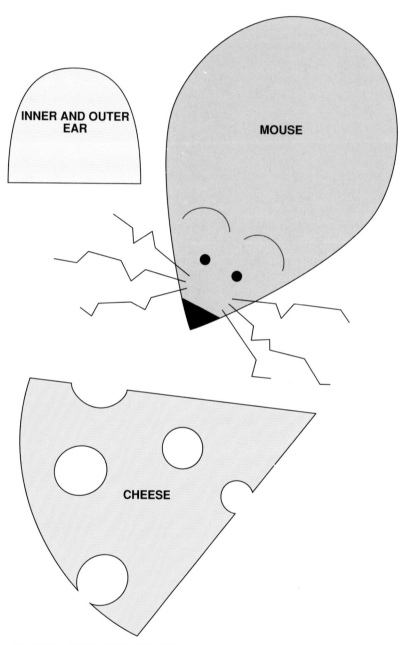

INNER AND OUTER EAR

MOUSE

CHEESE

PLAYFUL MICE SWEATSHIRT

106

N is for *Novelty Neckties*

Necktie Vest

Rich in color and pattern, men's neckties combine to make our feminine vest. A prairie point edge separates the panels created by piecing the patterned ties. We've used a double-breasted-style vest with princess seams, but this idea can be adapted to another favorite vest pattern. Instructions are on page 110.

DESIGNER: MARGARET SINDELAR ● PHOTOGRAPHER: SCOTT LITTLE

Cravat Pillow

Our cravat pillow is a simple way to preserve someone's special neckties. Seven ties make a 9x11-inch pillow, but the size can be adjusted using more or fewer ties. Add more keepsakes in the form of treasured stick pins or tie tacks. Instructions are on page 110.

DESIGNER: JIM WILLIAMS ● PHOTOGRAPHER: HOPKINS ASSOCIATES

Curtain Tieback

Perfect for a den or masculine room, this curtain tieback requires only two neckties,
a few strands of pearl cotton, and some colorful buttons. Tie a Windsor knot and slip the
finished tieback over curtains for an eye-catching accent. Instructions are on page 110.

DESIGNER: PHYLLIS DUNSTAN ● PHOTOGRAPHER: HOPKINS ASSOCIATES

NECKTIE VEST

Vest shown on page 107 has a front princess seam approximately 23 inches long. Adjust the number of neckties for a longer or shorter vest pattern.

MATERIALS

Approximately 24 neckties

Cotton fabric in amount specified on pattern envelope for vest front

Purchased vest pattern with princess seams

Jacquard or other silky fabric in amount specified on pattern envelope for vest back and lining or facing

Notions as specified on pattern envelope

Sewing thread

INSTRUCTIONS

Remove the stitching and the interfacing from ties; press flat. Hand-wash and line dry or dry clean ties. (If silk ties are washed, colors may water-spot or bleed.)

From tie fabric, cut thirty 3x3-inch squares for prairie points. Cut remaining tie fabric into long piecing strips, 1½- to 3-inches wide. From cotton fabric, cut front vest panels. From jacquard fabric, cut vest back, all lining, and additional pieces called for in pattern instructions.

To piece vest front, begin with one side-front panel. Baste one tie strip, right side up, horizontally across the top of the panel, with the top and the side edges of tie extending beyond edges of vest panel. Stitch a contrasting strip to the bottom edge of first strip, with right sides together and using ¼-inch seam. Press second strip right side up and away from first strip, covering seam. Continue sewing strips until vest shape is completely covered. Trim excess

tie fabric even with cut edges of vest panel.

Baste around perimeter ¼ inch from edges to secure strip ends. Repeat for remaining side-front panel. Set both panels aside.

Piece each center-front panel of vest in same manner *except,* sew tie strips vertically, joining strips end to end as necessary to make strips long enough. Cut out; baste edges as for side-front panels.

For prairie points, press each fabric square in half diagonally twice to form a triangle. Baste triangles in a line along princess seam of each side-front panel, right sides together with raw edges even. Alternate fabrics and overlap triangles, with end of first and last triangles inside seam allowance of panel.

Assemble vest according to pattern directions.

CRAVAT PILLOW

As shown on page 108, pillow measures 9x11 inches.

MATERIALS

Seven vintage-patterned neckties

Sewing thread

8x10-inch piece of fabric for pillow back

Polyester fiberfill

1⅛ yards of ½-inch-diameter metallic gold cord

Crafts glue

INSTRUCTIONS

Cut 12-inch lengths from the narrow ends of ties. Lay the strips side by side, alternating the wide and the narrow ends to make an 8x10-inch rectangle. Use a ladder stitch (diagram, *page 23*) to join the pieces together along the folds of the strips.

Sew pillow back to pillow front, right sides together using ½-inch

seams, leaving an opening for turning. Trim seams and clip the corners; turn. Stuff pillow and sew opening closed, leaving a ¾-inch opening at center.

Apply glue to both ends of cord to prevent raveling. Insert one end of cord into pillow opening. Hand-stitch cord around pillow over seam line. Insert other end of cord into pillow opening, and sew opening closed.

CURTAIN TIEBACK

As shown on page 109.

MATERIALS

For one tieback

Two neckties

Pearl cotton in assorted colors

Tapestry needle

Sewing thread to match ties

Six or seven ½-inch-diameter decorative metal buttons

INSTRUCTIONS

Lay the ties side by side, overlapping the folded edges and crossing the ties 21 inches from narrow ends; pin.

Use one strand of pearl cotton to work feather stitches along overlapped edges, stitching through all layers of both of ties.

Add random groupings of French knots using one strand of pearl cotton in desired colors.

Work machine buttonholes in a random pattern on wide portion of each tie. Sew one button in center of each buttonhole.

Wrap wide end of joined ties around narrow end once. Bring wide end through loop formed, and under wrapped horizontal fold of tie.

Slip curtain through loop. Pull narrow end of tie to tighten knot. Adjust the curtain folds; secure tieback to side of window frame.

O is for *Outstanding Ornaments*

Cotton Batting Friends

Christmas is the season when ordinary things become extraordinary in the hands of crafters. Even humble cotton batting takes on a turn-of-the-century air when stitched, stuffed, and embellished with puffy paints to resemble tiny bears and snowmen. Instructions begin on page 114.

DESIGNER: KAREN TAYLOR ● PHOTOGRAPHER: SCOTT LITTLE

Twinkling Winter Trims

Sparkling stars, glittering snowflakes, and shimmering icicles have everyday origins—the foam trays so often discarded. Let the whole family help create these ornaments (or last-minute gifts) using glitter paint and imagination. Instructions begin on page 116.

DESIGNERS: SNOWFLAKES AND ICICLES, KAREN TAYLOR; STARS, PHYLLIS DUNSTAN
PHOTOGRAPHER: SCOTT LITTLE

Church Window Ornaments

Tiny bits of felt glued to Christmas shapes create the look of stained glass. These bright ornaments were designed for creativity—vary the colors using three basic patterns for dozens of festive ornaments. Patterns and instructions begin on page 118.

DESIGNER: KAREN TAYLOR ● PHOTOGRAPHER: SCOTT LITTLE

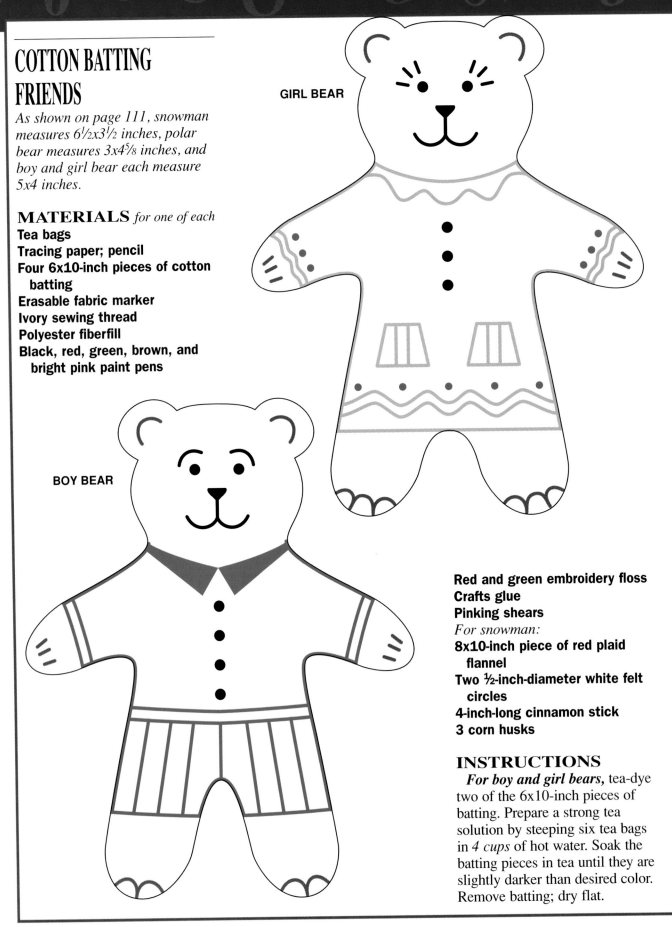

COTTON BATTING FRIENDS

As shown on page 111, snowman measures 6½x3½ inches, polar bear measures 3x4⅝ inches, and boy and girl bear each measure 5x4 inches.

MATERIALS *for one of each*
Tea bags
Tracing paper; pencil
Four 6x10-inch pieces of cotton batting
Erasable fabric marker
Ivory sewing thread
Polyester fiberfill
Black, red, green, brown, and bright pink paint pens

GIRL BEAR

BOY BEAR

Red and green embroidery floss
Crafts glue
Pinking shears
For snowman:
8x10-inch piece of red plaid flannel
Two ½-inch-diameter white felt circles
4-inch-long cinnamon stick
3 corn husks

INSTRUCTIONS
For boy and girl bears, tea-dye two of the 6x10-inch pieces of batting. Prepare a strong tea solution by steeping six tea bags in *4 cups* of hot water. Soak the batting pieces in tea until they are slightly darker than desired color. Remove batting; dry flat.

POLAR BEAR

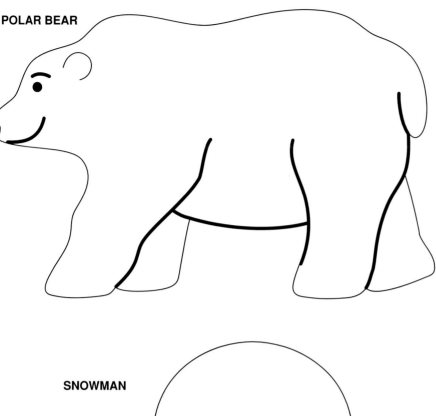

SNOWMAN

ARM

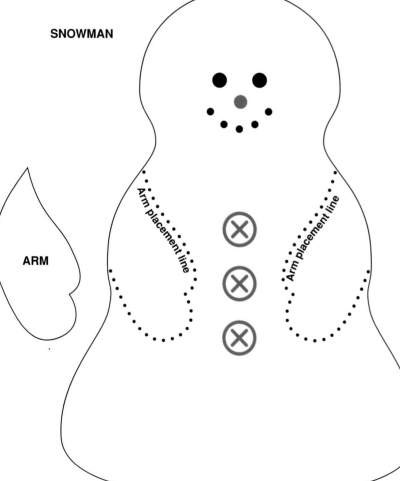

Trace patterns, *opposite and left,* onto tracing paper; cut out. From the batting, cut one front and one back for each ornament. Cut four arm pieces for the snowman. Transfer markings from the patterns to body fronts.

From the flannel, cut a ½x10-inch scarf strip and a 6x6-inch square hat piece for the snowman.

Whipstitch the snowman's arms together in pairs with sewing thread, leaving openings for stuffing. Stuff arms lightly and whipstitch the openings closed. Pin the arms in place on the snowman front. (Arms are joined to body when front and back pieces are sewn together.)

For each ornament, whipstitch front to back around perimeter; leave opening for stuffing. Stuff ornament and whipstitch opening closed. Paint details with paint pens in colors shown on patterns.

For snowman, tie scarf strip around neck. Fold hat square in half and draw a diagonal line from one corner to the opposite corner. Sew along drawn line. Trim seam allowance to ¼ inch. Turn hat right side out and press. Using pinking shears, trim hat to measure 5 inches tall. Glue a felt circle to each side of hat point. Glue hat to head at an angle. Fold top 3 inches of hat to back.

For broom, cut two or three 3-inch-long pieces from corn husks. Join pieces and wrap three quarters of way around one end of cinnamon stick. Wrap red floss several times around top of husks to secure them to stick. Cut husks below floss into narrow strips to resemble broom straw. Use pinking shears to trim bottom of broom. Glue broom to snowman, with top of stick under one arm.

For hanging loops, thread a six-ply strand of floss through top of ornament; knot floss ends.

FOAM TRAY SNOWFLAKES AND ICICLES

As shown on page 112, ornaments vary from 4⅛ to 5 inches long.

MATERIALS
Cardboard or quilter's template plastic
Ballpoint pen
Tape
Foam produce trays
Crafts knife
Cutting mat
Silver and gold glitter paint pens
Large needle
Monofilament

INSTRUCTIONS

Trace the patterns, *right and opposite,* on the cardboard or template plastic; cut out. Tape the pattern to a foam tray. Trace around each pattern piece, pressing firmly with the ballpoint pen. Remove the pattern and cut out the piece along the indented outlines using the crafts knife.

Paint the designs on each ornament freehand using the gold or silver paint pen. When the paint is dry, thread a needle with 6 inches of monofilament and poke it through the top of the ornament. Remove the needle and knot the monofilament ends to make a hanging loop.

**FOAM TRAY SNOWFLAKES
AND ICICLES**

FOAM TRAY STAR ORNAMENTS

As shown on page 112, stars measure 3 inches and 4 inches across.

MATERIALS
Tracing paper
Cardboard; tape
Ballpoint pen
Foam produce trays
Crafts knife and cutting mat
Gold or silver metallic acrylic
   paint and brush
Gold and silver paint pens
Gold metallic tinsel stems
½-inch-long gold flat-head pins
3-millimeter round gold beads
Gold metallic thread

INSTRUCTIONS
   Trace both sizes of star patterns, *right*. Draw around each on cardboard; cut out. Tape patterns to foam tray and draw around each, pressing firmly with ballpoint pen.
   Remove pattern and cut out pieces along indented outlines using crafts knife. Paint stars as desired using silver and gold paint and/or use paint pens to outline edges of stars. If desired, push pins through beads and into foam around edges of each star.
   For tinsel stem ornament, cut two smaller stars. Poke each end of a tinsel stem into one side of each. To hang on tree, twist stem around branch.
   For alternating star ornament, cut two stars of equal size. From foam scraps cut 1x1-inch square. Glue foam square between the two stars, positioning stars so points alternate. Make hanging loop from gold thread.
   For hanging star ornament, center a small star atop a large star and glue. Make hanging loop from gold thread.

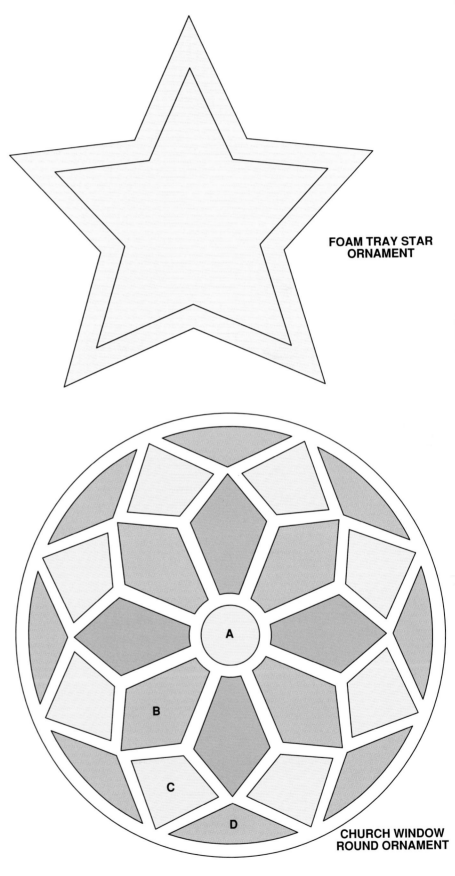

FOAM TRAY STAR ORNAMENT

CHURCH WINDOW ROUND ORNAMENT

CHURCH WINDOW ORNAMENTS

As shown on page 113, star measures 5¹/₄x5¹/₄ inches; candle measures 5¹/₂x4¹/₂ inches; and circle is 4⁵/₈ inches in diameter.

MATERIALS *for one of each*
Tracing paper
Cardboard
Erasable fabric marker
Scraps of felt in assorted colors
Crafts glue
Embroidery floss

INSTRUCTIONS

For each ornament, trace one of each lettered shape plus outline shape from pattern, *left, below, or right,* onto tracing paper; cut out. Draw around each paper shape on cardboard; cut out.

For round ornament, from the desired colors of felt, cut one A, eight Bs, eight Cs, eight Ds, and one outline, referring to the pattern and

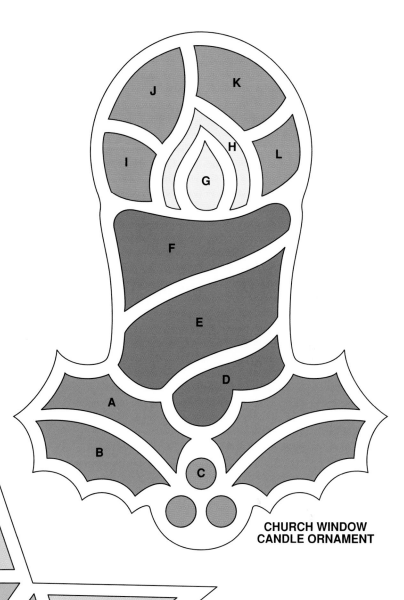

CHURCH WINDOW CANDLE ORNAMENT

CHURCH WINDOW STAR ORNAMENT

the photograph, *page 113,* for color combination ideas.

For candle ornament, from desired colors of felt, cut two As (one reversed), two Bs (one reversed), three Cs, one each of D–L, and one outline.

For star ornament, from desired colors of felt, cut five As, five Bs, and one outline.

Glue each lettered piece in place on outline shape, referring to patterns for placement.

Use a six-ply strand of floss to make a hanging loop.

P is for *Pretty* *P*illows and *P*incushions

Jeweled Star Pillow

Bits of taffeta and velveteen turn old-fashioned patchwork into a work of art. With masterful placement of the clear, jewel-like colors, the solid fabrics in this pillow create a stained-glass effect that seems to catch the sun. Button tufting and a double-fabric ruffle complement the colorful design. Instructions and patterns begin on page 124.

DESIGNER: MARGARET SINDELAR ● PHOTOGRAPHER: HOPKINS ASSOCIATES

Crazy Quilt Pillow

This heart pillow adds an elegant touch to a settee, sofa, or window seat.
Gather up all your scraps of satin, ribbon, and trims for the crazy-quilt front, then
add a lacy edging to the ruffle and embellish the pillow with your best embroidery
stitches, using metallic threads for extra sheen. Instructions begin on page 125.

DESIGNER: LAURA COLLINS ● PHOTOGRAPHER: PERRY STRUSE

High Button Shoe Pincushion

Grandma would love this crazy-quilt pincushion, fashioned after a turn-of-the-century-style shoe. Use scraps of fancy fabrics—velveteen, taffeta, and satin—plus a variety of flowery embroidery stitches to create the quilted front. Instructions and pattern begin on page 127.

DESIGNER: MARGARET SINDELAR ● PHOTOGRAPHER: HOPKINS ASSOCIATES

Heart-in-Hands Pincushion

This unique pincushion is a symbol of affection, with loving hands cradling a beribboned heart. Sure to become an heirloom, it's actually simple to make. Craft the heart with ribbon roses and lace, then shape a pair of gloves into hands with fiberfill and cardboard. Instructions begin on page 128.

DESIGNER: SALLY PAUL ● PHOTOGRAPHER: SCOTT LITTLE

JEWELED STAR PILLOW

As shown on page 120, pillow is 16x16 inches, with a 4¼-inch-wide ruffle.

MATERIALS
Quilter's template plastic
9x11-inch piece *each* of mauve, purple, light pink, and bright pink taffeta
4½x11-inch piece *each* of burgundy, royal blue, dark navy, and teal velveteen
4½x11-inch piece *each* of burgundy, royal blue, dark navy, and teal taffeta
Sewing thread
2 yards of ⅜-inch-diameter navy satin piping
⅝ yard of 45-inch-wide emerald green satin
⅜ yard of 45-inch-wide burgundy satin
3¾ yards of 2-inch-wide flat lace
16x16-inch piece of fabric for back
Thirteen ¾-inch shank buttons
Pillow form; pearl cotton thread

INSTRUCTIONS

Trace pattern pieces A–D, *above,* onto template plastic; cut out. Templates and measurements include ¼-inch seam allowances. Sew seams with right sides facing.

From mauve and purple taffeta, cut eight As. From light pink and bright pink taffeta, cut eight Bs. From each velveteen, cut four Cs. From burgundy, royal blue, dark navy, and teal taffeta, cut four Ds. Divide pieces into four groups containing equal amounts of each color. (One group of pieces will be used for each of the four large blocks that make up the pillow.)

For each large block, make four small blocks by sewing pieces C and D of matching color together. Stitch the mauve A pieces to the

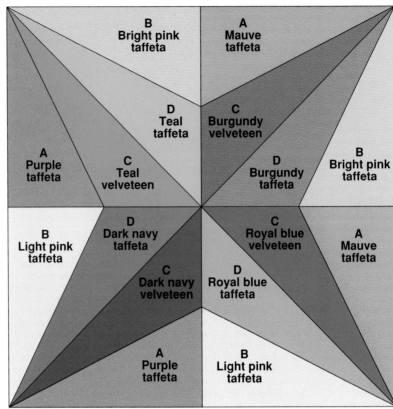

JEWELED STAR PILLOW DIAGRAM 1

royal and burgundy C pieces and the purple A pieces to the navy and teal C pieces. Stitch the light pink B pieces to the royal and navy D pieces and the bright pink B pieces to the teal and burgundy D pieces. Sew the four small blocks together, referring to Diagram 1, *above.*

Sew the four large blocks together, referring to Diagram 2, *right.* Sew piping to outside edge of completed pillow top, right sides facing.

For ruffle, cut three 6½x45-inch strips of green satin and three 3x45-inch strips of burgundy satin. Stitch short ends of each color together. Stitch ends of lace together. Pin lace, then green strip to burgundy strip, right sides facing and raw edges even. Stitch three layers together. Press lace toward green strip, then press the pieced ruffle in half lengthwise, wrong sides facing. Sew a gather-

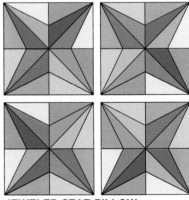

JEWELED STAR PILLOW DIAGRAM 2

ing thread through both layers close to raw edges. Pin ruffle to pillow top; adjust gathers evenly.

Trim back fabric to same size as front. Stitch pillow front to back, right sides together and leaving an opening for turning. Trim corners. Turn right side out and insert pillow form. Slip-stitch closed.

Stitch buttons at points and centers of star shapes, using pearl cotton thread and pulling tightly.

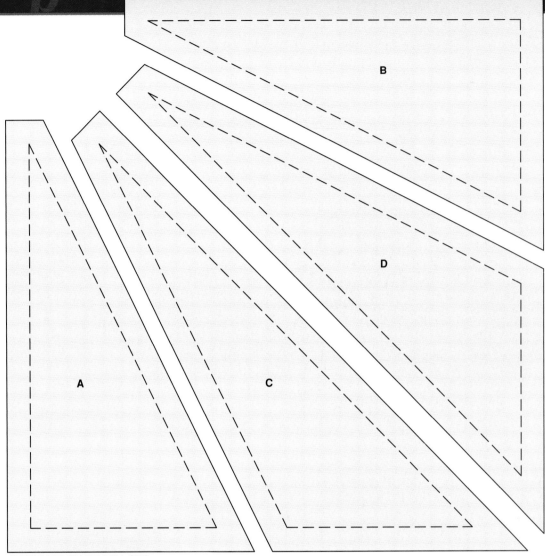

JEWELED STAR PILLOW

CRAZY QUILT PILLOW

As shown on page 121, pillow is 17x15 inches.

MATERIALS
Graph paper
14x14-inch square of muslin
½ yard of 45-inch-wide burgundy fabric
Sewing thread
Erasable fabric marker
Scraps of velvet, satin, brocade, and tapestry fabric or ribbon
Assorted embroidery threads
Small glass and metallic beads
1⅛ yards of satin piping
2 yards of 2-inch-wide white lace
Polyester fiberfill

INSTRUCTIONS

Enlarge heart pattern, *page 126*, cut out. Draw around pattern on muslin and burgundy fabrics. Cut out burgundy heart ¼ inch beyond outline. Also from burgundy, cut enough 4½-inch-wide strips to make a 72½-inch ruffle.

Machine-stitch outline of heart on muslin using contrasting thread. Cut velvet and other fancy fabrics into three- or four-sided pieces, each 3 to 4 inches long. Baste one piece to center of muslin heart. Stitch another piece to one side of first, right sides facing, using a ¼-inch seam. Hand-press pieces to right side, trimming excess.

Repeat process, continuing clockwise around first piece until the heart shape is completely covered. (Some pieces will overlap the stitched outline.)

Machine-stitch again over heart outline on wrong side of muslin, marking outline on both sides.

Work assorted embroidery stitches in various colors and threads on all seams, referring to photograph, *page 121*, for ideas. Embroider simple motifs in center of selected pieces and attach beads, if desired. Cut out heart ¼ inch beyond outline. Sew piping to heart edge, raw edges even.

Sew short ends of ruffle strips together, right sides facing, using

CRAZY QUILT PILLOW

1 Square = 1 Inch

¼-inch seam to form a circle. Fold strip in half, wrong sides facing, matching raw edges. With straight edge of the lace aligned to raw edge of the ruffle, sew a gathering thread along raw edge. Pin ruffle to pillow top, aligning raw edges. Adjust gathers evenly.

Sew pillow back and front together, right sides facing, using a ¼-inch seam allowance and leaving a 5-inch opening along one side for turning. Turn pillow right side out and stuff firmly with fiberfill. Sew opening closed.

HIGH BUTTON SHOE PINCUSHION

As shown on page 122, pincushion measures 7x8½ inches.

MATERIALS
Tracing paper
Erasable fabric marker
8x10-inch piece of cotton batiste
8x10-inch piece of satin
Contrasting and matching sewing thread
Scraps of velvet, satin, taffeta, brocade, polished cotton, and tapestry fabric or ribbon
¼ yard of narrow lace
½ yard of 1-inch-wide satin ribbon
Assorted embroidery floss
Assorted pearl cottons
Embroidery needle
Three small metallic shank buttons
Polyester fiberfill

INSTRUCTIONS
Trace the shoe pattern, *left;* cut out. Use erasable marker to draw around pattern on batiste and satin fabrics. Cut out satin shoe ½ inch beyond shoe outline.

HIGH BUTTON SHOE PINCUSHION

Machine-stitch the outline of the shoe on the batiste using contrasting thread. Cut the velvet and other fancy fabrics into three- or four-sided pieces, each 2 to 3 inches long. Baste one piece to the center of the batiste shoe. Stitch another piece to one side of first, with right sides together and using a ¼-inch seam. Hand-press the pieces to the right side, trimming excess fabric.

Repeat the process, continuing clockwise around the first piece. Add more pieces, following same method, until the shoe shape is completely covered. (Some of the fabric pieces will overlap the stitched outline.)

Machine-stitch again over the shoe outline on the wrong side of the batiste, marking the shoe shape on the pieced side.

Work assorted embroidery stitches in assorted colors and threads on all seams, referring to photograph, *page 122,* for ideas.

Sew the patchwork front and satin back together along the stitched outline, right sides together and leaving the top of the shoe open. Trim the seam allowance to ¼ inch; clip the curves and turn right side out.

Sew a gathering thread along one long edge of the lace. Pull up the gathers to fit along the outline on the top front of the shoe. Hand-stitch in place. Turn under the raw ends of the ribbon and stitch. Sew a gathering thread along one long edge of the ribbon. Pull up the gathers to fit behind the lace at the top of the shoe. Hand-sew the ribbon next to the lace. Referring to the photograph, *page 122,* sew the three shank buttons down the side of the shoe.

Stuff the shoe with fiberfill. Turn under the raw edges at the top of the shoe; slip-stitch the top opening closed.

HEART-IN-HANDS PINCUSHION

As shown on page 123, pincushion is 7 inches wide.

MATERIALS
One pair of cotton gloves
Fabric dye in color to coordinate with striped fabric (optional)
Tracing paper
9x12-inch piece of striped brocade or other fabric
Sewing thread to match striped fabric
Polyester fiberfill
½ yard of 1-inch-wide black pre-gathered lace
Antique gold spray paint (optional)
⅝ yard of ⅜-inch-wide picot-edged ribbon in color to coordinate with striped fabric
Embroidery floss in gold and color to match picot-edged ribbon
⅜-inch-diameter gold shank buttons
Purchased ribbon roses in colors to coordinate with striped fabric
Small pieces of ½-inch-wide ribbon in colors to match ribbon roses
¾-inch-wide ribbon in color to coordinate with striped fabric
20-inch piece of ⅛-inch-diameter black satin cord
White crafts glue
Toothpick
20-inch piece of ⅛-inch-diameter antique gold cord
Pencil or knitting needle
6x6-inch piece of cardboard

INSTRUCTIONS
Dye gloves to coordinate with the striped fabric color, following package directions, if desired.

Trace the heart pattern, *opposite,* onto tracing paper; cut out.

Use the heart pattern to cut two heart shapes from the striped fabric, positioning the pattern so the stripes run vertically through the hearts. From the remaining striped fabric, cut two 1½x11-inch strips for boxing welt. Set the excess fabric aside.

Sew the two welt strips together, end to end and right sides facing, using a ¼-inch seam, to make one 21½-inch-long strip. Press the seam open.

Match the center seam of the pieced welt strip with the top center of the heart front, right sides together. Pin the strip around the heart, letting both ends hang past the bottom of the heart. (Strip will be longer than needed, but *do not* trim the excess.)

Stitch the strip to the heart, starting at the bottom point and using a ¼-inch seam. Press the seam; sew the ends of the strip together, with the seam directly at the tip of the heart. Trim the seam allowance to ¼ inch.

Pin the heart back to the remaining long edge of the welt strip in the same manner. Sew the heart back to the raw edge of the boxing strip, beginning at the bottom point and leaving a 3-inch opening for turning. Turn the heart right side out. Stuff heart firmly with polyester fiberfill and slip-stitch the opening closed.

Spray the black lace lightly with gold paint, if desired. Allow the paint to dry completely. Beginning at the bottom of the heart, hand-sew the gathered edge of the lace around the heart about ¼-inch inside the front seam, overlapping the ends.

Use two plies of matching embroidery floss to couch the picot-edged ribbon over bottom edge of the black lace, so the picots just cover the seam. Allow the ribbon to lie loosely on the

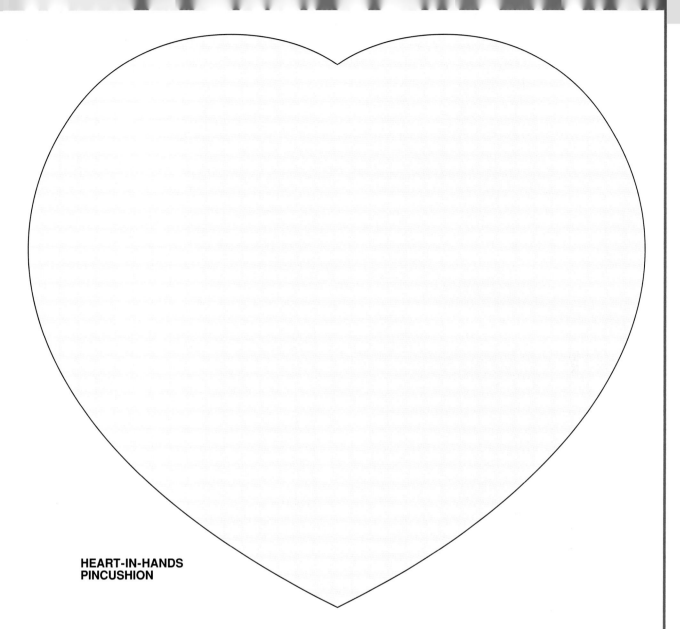

HEART-IN-HANDS PINCUSHION

fabric and pull the floss stitches firmly so the ribbon puffs slightly between stitches. Overlap the ribbon ends at the bottom point of the heart.

For ribbon flowers, cut the ¾-inch-wide ribbon into 5- to 6-inch lengths. Sew a gathering thread along one long edge of each piece; pull up gathers tightly and secure. Sew a gold button in center of each gathered flower.

Cut the black satin cord in half. To prevent fraying, lightly apply glue to cut ends with a toothpick. Tie into two bows.

Arrange the ribbon flowers, ribbon roses, small pieces of ribbon, and bows in a small bouquet as desired, tacking each piece in place on the left side front of the heart. Make a bow in the middle of the gold cord. Sew the bow in place on the bouquet. Use one ply of the gold embroidery floss to couch the tails onto the heart in a random curly pattern.

Stuff the gloves firmly with polyester fiberfill. Use a pencil or the flat end of a knitting needle to push stuffing into the fingertips of the gloves.

Cut two oval shapes from the cardboard to fit securely into the wrist openings of the gloves. Lay the ovals on the reserved striped fabric. Cut around the ovals ½ inch beyond the edges of the cardboard. Cover one side of each cardboard oval with a fabric oval, gluing the excess fabric to the back of the cardboard. Slip the ovals into the gloves to keep the fiberfill from coming out. Glue the ovals in place. Position gloves side by side and tack together. Tack the completed heart into the palms of gloves.

Q is for Quaint Quilts

Housedress Quilt

Made from real feed sack prints, this charming housedress quilt sports an old-fashioned look that's right in style today. Trimmed with vintage buttons, ribbon, and rickrack, this delightful pattern is the ideal way to display and enjoy a collection of heirloom fabrics or buttons. This quilt was pieced from authentic depression fabrics, but you can find reproductions in quilting specialty shops—or explore flea markets, second-hand stores, garage sales, and Grandmother's attic for real housedresses. If a whole quilt exceeds your stock of sentimental fabrics, turn the page for a closer view of the days-of-the-week tea towels and other housedress quilt accessories. Instructions begin on page 134. Patterns are on pages 136–137.

DESIGNER: MARGARET SINDELAR
PHOTOGRAPHER: SCOTT LITTLE

Housedress Quilt Accessories

An ample supply of tea towels was a must for the well-stocked kitchen of yesteryear. This collection contains a triple dose of nostalgia—depression-era feed sack fabrics are shaped as classic housedresses and embroidered with the traditional chore assignments for each day of the week. Use the same fanciful shape for hot pads, piece tiny scraps from the housedress fabrics for a charming tea cozy, and add buttons and bows for a unique contemporary kitchen. Instructions and patterns are on pages 134–137.

DESIGNER: MARGARET SINDELAR ● PHOTOGRAPHER: SCOTT LITTLE

Quilted Tulips

Every day is the first day of spring with these tulip-quilted designs. Add a bright bloom to any room with a simple headboard and pillow. This flower garden will expand to fit over a larger bed or add extra blocks to the pillow for a sham. If the room belongs to a young lady, create a matching apron that's perfect for a tea party. Instructions and patterns begin on page 137.

DESIGNER: MARGARET SINDELAR ● PHOTOGRAPHER: HOPKINS ASSOCIATES

HOUSEDRESS QUILT

As shown on page 130–131, finished size is 68x84 inches.

MATERIALS

Tracing paper
Quilter's template material
14x14-inch piece of 20 different feed sack or other print fabrics
11x5-inch scraps of 20 different coordinating solids
¾ yard of 45-inch-wide white cotton fabric
3 yards of 45-inch-wide print fabric for sashing and binding
4 yards of 45-inch-wide fabric for back
Polyester batting
Assorted buttons, rickrack, ribbon, buckles, narrow flat lace or other trims for dresses

INSTRUCTIONS

Trace pattern, *pages 136–137.* Cut apart on solid lines. Draw around pieces on template material, joining the F pieces and adding ¼-inch seam allowances. From each of the 20 print fabrics, cut one A, B, and C piece. Turn templates over; cut one more of each piece. From coordinating solid, cut one E and F piece. Turn template over; cut one more F. From white fabric, cut 40 D pieces.

For sashing, cut forty-nine 4½x12½-inch print strips and thirty 4½x4½-inch white blocks. Cut remaining print into 2-inch-wide binding strips. (Measurements include ¼-inch seam allowances.)

For each block, referring to diagram, *below,* sew A to B and B to C; set in F. Repeat for other side of dress. Stitch halves together along center front. Stitch D pieces to E; stitch to dress.

Arrange blocks in five rows of four blocks each. For each row, sew long side of a sashing strip to each side of the left-hand block. Sew second block to right sashing. Continuing to work from left to right, sew another sashing, third block, another sashing, fourth block, and another sashing.

For horizontal sashing, sew a white block to each short end of a sashing strip, then sew another sashing to the right of the right-hand block. Continuing to work from left to right, sew third block, another sashing, fourth block and another sashing, and a fifth block. Make six. Sew a horizontal sashing between rows of blocks and at top and bottom, matching seam lines. Layer quilt top, batting, and back (pieced as necessary). Baste. Machine-quilt along seam lines of sashing.

Trim batting and back ½ inch beyond quilt top. Sew enough 2-inch-wide strips together to fit around edge of quilt. Pin binding to quilt top, right sides together; stitch through all layers, using a ¼-inch seam and mitering corners. Turn binding to back of quilt and turn under ¼ inch along raw edge. Blindstitch in place. Add buttons and trims to decorate dresses, stitching through all layers.

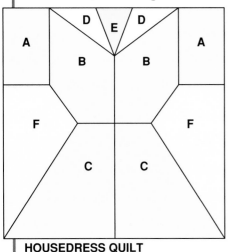

HOUSEDRESS QUILT ASSEMBLY DIAGRAM

HOUSEDRESS TEA TOWEL

HOUSEDRESS TEA TOWELS

As shown on page 132, appliquéd design measures 6x6 inches.

MATERIALS *for each towel*

Tracing paper
Paper-backed iron-on adhesive
7x7-inch piece of print fabric
Scrap of white fabric
Scrap of contrasting solid fabric
Muslin tea towel; sewing thread
Dressmaker's carbon paper
Embroidery floss in desired color
Erasable fabric marker
Narrow ribbon; rickrack

INSTRUCTIONS

Trace pattern, *above,* on folded tissue paper; cut out and unfold.

Draw outline of complete pattern onto paper side of iron-on adhesive. Cut pattern apart between B and D pieces. Draw outline of smaller portion on adhesive. Cut D pieces off pattern; trace around E on iron-on adhesive. Cut out all three pieces. Following manufacturer's instructions, fuse dress to print, collar to white fabric, and center (E piece) to solid fabric. Cut out pieces.

Fuse dress to towel, positioning bottom 1¼ inches above edge and centering left to right. Fuse collar and center piece onto dress. Transfer piecing lines (center front, waist, and sleeve seams) to dress. Machine-satin stitch along all edges and piecing lines.

Use fabric marker to write desired day of week and chore centered above dress. Stem-stitch writing using two plies of floss.

Tie ribbon in a small bow and tack to front of dress. Machine-stitch rickrack to hem of towel.

HOUSEDRESS HOT PADS

As shown on page 132, hot pads are 9x9¼ inches.

MATERIALS
For each hot pad
Tracing paper
12x20-inch piece of print fabric
Scrap of white fabric
Scrap of contrasting solid fabric
Thread to match print fabrics
10x10-inch piece of extra-loft polyester fleece
1¼ yards of purchased piping
Scraps of narrow rickrack, lace, and ribbon

INSTRUCTIONS
Trace pattern, *right,* onto tracing paper twice; cut out. Cut *one* pattern apart. Draw around pieces on template material, adding

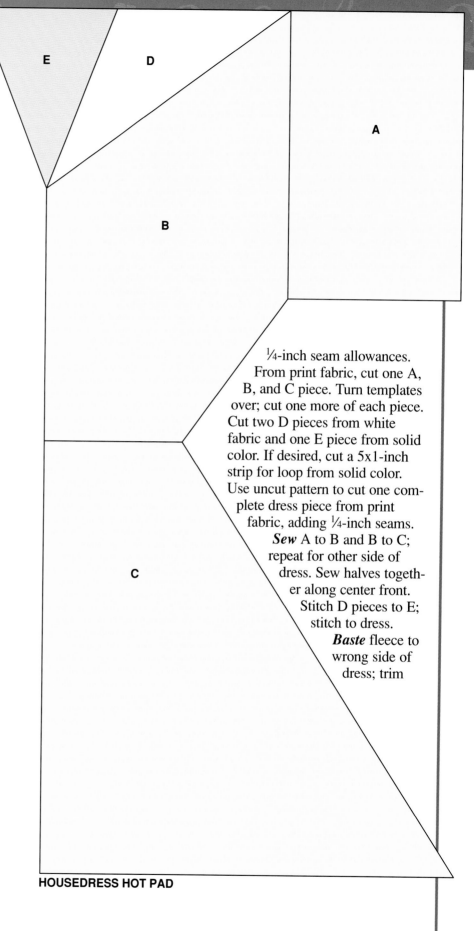

¼-inch seam allowances. From print fabric, cut one A, B, and C piece. Turn templates over; cut one more of each piece. Cut two D pieces from white fabric and one E piece from solid color. If desired, cut a 5x1-inch strip for loop from solid color. Use uncut pattern to cut one complete dress piece from print fabric, adding ¼-inch seams.

Sew A to B and B to C; repeat for other side of dress. Sew halves together along center front. Stitch D pieces to E; stitch to dress.

Baste fleece to wrong side of dress; trim

HOUSEDRESS HOT PAD

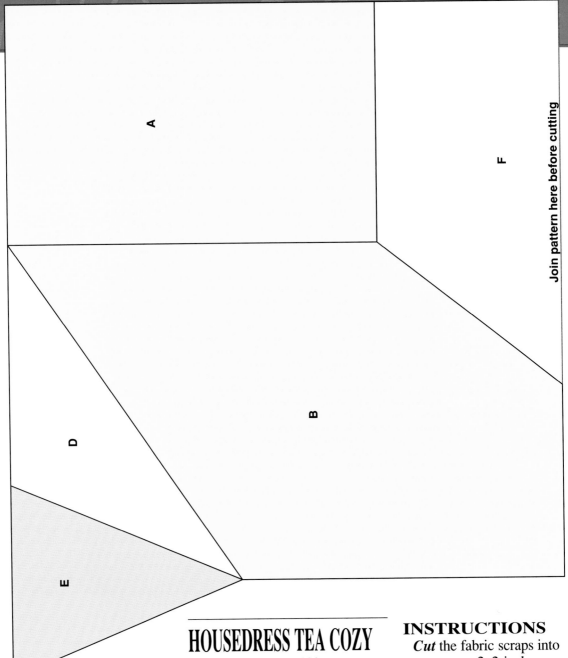

A

F

Join pattern here before cutting

D

B

E

HOUSEDRESS QUILT

edges even. Stitch piping to outer edges of dress, raw edges even. If desired, sew long edges of loop strip together using a ¼-inch seam. Turn right side out. Fold in half and pin to top of dress, raw edges even. With the right sides facing, stitch dress front to back, leaving an opening for turning. Trim the corners and clip curves. Turn right side out. Slip-stitch the opening closed. Stitch lace or rickrack to edge of collar. Add buttons and bow trim as desired.

HOUSEDRESS TEA COZY

As shown on page 132, tea cozy measures 11x12½ inches.

MATERIALS

Scraps of assorted print fabrics, each at least 2x2 inches
Sewing thread
12x14-inch piece of fabric for back
Two 12x14-inch pieces of quilt batting
Two 12x14-inch pieces of fabric for lining
2 yards of purchased piping
Cording to match piping
Pearl buttons in assorted sizes
Pearl cotton in assorted colors

INSTRUCTIONS

Cut the fabric scraps into seventy-two 2x2-inch squares. With right sides together and using ¼-inch seams, sew squares together in eight rows of nine squares each. Stitch rows together. Press seams to one side.

Layer top and one piece each of batting and lining. Baste. Trim excess fabric and lining to same size as top.

Fold basted fabric in half to form a 12x6¾-inch rectangle. Trim raw edges of one corner away to shape rounded top of cozy. Stitch piping along side and top edges, raw edges even. Add loop of cording at center top.

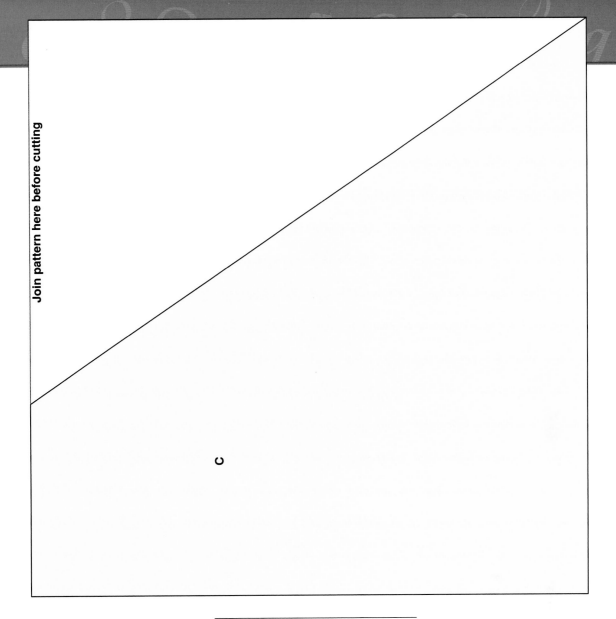

Join pattern here before cutting

C

For back of cozy, layer, baste, and trim back fabric, remaining batting, and lining fabric to same size as front of cozy. Machine-quilt in horizontal and vertical rows, 1½ inches apart.

Stitch cozy front to back, right sides facing, along piping line, leaving bottom open. Turn right side out and press.

Stitch piping to right side of cozy with raw edge ¾ inch above bottom edge. Turn raw edge of fabric to wrong side along the stitching line. Topstitch through all layers, ¼ inch above piping.

Use pearl cotton to sew a button at corner of each square. Tie ends together on front of cozy and trim to ½ inch.

TULIP HEADBOARD AND PILLOW

As shown on page 133, head-board measures 16x58 inches; pillow measures 16x17 inches.

MATERIALS
For headboard
6x12-inch pieces of polished cotton, chintz, or other fabric in 14 pastel colors
¼ yard *each* of dark and light green polished cotton, chintz or other fabric
½ yard of cream-colored fabric
1 yard of pink fabric for sashing strips and back
1⅝ yards of polyester fleece

For pillow
6x12-inch pieces of polished cotton, chintz, or other fabric in four pastel colors
16x12-inch piece *each* of dark and light green polished cotton, chintz, or other fabric
⅜ yard of cream-colored fabric
⅝ yard of purple fabric for sashing strips and back
Polyester fleece; pillow form
For quilt and pillow
Tracing paper
Quilter's template material
White sewing thread
Transparent nylon thread

INSTRUCTIONS
Trace patterns, *pages 138–139,* onto tracing paper. Cut apart on

solid lines. Draw around pieces on template material, adding ¼-inch seam allowances.

For headboard, sort pastel colored fabrics, pairing colors for each tulip. Cut A pieces from seven colors for centers, one D and E piece from remaining seven colors for petals, seven each of B, G, and N pieces from dark green, seven each of C, F, L, and M from light green, 28 each of H and K pieces from cream

fabric, and 14 each of I and J from cream.

From pink fabric, cut two 28½x16½-inch rectangles for back, fourteen 1½x7½-inch horizontal sashing strips, and eight 1½x16½-inch vertical sashing strips. From scraps of all fabrics, cut seventy 3x3-inch squares. (Measurements include ¼-inch seam allowance.)

For each flower block, sew B strip to A square and C strip to

AB, referring to pattern, *below.* Continue until pieces D–G have been sewn. Sew H pieces to each edge of flower to complete block.

For each stem block, sew two K pieces to each M and L piece, referring to pattern, *opposite.* Stitch resulting strips to I and J pieces, then stitch them to N.

To assemble each tulip, stitch flower block to stem block. Stitch horizontal sashing strips to top and bottom of tulip. Sew the

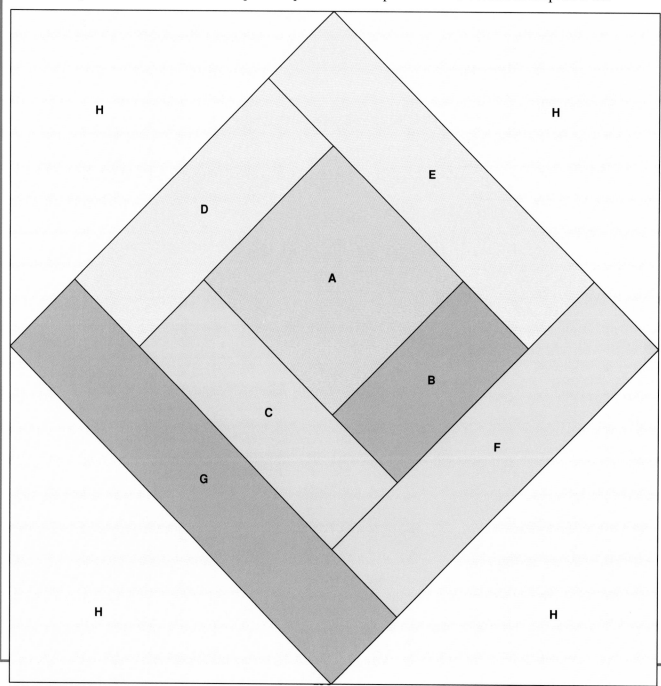

TULIP HEADBOARD AND PILLOW – FLOWER BLOCK

seven tulips together with vertical sashing between each square and on ends. Baste fleece to wrong side of quilt top and trim edges even with quilt top.

For prairie points, press colored 3-inch squares in half diagonally, wrong sides together. Press in half again, matching raw edges. Pin 8 prairie points on each end and 27 along top and bottom edges of quilt, raw edges together, overlapping points slightly.

Sew short ends of back rectangles together. Stitch front to back, right sides together, leaving an opening. Trim corners; turn. Stitch opening closed. Machine-quilt through all layers along edge of flowers and stems, and along sashing strips. Remove basting.

For pillow, pair pastel fabrics as directed for headboard. Cut two A pieces and two each of D and E pieces. Cut two each of B, G, and N pieces from dark green, two

each of C, F, L, and M pieces from light green, eight each of H and K pieces from cream fabric, and four each of I and J from cream. From purple fabric, cut a 17½x17½-inch back, four 1½x7½-inch horizontal sashing strips, and three 1½x16½-inch vertical sashing strips. For prairie points, cut thirty-six 3-inch squares from all colors of fabrics.

Assemble two tulips in same manner as for headboard. Stitch

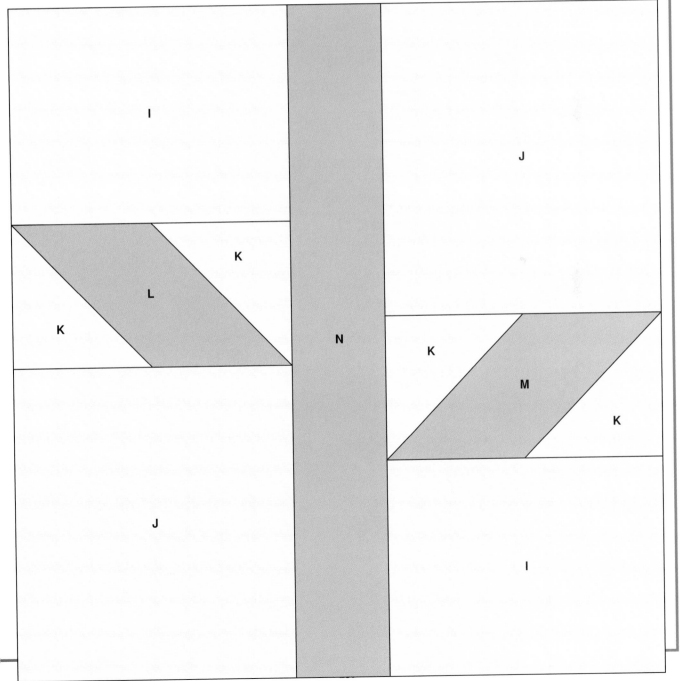

TULIP HEADBOARD AND PILLOW – STEM BLOCK

horizontal sashing strips to top and bottom of tulips; sew together with vertical sashing strips between tulips. Layer pillow front and fleece; machine-quilt as directed for headboard. Fold prairie points as directed for headboard; pin evenly around edge of pillow, overlapping slightly.

Sew pillow front to back, leaving an opening for turning. Insert pillow form and slip-stitch closed.

TULIP APRON

As shown on page 133.

MATERIALS

- Tracing paper
- Quilter's template material
- Scraps of pastel print calico fabrics in at least six colors
- 6x6-inch piece *each* of dark and light green calico
- 1½ yards of 44-inch-wide peach fabric
- Sewing thread
- 12x12-inch piece of fleece

INSTRUCTIONS

Trace patterns, *below*. Cut apart on solid lines. Draw around pieces on template material, adding ¼-inch seam allowances.

Sort pastel fabrics, pairing colors for each tulip. Cut A pieces from each of three colors for centers, one D and E piece from remaining three colors for petals. Cut two each of B, G, and N pieces from dark green, two each of C, F, L, and M pieces from light green, eight each of H and K pieces from peach fabric, and four each of I and J from peach. From calico fabrics, cut forty-three 3x3-inch squares for prairie points.

From peach fabric, also cut an 18x45-inch skirt, two 2½x20-inch strips for waistband, two 5½x36-inch strips for ties, one 2½x18-inch neckband, one 7½x11-inch bib lining, and four 4½x4½-inch pockets. (Measurements include ¼-inch seam allowances.)

Assemble three calico flowers as for tulip headboard. Stitch flowers together for apron bib. Baste fleece to wrong side of bib. Fold prairie points as directed for headboard. Pin four prairie points along sides of bib and six prairie points along top of bib.

Fold neckband in half lengthwise, right sides together, and stitch, leaving short ends open. Turn and press. Pin ends of the neckband to top of bib, ¼ inch from each side. Stitch bib lining to bib front along sides and top, right sides together. Turn right side out. Baste along bottom edge of bib. Machine-quilt bib as desired. Pin center front of bib to center front of waistband.

Narrow-hem short edges of skirt. Stitch twenty-three prairie points to bottom edge of apron, raw edges together. Clean-finish raw edge; turn on stitching line and topstitch through all layers.

For pockets, pin three prairie points to top edge of two pocket squares. Stitch pocket linings to pockets, right sides facing, leaving an opening. Trim corners, turn, and slip-stitch openings. Topstitch to skirt 5 inches from top and 12 inches from sides.

Gather top of skirt; stitch to bottom of waistband. Fold ties in half lengthwise, right sides facing; stitch along two sides. Turn and press. Pleat open ends; sew to sides of waistband, right sides facing. Stitch waistband facing to top and sides of waistband; turn. Fold raw edge under and sew.

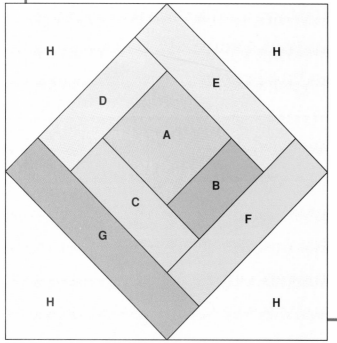

TULIP APRON – FLOWER BLOCK

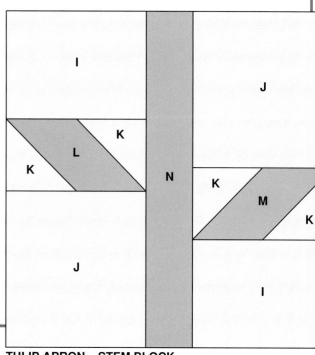

TULIP APRON – STEM BLOCK

R is for *R*azzle-Dazzle *R*ugs

Stars and Stripes Rug and Pillow

Small squares of wool are folded and stitched to create this flurry of fabric in patriotic designs. The rug and coordinating pillows use pillow ticking as a base, which provides guidelines for creating the stars-and-stripes designs. Instructions and pattern begin on page 144.

DESIGNER: MARGARET SINDELAR ● PHOTOGRAPHER: HOPKINS ASSOCIATES

Circles of Color Rug

This charming rug is a scrap saver's dream come true. Collect all those little sewing scraps or clean out the closets and select brightly colored used garments. Cut them into strips to make "yarn." Then use a simple single crochet stitch to create this colorful colonial-style home accessory. Centers and borders of black make the finished rug a real attention-getter. Instructions begin on page 145.

DESIGNER: ADAPTED FROM AN ANTIQUE RUG ● PHOTOGRAPHER: HOPKINS ASSOCIATES

Folk Heart Table Rug

A peach linen background is the perfect pastel backdrop to this pretty hooked design. Use strips of wool fabric to create the motif, then finish the edges and enjoy the end result as a diminutive rug, wall hanging, or table mat.
Instructions and pattern begin on page 146.

DESIGNER: MARGARET SINDELAR ● PHOTOGRAPHER: HOPKINS ASSOCIATES

STAR RUG

As shown on page 141, rug measures 29½x40 inches.

MATERIALS
Graph paper
Erasable fabric marker
1¼ yards of 45-inch-wide striped pillow-ticking fabric
1 yard of fusible polyester fleece
1½ yards of 56-inch-wide white wool fabric or equivalent in scraps
1¼ yards of 56-inch-wide red wool fabric or equivalent in scraps
1 yard of 56-inch-wide blue wool fabric or equivalent in scraps
Rotary cutter; cutting mat
White sewing thread
Liquid latex rug backing

INSTRUCTIONS
Cut a 32½x43-inch rectangle from ticking and fleece. Fuse fleece to wrong side of ticking. Clean finish edges. Enlarge star pattern, *below;* cut out. Draw around pattern on ticking. Also draw lines extending from points of star to indicate blue/red color change. (See diagram, *below.*)

Cut wool fabrics into 2-inch squares, using rotary cutter. Cut 752 white squares, 588 red squares, and 504 blue squares.

For first row, fold the two opposite edges of each of about 40 blue squares to center and finger-press. Pin folded squares side by side with one short edge aligned to ticking stripe 2½ inches from edge; leave 1½ inches on each end empty. Machine-stitch squares to ticking, sewing across center of each folded square.

STAR RUG

(See stitching diagram, *opposite.*) Finger-press stitched squares toward outside of rug. Fold and align a second row of blue squares with next ticking; stitch.

Continue adding rows, changing colors as indicated by star outline. Last row of stitching should be 1½ inches from edge.

Turn seam allowance to wrong side, mitering corners, and whip-stitch in place. Paint back of rug with liquid latex rug backing.

STRIPED PILLOWS

As shown on page 141, pillows measure 16x16 inches.

MATERIALS *for each pillow*
19x19-inch piece of fusible fleece
19x19-inch square of striped pillow-ticking fabric
½ yards of 56-inch-wide white wool fabric or equivalent in scraps
½ yard of 56-inch-wide red wool fabric or equivalent in scraps
½ yard of 56-inch-wide blue wool fabric or equivalent in scraps
19x19-inch piece of red fabric
Rotary cutter; cutting mat
White sewing thread
Polyester fiberfill

INSTRUCTIONS
Fuse fleece to back of ticking. Use fabric marker to draw wavy or bunting striped pattern on ticking, referring to illustrations, *below.* Make wavy pattern stripes about 5 inches wide. Make blue rectangle in bunting pattern about 16x6 inches and red and white stripes about 2⅝ inches wide.

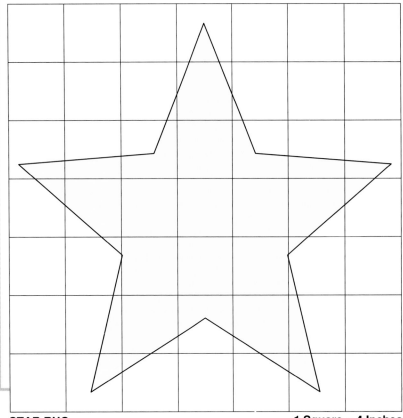

STAR RUG

1 Square = 4 Inches

WAVY STRIPES PILLOW

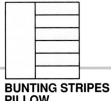

BUNTING STRIPES PILLOW

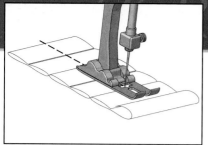

STITCHING DIAGRAM

Cut wool fabrics into 2-inch squares, using rotary cutter.

For first row, fold two opposite edges of each of about 16 squares (all red for wavy pattern, 6 blue and 10 red for bunting pattern) to center and finger-press. Pin folded squares side by side with one short edge aligned to ticking stripe 2½ inches from edge; leave 1½ inches on each end empty. Machine-stitch squares to ticking, sewing across center of each folded square. (See diagram, *above.*) Finger-press stitched squares toward outside of pillow. Fold and align a second row of squares with next ticking; stitch.

Continue adding rows, changing colors as indicated by stripe markings. Last row of stitching should be 1½ inches from edge.

To assemble, sew pillow fronts to backs, right sides facing, about ½ inch beyond last row of wool squares, leaving an opening for turning. Trim corners; turn right side out. Stuff pillows with fiberfill; slip-stitch closed.

CIRCLES OF COLOR RUG

As shown on page 142, rug measures 36 inches in diameter. Crochet abbreviations, page 17.

MATERIALS
SUPPLIES
Cotton and cotton blend dress fabrics in assorted colors
Rotary cutter; cutting mat
Size K crochet hook or size to obtain gauge
Carpet thread; tapestry needle
GAUGE: 5 sc = 2 inches

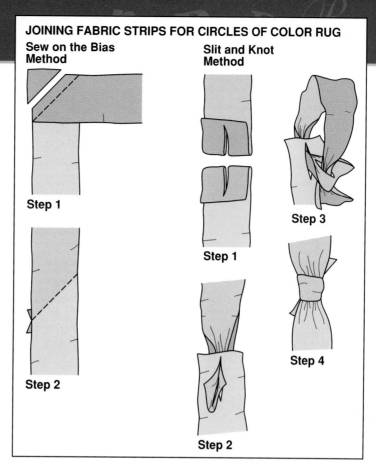

JOINING FABRIC STRIPS FOR CIRCLES OF COLOR RUG

Sew on the Bias Method
Step 1
Step 2

Slit and Knot Method
Step 1
Step 2
Step 3
Step 4

INSTRUCTIONS

Cut all fabric into strips ¾- to ⅞-inch wide. Sew or slit and knot strips together (see diagrams, *above*) and roll into balls. Sort balls by color. Both circles have black centers and borders. Work each round between center and border of small circle in shades of same color or complimentary colors, referring to photograph, *page 142,* for ideas. Work each round between center and border of central circle in random colors. To change colors, use new color for last yarn over of last st in previous color.

For small circles, black, ch 2.
Rnd 1: 7 sc in second ch from hook, changing to lightest shade in one color on last st—7 st.
Rnd 2: Inc in each st around—14 sts.
Rnd 3: *1 sc, inc in next st; rep from * around—21 sts.
Rnd 4: *2 sc, inc in next st; rep from * around—28 sts.
Rnd 5: *3 sc, inc in next st; rep from * around—35 sts.

Rnd 6: *4 sc, inc in next st; rep from * around, changing to black in last st—42 sts.
Rnd 7: *5 sc, inc in next st; rep from * around, end with sl st in next st—49 sts. End off.
For center, with black, ch 2.
Rnd 1: 7 sc in second ch from hook—7 sts.
Rnd 2: Inc in each st around, changing to desired color on last st—14 sts.
Rnds 3–7: Work as directed for Rnds 3–7 of small circles, except change to a different color at end of each round.

Work 17 more rnds, continuing to inc 7 st in each rnd—168 sts. Change to black in last st.
Rnd 25: *Hdc, dc, tr, dtr, tr, dc, hdc, 6 sc, hdc, dc, tr, dtr, tr, dc, hdc, 6 sc, inc in next st; rep from * 5 times. Hdc, dc, tr, dtr, tr, dc, hdc, 5 sc. End with sl in first hdc. End off.

Place 13 small circles in a ring; sew 4 sts of each to the next one together where circles touch. Sew the outer ring to Rnd 25 of center.

FOLK HEART TABLE RUG

As shown on page 143, rug measures 14x14 inches.

MATERIALS
Tracing paper
Dressmaker's carbon paper
16x16-inch piece of 28-count peach-color linen
Scraps of wool fabric in the following colors: taupe, hot pink, green, turquoise, purple
Hoop or frame; hook
16x16-inch piece of print fabric for border and back
14x14-inch piece of paper-backed iron-on adhesive
Sewing thread

INSTRUCTIONS

Trace pattern, *below.* Fold linen into quarters and finger-press creases; unfold. Transfer pattern to each quarter of linen, aligning the center lines to creases and repeating it three times to complete the pattern. Cut the wool into ¼-inch-wide strips following lengthwise grain of fabric.

To hook designs, mount linen in hoop. Hold one end of a wool strip under linen. Push hook between threads from top and pull end of wool through to right side. Move two threads and repeat, pulling a loop to right side. Keeping loop on hook, pull on wool from underside until loop is ¼-inch tall. Referring to patterns, *below,* for colors, continue pulling up loops until entire area is covered. Trim ends even with loops.

Trim hooked design to a 14x14-inch square with design centered. Fuse iron-on adhesive to back of design. Center on back fabric; fuse. Turn under ¾ inch along all sides of backing fabric; press. Repeat, turning under another ¾ inch. Slip-stitch in place.

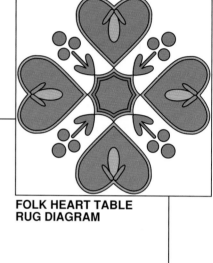

FOLK HEART TABLE RUG DIAGRAM

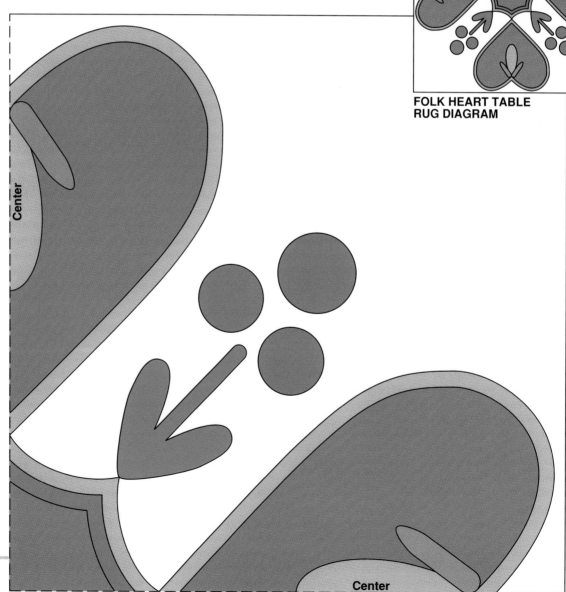

Center

Center

S is for *Sensational Stockings and Santas*

Scrap Yarn Stocking

This rustic stocking finds a home for all those little scraps of Persian wool that are "too good" to throw away. Work simple cross-stitches on needlepoint canvas, creating a color scheme as you work. Instructions are on page 150.

DESIGNER: JIM WILLIAMS ● PHOTOGRAPHER: HOPKINS ASSOCIATES

Country Cabin Stockings

A variety of blue and white fabrics lend country charm to these primitive holiday stockings. One features a lace cuff and button-trimmed heart, while the other is adorned with a grid of running stitches and pearl buttons. Instructions and pattern begin on page 151.

DESIGNER: SUSAN CAGE-KNOCH ● PHOTOGRAPHER: SCOTT LITTLE

Corncob Santa

A few corncobs and bits of fabric are all you need to fashion this adorable rustic Santa. He stands on a block of wood, as well-dressed as you please. The colors and prints of his clothes and jaunty cap give him a festive look, and his marking-pen face features an elf-like expression. Instructions and pattern begin on page 153.

DESIGNER: PHYLLIS DUNSTAN ● PHOTOGRAPHER: SCOTT LITTLE

Santa Pins

These cute-as-a-button diminutive pins will brighten up a holiday wardrobe or secret Santa exchange in no time at all. Use your smallest scraps of fabrics, ribbon, and yarn to craft the Santas, then add an assortment of bells, beads, and miniature ornaments to make each one unique. Complete instructions and patterns are on page 155.

DESIGNER: BETTY AUTH
PHOTOGRAPHER: HOPKINS ASSOCIATES

SCRAP YARN STOCKING

As shown on page 147, stocking is 15½ inches tall.

MATERIALS
FABRICS
20x14-inch piece of 10-count interlock mono needlepoint canvas
18x12-inch piece of fabric for stocking back
18x24-inch piece of lining fabric
THREADS
Scraps of various colors of 3-ply Persian wool equal to about 110 yards
SUPPLIES
Tapestry needle
Graph paper
2 yards of decorative upholstery cord
Sewing thread

INSTRUCTIONS
Enlarge the pattern, *opposite,* onto graph paper. Cut out.

Tape or zigzag the edges of the needlepoint canvas to prevent fraying. Beginning ½ inch below top of canvas, draw around the outline of the stocking; *do not* cut out. Cut the yarns into varied lengths. Randomly select colors to work cross-stitches over two threads of the canvas within the stocking outline. Work first row from left to right, then second row right to left to minimize the canvas distortion.

When stitching is complete, pin canvas to ironing board or other firm surface, right side down, and steam with a medium-hot iron and a damp press cloth to reshape.

Center canvas on back fabric, right sides together. Machine-stitch on stocking outline around

sides. Trim excess canvas and fabric, ½ inch beyond seam and ½ inch beyond top row of cross-stitches. Use cut piece to cut two lining pieces. Sew lining pieces together, right sides facing, leaving an opening at top and in toe. Set the lining aside.

Clip curves, and turn stocking right side out. Knot one end of the decorative cord, leaving a loop for hanging and a ½-inch-long piece below knot to attach to the inside of the stocking. Position knot at top of stocking on the right-hand side (heel side) leaving short end free. Hand-sew the remaining cord to stocking edge along seam.

Slip the lining inside stocking. Sew stocking and lining together around top, catching ends of cord in seam. Turn right side out through opening in toe. Tuck the lining into the stocking.

COUNTRY CABIN STOCKINGS

As shown on page 148, stockings measure 12½ inches tall.

MATERIALS

For heart stocking

14x24-inch piece of blue and white striped chambray

5¼x13-inch piece blue and white ticking fabric

6½-inch piece of 3-inch-wide white cotton lace

3 antique metal buttons

For plaid stocking

14x24-inch piece of dark blue wool

4x12-inch piece of blue and white striped chambray

Ruler; white chalk

6 pearl or plastic buttons

For either stocking

Graph paper; tracing paper

String; large darning needle

INSTRUCTIONS

Enlarge the pattern, *page 152,* then trace the heart, heel, and toe shapes; cut out. Cut the pattern pieces from the fabrics indicated in the materials list. Work all stitches using a darning needle and string unless otherwise noted.

For heart stocking, cut two stockings from chambray. From ticking cut heart, heel, toe, and a 1¼x5½-inch binding strip, and a 5x½-inch hanging loop.

Center the heart on the right side of the stocking front piece as indicated on the pattern. Stitch the heart to the stocking by working a featherstitch around the perimeter and a chain stitch ¼ inch inside of the heart perimeter.

Place lace cuff piece wrong side down on the stocking front with the top edges aligning. Baste the sides and the top edge of the lace cuff piece to the stocking. With

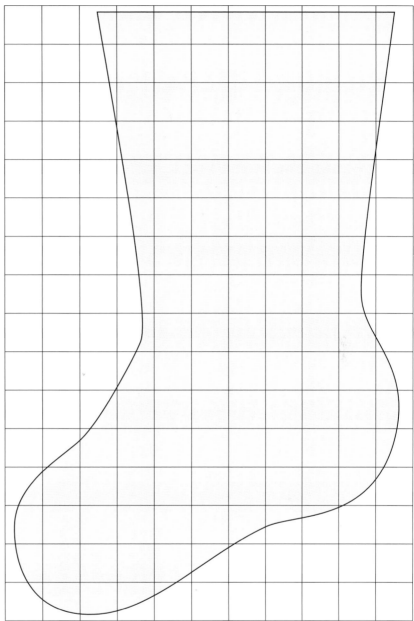

SCRAP YARN STOCKING　　　　　　**1 Square = 1 Inch**

right sides facing, sew the binding strip to the top of the stocking using a ¼-inch seam. Fold under ¼ inch along the raw edge. Turn the binding to the wrong side and slip-stitch to the seam. Work a featherstitch across the seamline of the binding on the right side.

Sew heel and toe pieces in place on stocking front using feather-stitches around the edges. Stitch buttons on the heart referring to the photograph, *page 148.* With *wrong* sides facing, sew stocking

front to back using buttonhole stitches around edges.

Whipstitch along both long edges of the hanging strip. Fold the strip in half and secure the ends inside the stocking top.

For plaid stocking, cut two stocking pieces and a 5x½-inch hanging loop from blue wool. From chambray, cut heel, toe, and a 2x5-inch cuff.

Make a grid pattern on stocking front by drawing chalk lines hori-zontally and vertically, spacing

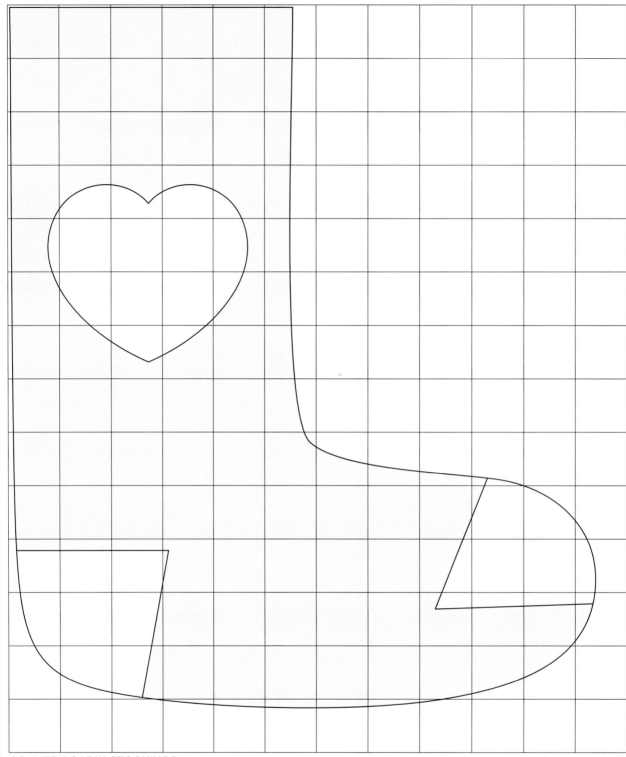

COUNTRY CABIN STOCKINGS

1 Square = 1 Inch

lines approximately 1¼ inches apart. Work running stitches along chalk lines. Tie buttons to centers of random grid squares. Stitch down and then up through button holes and knot string at top.

Place cuff wrong side down on stocking front, aligning top edges. Work buttonhole stitches across top, securing cuff to stocking. Sew heel and toe pieces in place on front using a buttonhole stitch.

Sew stocking front to back using featherstitches inside cut edges.

Work running stitches ⅛ inch from each long edge. Fold hanging strip in half; secure ends inside the stocking top.

CORNCOB SANTA

As shown on page 149, Santa is approximately 11 inches high.

MATERIALS
Tracing paper
Pencil
12x6-inch piece of solid red
   fabric
12x12-inch piece of red print
   fabric
4 corncobs, each approximately
   6 inches long and 1 inch in
   diameter
Slice of a tree branch, 3 inches
   in diameter and ½-inch thick
Two 1-inch-long finishing nails
Hammer; hot glue gun
Sewing thread
Polyester fiberfill
Corn husks
Drill and small bit
Two ½-inch-diameter black
   wooden beads
Scrap of muslin
Dressmaker's carbon paper
Permanent fine-point black
   marker
Approximately 30 to 35 white
   buttons of different sizes
Powdered rouge
Lengths of raffia
5½-inch-long pipe cleaner
White glue

INSTRUCTIONS

Trace the patterns, *page 154;* cut out. Cut the body pieces from solid red fabric. Transfer markings. Cut the hat pieces, two 4½x5-inch pant rectangles, and a 1x12-inch body trim strip from the print fabric. Pattern pieces and measurements include a ¼-inch seam allowance.

For feet, cut 1 inch off the rounded ends of two corncobs. Position the two corncobs on the wood slice for legs, standing them flat side down, and leaving approximately ⅜ inch between

them. Mark their position on the wood, drawing around them with a pencil. Pound a finishing nail into the center of each mark. Push the ends of each corncob leg onto a nail and hot-glue them to the wood. Hot-glue the corncob feet, pointed ends to the outside, in front of the legs.

For pants, fold each pant rectangle in half lengthwise, right sides together, and stitch the long raw edges together using a ¼-inch seam. Turn right side out and hem one short edge. Slip one rectangle over each leg, with the raw edge to the top and the hemmed edge 1 inch above the foot. Glue the top edge to the leg.

For body, sew the body pieces together, right sides facing, leaving an opening on one end as indicated on the pattern. Turn right side out. With the opening at the top, push the bottom half of the body up into top half, creasing along the fold line. Stuff the body with fiberfill through the opening, pushing small amounts of fiberfill to the fold edge and gradually filling the body to the top. Blind-stitch the opening closed and flip the body inside out, so opening is inside. Slip the folded edge of the body over the top of the legs until tops of pants are covered. Hot-glue the inside of the body to tops of the legs.

Fold one corn husk into a band approximately 1-inch wide and hot-glue it around the bottom edge of the body. Fold the long edges of the body trim strip to the center and press. Center folded strip, raw edges in on top of the corn husk strip and glue in place, overlapping the edges.

For arms, cut a 4-inch length from the two remaining corncobs. Drill a hole through each corncob ¾ inch below from the flat end. Thread a needle with a double

length of thread; knot the ends. Loop the thread through a large bead, then pass the needle through the hole on the outside of one corncob arm. Push the needle into the body at the X indicated on the pattern and out the X on the other side of the body. Tie the thread snugly against the body. Repeat for the other arm.

For head, draw around the head pattern on a double thickness of muslin. Stitch along the outline, leaving the top open. Trim away the excess fabric ⅛ inch beyond stitching and turn right side out. Use dressmaker's carbon paper to transfer the facial features to the head. Trace over the features, using the felt pen. Stuff the head with fiberfill and slip-stitch the opening closed. For the beard, sew the buttons to the beard section indicated on pattern, overlapping buttons slightly. Brush cheeks lightly with rouge. Tie ten 2½-inch lengths of raffia together and tack under the nose for a mustache.

For hat, sew the front and back pieces together, with right sides facing and leaving the bottom open. Stitch one end of the pipe cleaner to the wrong side of the tip of the hat. Turn the hat right side out with pipe cleaner inside. Turn under ½ inch along bottom edge and glue in place. Make a loop in the free end of the pipe cleaner and stitch it to the bottom back edge of the hat. Slip the hat over Santa's head, pulling it down over most of the back of the head. Blind-stitch the hat to the back of the head. Bend the pipe cleaner and gather the fabric along it to arrange the end of the hat.

To finish, hot-glue head to top of body. Tuck fiberfill under front edge of hat for hair; glue. Tie a length of raffia around middle of the body for a belt.

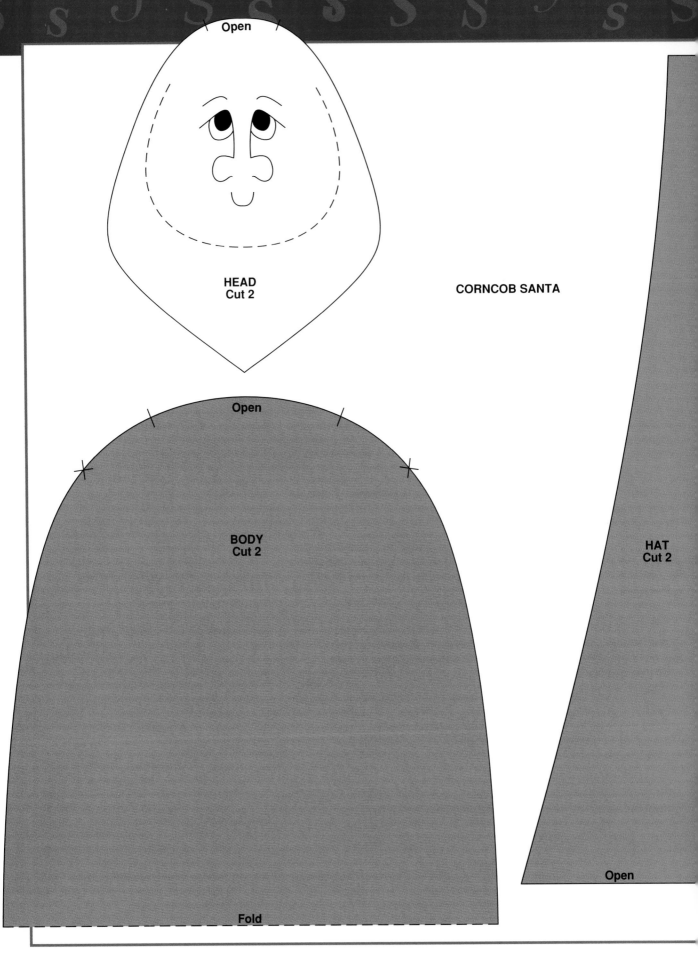

Open

HEAD
Cut 2

CORNCOB SANTA

Open

BODY
Cut 2

HAT
Cut 2

Open

Fold

SANTA PINS

As shown on page 150, pins are 3½ inches long.

MATERIALS

For one pin

Tracing paper
Two 3¼x4-inch pieces and one 3x3-inch piece of medium-weight holiday print fabric
Two 2¼x4-inch pieces of unbleached muslin
Heavy-duty thread
Polyester fiberfill
Sewing thread
Scraps of narrow ribbon
One 2½-inch-long white silk rose leaf, long-nap fake fur, or scraps of any white yarn
Assorted embellishments, including jingle bells, beads, brass charms, and miniature ornaments
Black extra-fine permanent marker
Gold paint pen (optional)
Hot glue gun and glue sticks or crafts glue
One ¾-inch-long pin back
All-purpose cement

INSTRUCTIONS

Trace the patterns, *right,* onto tracing paper and cut out.

Sew one 4-inch edge of each print rectangle to the 4-inch edge of a muslin rectangle with right sides together and using a ¼-inch seam allowance. (If desired, use a 4x5-inch piece of holiday print for back of the pin, omitting one muslin rectangle.) Press seam allowances toward darker fabric. Pin rectangles together, right sides facing, matching seams together. Trace around body pattern on top of layered fabric, matching dashed neckline to seam.

Stitch twice along traced lines, using heavy-duty thread and tiny stitches. *Do not* leave an opening.

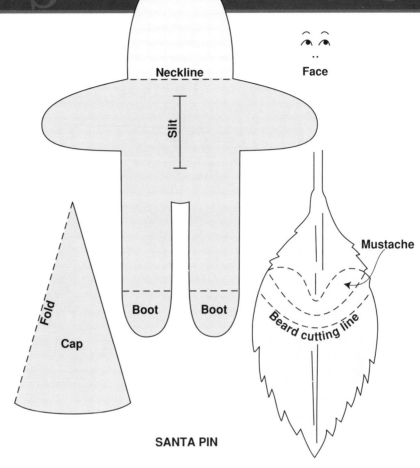

SANTA PIN

Cut out ⅛ inch beyond the stitching and clip curves.

Pull two layers at center of the Santa apart. Carefully cut a ¾-inch-long slit through back layer (see the pattern for position). Turn Santa right side out through slit. Stuff with polyester fiberfill, using flat end of a knitting needle or a pencil to push fiberfill into arms and legs. Hand-stitch the slit closed.

For cap, fold the 3-inch square of holiday print fabric in half, right sides together. Place cap pattern along the fold; trace around the pattern. Cut out along curved line only. Sew through both layers along straight edge. Cut out ⅛ inch from stitching; turn right side out. Tack or glue the cap to head, folding the point down and to one side. Glue narrow ribbon over the raw edge. Sew a white bead, bell, miniature ornament, or charm to the point of cap.

For beard, cut the beard and mustache from the silk leaf as shown on the pattern. Or, cut the beard from fake fur and omit the mustache. Glue in place. Or, use yarn for the beard, hand-sewing small loops along the bottom of the face. Sew loops just below the hat for hair.

Draw Santa's face with marking pen. If desired, use a red bead for the nose. For ears, hand-sew tiny stitches through each side of the head, pulling the thread taut with each stitch to create small indentations. Secure thread on back.

Color the boots as indicated on the pattern, using black marking pen or gold paint pen. Trim the body with white ribbon to resemble fur on Santa's jacket, or add a tiny charm or ornament to his chest. Tack or glue bells, miniature ornaments, or charms to hands. Cement the pin back over the slit in back.

T is for *Treasured Tote Bags and Toys*

Ice Cream Tote

What a perfect gift for any friend—a tote decorated with ice cream cone blocks that are easy to appliqué. Use brown calico fabrics to piece the cones, pastel calicos for ice cream, and wooden beads for colorful accents. The bag is easy to assemble and roomy enough for all kinds of treasures. Instructions and patterns begin on page 160.

DESIGNER: MARGARET SINDELAR
PHOTOGRAPHER: HOPKINS ASSOCIATES

Flowered Satchel

This sophisticated satchel is made from floral print upholstery fabric. With braided handles for extra strength, simple pleats for roominess, and a contrasting flap sporting covered buttons and tassels, it's just the thing for a mom, a student, or an overnight traveler. Instructions are on page 161.

DESIGNER: MARGARET SINDELAR
PHOTOGRAPHER: HOPKINS ASSOCIATES

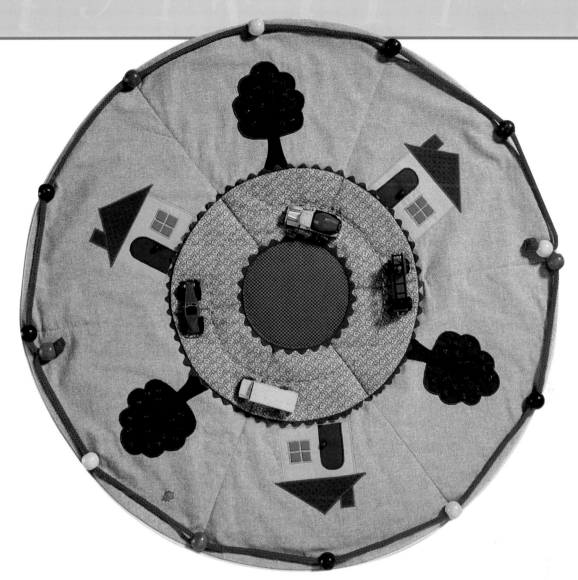

Toy Car Tote

What a clever way to bundle up a toddler's toys! This tote is a game in itself, featuring appliqués that form a neighborhood and street—complete with pockets to park a fleet of miniature cars. Using the colorful beaded drawstring, simply gather up edges to tow the toys in style. Instructions and patterns begin on page 162.

DESIGNER: MARGARET SINDELAR
PHOTOGRAPHER: HOPKINS ASSOCIATES

Puff and Shuffle
Game

What to do indoors on those rainy days? Make a shuffleboard game from a felt rectangle and acrylic paints. You can make this game in minutes—for hours of family fun. Our complete instructions include game-playing directions, too. Pattern is on page 163, instructions begin on page 164.

DESIGNER: KAREN TAYLOR ● PHOTOGRAPHER: HOPKINS ASSOCIATES

Star Fishing Toy

For a child's birthday party, this star fishing game makes an entertaining treat. It starts with a few basics—a wooden dowel, a block of wood, and a length of kite string. With the addition of beads, paint, and colorful plastic stars, it becomes an irresistible toy for children of all ages. Instructions and pattern are on page 164.

DESIGNER: MARGARET SINDELAR ● PHOTOGRAPHER: HOPKINS ASSOCIATES

ICE CREAM TOTE

As shown on page 156, tote measures 19x19x3½ inches.

MATERIALS

Tracing paper
Paper-backed iron-on adhesive
Six 6x6-inch squares of pastel calico fabrics
Scraps of nine different brown calico fabrics
¼ yard of 45-inch-wide white-on-white print fabric
1 yard of 45-inch-wide pink calico
1 yard of 45-inch-wide lining fabric
1 yard of fusible fleece
2 yards of pink jumbo rickrack
Six ½-inch-diameter wooden beads
Matching sewing threads

INSTRUCTIONS

Trace ice cream pattern and all markings, *right;* cut out. Draw around ice cream pattern six times on paper side of iron-on adhesive; cut out. Fuse each ice cream shape to a pastel calico fabric, following manufacturer's directions; cut out. Transfer markings to right side of ice cream shapes; set aside.

Trace the cone outline and cut out. Trace the A piece outline, adding ¼-inch seam allowances to all three edges; cut out. Cut six A pieces and a total of twenty-four 1-inch-wide strips from the brown calico fabrics.

From white print fabric, cut six 5½x5½-inch squares, and six 3½x5½-inch rectangles. From pink calico, cut eight 1½x8½-inch vertical sashing strips, three 1½x19½-inch horizontal sashing strips, one 19½x19½-inch back, two 4x28½-inch boxing strips, and two 2½x14-inch handles. From fusible fleece, cut two

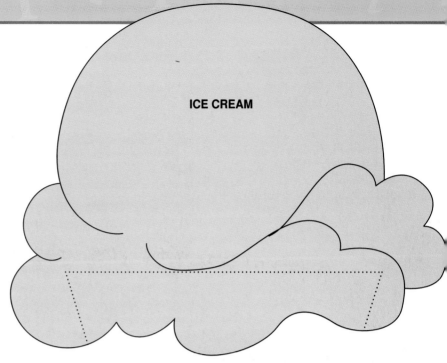

ICE CREAM

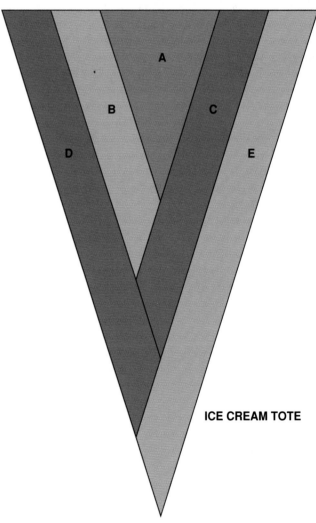

ICE CREAM TOTE

19½x19½-inch squares for front and back and two 4x28½-inch boxing strips.

From lining fabric, cut two 19½x19½-inch squares, and two 4x28-inch boxing strips. All patterns and measurements include ¼-inch seam allowances. Sew all seams with right sides facing unless otherwise specified.

For each cone block, trace cone shape, centered, on one end of a 5½x5½-inch square of white fabric. Referring to pattern, *opposite,* position A piece at center of traced outline with raw edges even with top of square; baste.

Select one brown calico strip as the B piece. Stitch to left side of triangle using ¼-inch seam. Press strip over seam. Sew strip C to right side of A piece in same manner. Continue with D and E strips. Trim D and E pieces even with edge of cone outline. Work machine-satin stitches around sides of cone. Make six blocks.

For each ice cream block, stitch a 3½x5½-inch white rectangle, right sides together, to top of each 5½-inch square. Press seam toward rectangle. Position ice cream shapes on top of cone, matching dotted lines indicated on pattern and fuse.

Work machine-satin stitches around edges of ice cream and swirls in ice cream using matching thread.

Arrange blocks in two rows of three. For each row, sew long side of a sashing strip to each side of the left-hand block. Sew second block to right sashing. Continuing to work from left to right, sew another sashing, third block, and another sashing.

Sew one vertical sashing strip between the two rows. Sew another vertical sashing strip above top row. Sew remaining sashing strip below bottom row.

For bag, join ends of pink fabric and of fleece boxing strips to make each one long piece. Fuse fleece to boxing strip and bag front and back. Beginning at one corner, sew one long edge of the boxing strip to sides and bottom of bag front, clipping and pivoting strip at corners. Sew remaining long edge of strip to bag back. Sew lining pieces together in same manner except, leave an opening in one bottom seam, but *do not* turn.

Fold each handle piece in half lengthwise. Sew long edge, turn, and press. Topstitch ⅛ inch from each long edge. Center and sew rickrack to handles. Sew rickrack along top edge of bag, right sides together. With raw edges even, stitch ends of one handle to top of bag front, 6 inches from side seams. Repeat for other handle.

Sew top of bag and bag lining together, right sides facing, and matching seams; turn. Slip-stitch opening closed. Tuck lining into bag; press carefully. Topstitch around top edge of bag ¼ inch from edge. Sew a wooden bead to top of each ice cream.

FLOWERED SATCHEL
As shown on page 156, tote measures 19x22 inches.

MATERIALS
1½ yards of 48-inch-wide floral cotton upholstery fabric
1⅛ yards of cotton lining fabric
⅜ yard of contrasting fabric
Sewing thread to match fabric
1 yard of ⅛-inch-diameter cording
4⅛ yards *each* of heavy string and ¾-inch-diameter cording
Three 1¾-inch-diameter button forms
Three 3-inch-long tassels

INSTRUCTIONS
Cut a 24x40-inch front-back piece from floral fabric and lining fabric. For flap, cut one triangle with an 11-inch base and two 15-inch sides from contrasting fabric and lining fabric. Cut three 2½x48-inch handle strips and one 1x30-inch piping strip from floral fabric. All measurements include ¼-inch seam allowances. Sew all seams right sides facing unless otherwise specified.

Fold floral fabric in half, *wrong* sides facing, to form a 20x24-inch rectangle. Press the fold (bottom of bag). Refold fabric, *right* sides facing, 3 inches beyond first fold; press another fold. Repeat on other side of first fold. Form a pleat by pinning side folds together, sandwiching center fold between bag front and back. Sew side seams, raw edges even. Fold, press, and sew lining in the same manner, but *do not* turn.

Center narrow cording lengthwise on wrong side of piping strip. Fold fabric around cording, raw edges even. Use a zipper foot to sew through both layers of fabric close to cording. Sew piping to long edges of contrasting flap piece, raw edges even. Sew flap lining to flap along stitching line, raw edges even, leaving top edge open. Trim and turn. Baste across top edge of flap. Center flap, raw edges even, on bag back; stitch.

Sew short ends of handle strips together to make one long strip. Center string on right side of strip with 1 inch of string extending beyond one short edge of fabric. At same end, overlap 1 inch of the wide cording onto fabric. Fold fabric around string and sew across end where string and cording overlap, catching both in stitching. Stitch long edges of fabric together. Pull string from opposite end to turn fabric right

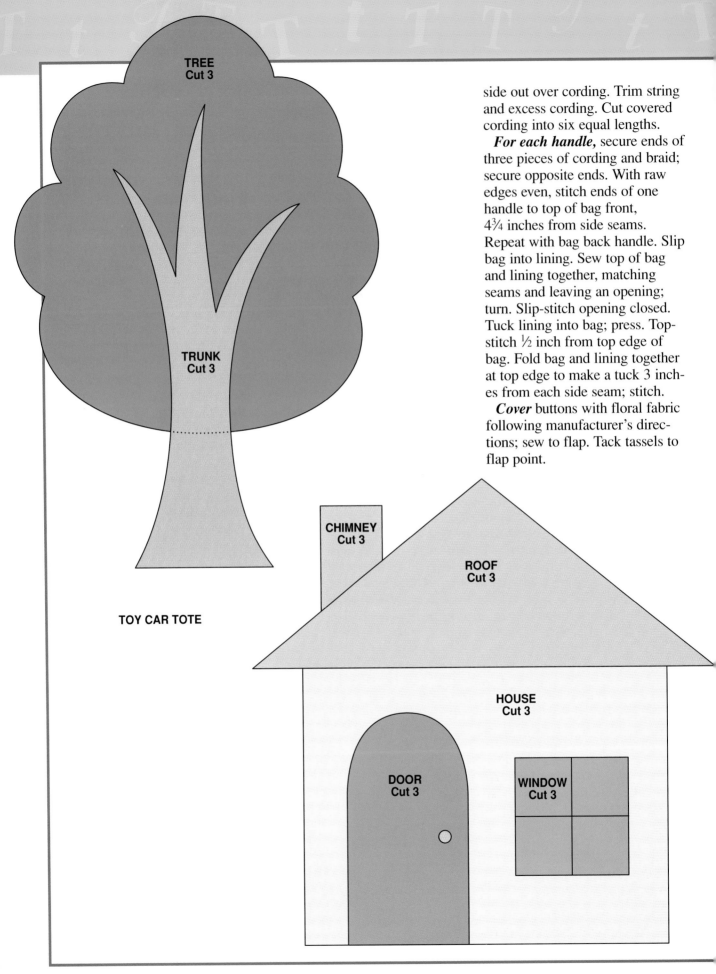

TREE
Cut 3

TRUNK
Cut 3

side out over cording. Trim string and excess cording. Cut covered cording into six equal lengths.

For each handle, secure ends of three pieces of cording and braid; secure opposite ends. With raw edges even, stitch ends of one handle to top of bag front, 4¾ inches from side seams. Repeat with bag back handle. Slip bag into lining. Sew top of bag and lining together, matching seams and leaving an opening; turn. Slip-stitch opening closed. Tuck lining into bag; press. Top-stitch ½ inch from top edge of bag. Fold bag and lining together at top edge to make a tuck 3 inches from each side seam; stitch.

Cover buttons with floral fabric following manufacturer's directions; sew to flap. Tack tassels to flap point.

TOY CAR TOTE

CHIMNEY
Cut 3

ROOF
Cut 3

HOUSE
Cut 3

DOOR
Cut 3

WINDOW
Cut 3

TOY CAR TOTE

As shown on page 157, tote measures 30 inches diameter.

MATERIALS
Tracing paper
Paper-backed iron-on adhesive
Scraps of brown, green, and red print fabric
Scraps of solid-colored green, turquoise, and yellow fabric
Erasable fabric marker
Sewing thread to match fabrics
31-inch-diameter circle of blue chambray fabric
1 yard of fusible polyester fleece
3 yards of ⅛-inch-diameter yellow piping
31-inch-diameter circle of red calico fabric
Two 15-inch-diameter circles of gray print fabric
Two 7-inch-diameter circles of green-checked fabric
2 yards of ½-inch-wide green rickrack
Gold pearl cotton
Fourteen 1-inch-diameter wooden beads
Three ¼-inch-diameter red beads
45 red pony beads
3 yards of ⅜-inch-diameter red cording

INSTRUCTIONS
Trace patterns, *opposite*, tracing tree trunk, branches, window, door, roof, chimney, and house separately; cut out. Draw around each shape three times on paper side of iron-on adhesive. Fuse tree trunks to brown print, branches to green print, doors to green solid, windows to turquoise, roofs and chimneys to red print, and houses to yellow fabric; cut out.

Use marker to divide chambray circle into six equal pie-shape wedges. Draw a 7-inch-diameter circle in center of chambray fabric. Arrange appliqués on chambray with bottoms on circle marking, centering each motif on a wedge shape. Fuse following manufacturer's directions. Machine satin-stitch pieces in place, using matching thread.

Cut a 31-inch-diameter circle of fleece; fuse to wrong side of chambray. Sew piping to circle, raw edges even. Sew chambray circle to red calico circle, right sides facing, leaving an opening. Turn and press. Sew opening closed. Assemble the two gray circles and the two green-checked circles in same manner, *except* substitute rickrack for piping.

For street detail, use two strands of pearl cotton to work running stitches 2 inches from outer edge of gray circle, stitching through all layers.

Center green-checked circle on gray circle and gray circle on chambray circle; baste. Machine-satin stitch around smallest circle. Topstitch, along wedge markings from outer edge of smallest circle to outer edge of chambray circle.

Sew small beads on doors of houses as indicated on pattern. Sew 15 red pony beads to each tree for apples. Sew 12 large wooden beads, evenly spaced, around edge of chambray circle.

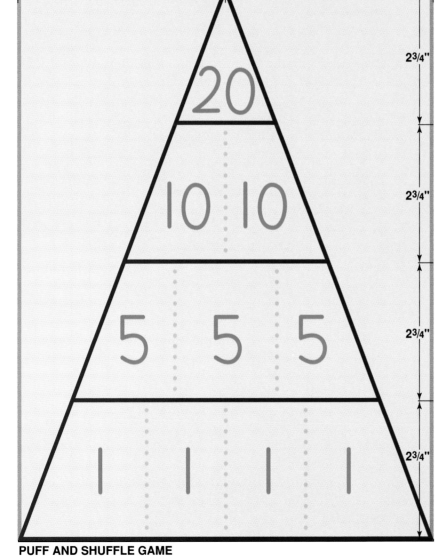

PUFF AND SHUFFLE GAME

For drawstring, cut cord in two equal pieces. Thread one piece through six large beads on one side of circle; thread other piece on opposite side. Slip each remaining bead over paired ends of cording; knot ends.

PUFF AND SHUFFLE GAME

As shown on page 158.

MATERIALS
8½x11½-inch piece *each* of paper-backed iron-on adhesive, pink felt, and poster board
Ruler; erasable fabric marker
Paint pens in desired colors
Pom-poms; straws; large buttons

INSTRUCTIONS
Fuse iron-on adhesive to felt, following manufacturer's instructions. Peel off paper backing and fuse felt to poster board.

Use pattern, *page 163,* ruler, and marker to draw triangle, horizontal and vertical lines, and numbers on felt. Use paint pens to trace over lines and numbers, referring to photograph, page 158. Finish remaining three edges of board with a line of paint; dry.

To play game, place game board on a flat surface and position button just below center bottom of board. Give each player a straw and three pom-poms. In turn, let each player place a pom-pom on button and, with straw, blow pom-pom onto board (only one puff through straw allowed). A pom-pom landing fully or partially within a row scores that row's points. A pom-pom on line between rows gets no score. Each player's turn consists of three tries to score. The first person to reach a total of 500 points wins.

STAR FISHING TOY

As shown on page 159.

MATERIALS
Tracing paper; graphite paper
5x5-inch piece of ¾-inch board
Jigsaw; sandpaper
Acrylic paints in assorted colors
18-inch-long ⅜-inch-diameter dowel
Four 1-inch-diameter round wooden beads with ⅜-inch hole
Two 1¼-inch-long wooden barrel beads with ⅜-inch hole
⅜-inch-diameter round wooden bead with ⅛-inch hole
Spray varnish
Ten ½-inch-diameter star-shaped acrylic jewels
Crafts glue
17-inch piece of kite string
⅝ yard *each* of two ⅜-inch-wide ribbons

INSTRUCTIONS
Trace pattern, *below,* onto tracing paper. Transfer the star shape and inner circle onto board. Cut out the star shape and center hole. Sand all edges.

Paint the star, dowel, and beads as desired. Seal with varnish. Glue the star-shaped jewels to the points of wooden star.

Glue three of the large round beads and the two barrel beads, alternately, at one end of the dowel for a handle. Glue the remaining large round bead at the opposite end of the dowel, securing one end of the kite string between the bead and the dowel.

Slip the small round bead onto the kite string and tie the star to the loose end of the string. Slide the small bead close to the knot and glue it to secure. Tie the ribbons into a bow around the dowel near the handle.

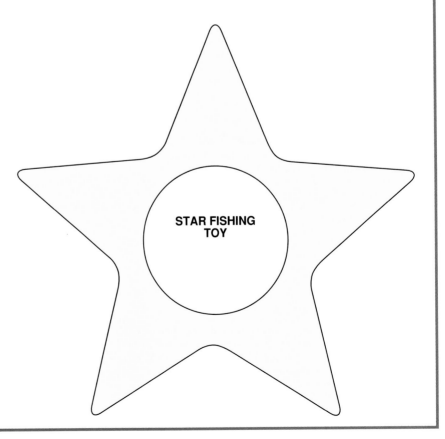

STAR FISHING
TOY

U is for *U*nique
*U*nicorn and *U*mbrellas

Dance Costume Unicorn

What could be lovelier for a special dancer than a lucky unicorn crafted from dance costume scraps. This fairy-tale friend has a mane of sparkling yarn and a gold sequined horn. Instructions begin on page 168, patterns begin on page 170.

DESIGNER: SANDI GUELY ● PHOTOGRAPHER: HOPKINS ASSOCIATES

Ladybug Umbrella

Enjoy those rainy days in style by embellishing an old umbrella with colorful painted ladybugs. These funny friends have buttons for spots and paint pen details. Complete instructions and pattern are on page 169.

DESIGNER: MARGARET SINDELAR ● PHOTOGRAPHER: HOPKINS ASSOCIATES

Pocket Express Umbrella

*Rain or shine you'll be chuggin' right along with our pocket express umbrella.
The pockets have been recycled from old jeans and filled with treasures that
any youngster would love. Instructions for this umbrella are on page 169.*

DESIGNER: MARGARET SINDELAR ● PHOTOGRAPHER: SCOTT LITTLE

167

DANCE COSTUME UNICORN

As shown on page 165, finished unicorn is approximately 18 inches tall.

MATERIALS

Tracing paper
Erasable fabric marker
Scraps of lamé, satin, or other firm fabric in desired colors
9x9-inch piece of lightweight fusible interfacing
Sewing thread to match fabrics
Polyester fiberfill
20-inch piece of gold sequin trim
Carpet thread
Two ½-inch-diameter acrylic jewels or buttons
Crafts glue
1/16-inch-wide black braid
7½-inch piece of silver sequin trim
Two ¼-inch-diameter black beads
24-inch piece of purple sequin trim
Gold jingle bell
Textured novelty yarn
Lightweight metal coat hanger
Fine gold tinsel or other dance costume trim (optional)
Two to four 16-inch lengths of 1/8-inch-wide ribbon

INSTRUCTIONS

Trace the patterns, *pages 170–173,* onto tracing paper and cut out. All patterns include ¼-inch seam allowances unless otherwise specified. Sew all of the seams with the right sides together. Backstitch at each end of all seams including the dot-to-dot seams.

Draw around ear piece twice, hoof eight times, and sole piece four times on interfacing; cut out. Fuse to wrong side of desired colors of lamé, following the manufacturer's instructions. Cut pieces from lamé.

Cut the remaining pieces as indicated on patterns. Transfer all markings to wrong side of fabrics using erasable marker.

For body, sew head gusset and one body piece together from A to B, matching dots and Xs. Clip the curves. Repeat with second body piece. Sew together body pieces from B to C and then from A to D. Clip the curves.

Sew together the underbody and one body piece from C to D. Clip the curves and repeat with the second body piece, leaving open between Xs. Turn right side out. Stuff firmly with fiberfill. Stitch the opening closed using ladder stitch (diagram, *page 23*).

For legs, sew one hoof to the bottom of each leg, matching Xs. Sew the legs together in pairs, leaving the bottom open. Sew one sole to the bottom of each hoof, matching dots. Clip curves. Cut an opening at the slit marking on each inner leg. Turn right side out through the slits. Stuff legs firmly. Whipstitch the slit closed. Cut gold sequin trim into four 5-inch pieces. Tack each piece around top of hoof, overlapping the ends. Thread needle with carpet thread and slip-stitch slit side of each leg to side of body.

For eyes, glue eyes to head sides. Fold each eyelid in half along dotted line and sew curved edges together using a *1/8-inch* seam allowance. Cut a slit in one side, taking care not to cut through both sides. Turn right side out through the slit. For the eyelashes, thread a needle with a double strand of black braid; knot ends. Insert the needle into the slit and exit at the fold. Cut the braid ½ inch beyond the fabric. Repeat making four eyelashes on each lid. Whipstitch the slit closed.

Slip-stitch the curved edge of each slit side to the head, partially covering the button eye and sewing the lid in place so eyelid curves outward from eye. Place a drop of crafts glue at point where each eyelash attaches to lid.

For nose, sew one bead nostril to each side of the unicorn's nose. Wrap the silver sequin trim around the nose 1½ inches above the seam. Overlap the ends and tack in place.

For ears, sew ear pieces together in pairs, leaving bottom open. Clip the curves and turn right side out. Turn the raw edges under and baste. Curve edges of the ear at the base to form an oval; slip-stitch onto head.

For horn, sew together straight edges using a ¼-inch seam allowance. Trim seam allowance at tip of cone. Sew gathering stitches along the raw edges, pull up slightly, and tie off. Stuff horn, turn raw edges under, and slip-stitch to forehead. Glue one end of purple sequin trim to tip of horn. Wrap trim diagonally around horn in stripes, spacing stripes about ¾ inch apart and circling base of horn; turn remaining end under and tack to horn. Sew jingle bell to tip of horn.

For mane, bend large loop of a coat hanger to form a rectangle about 8½x12 inches. Wrap novelty yarn around the 8½-inch width of hanger 80 times spreading threads over the 12-inch length of the hanger. Slip wrapped hanger loop under presser foot of sewing machine and machine-baste down the center of yarn. Cut the yarn loops at each wire edge. Pull up the basting stitches to measure 7 inches and tack to unicorn's head, matching stitches to seam of head back. If desired, cut tinsel into 8½-inch lengths and arrange in bundles of 20 to 25 strands. Tie the strands together at center of bundle. Tack two or three bundles along seamline of the mane.

For tail, wrap novelty yarn around the 8½-inch width of the hanger 25 times. Slip a length of ⅛-inch-wide ribbon under the yarn loops at one edge and tie firmly. Cut the loops at opposite edge and remove yarn from the hanger. Tie additional ribbons and tinsel around the yarn, if desired. Tack knot to the back of the unicorn, just above body gusset.

LADYBUG UMBRELLA

As shown on page 166.

MATERIALS
Tracing paper
Black fine-line permanent marker
Red and white check fabric umbrella
Red acrylic gloss fabric paint
Small paint brush; black paint pen
51 ½-inch-diameter black shank buttons
Black sewing thread
One skein *each* of six different colors of #3 pearl cotton
Tapestry needle

INSTRUCTIONS
Trace pattern, *right,* using marker. Position pattern on the inside of the opened umbrella. Hold pattern flat against umbrella and use marker to trace ladybug shape on right side of umbrella. Trace 17 ladybug shapes in random positions on umbrella.

Paint ladybug bodies with red paint; dry. Use black paint pen to color head area. Outline body, center stripe, legs, and antennae with black paint pen; dry. Thread needle with a doubled length of black thread and sew three buttons to the back of each ladybug.

Thread tapestry needle with two strands of one color of pearl cotton. Beginning at one umbrella spine, work buttonhole stitches around bottom edge of umbrella, stopping at the next spine. Change pearl cotton color and work next section of umbrella. Continue around, repeating first two pearl cotton colors for the last two sections of the umbrella.

POCKET EXPRESS UMBRELLA

As shown on page 167.

MATERIALS
Blue umbrella
½x2½-inch piece of cardboard
Red fine-line permanent marker
Red acrylic gloss paint
Small paint brush; gray paint pen
Denim jeans pockets
All-purpose cement
½- to 1½-inch-diameter buttons
Sewing thread in assorted colors
Assorted decorative buttons, glue-on acrylic jewels, and appliqués
Scraps of bandanna fabrics
Small toys

INSTRUCTIONS
For railroad ties, position the cardboard rectangle vertically at the edge of one umbrella spine with one short edge (bottom) of cardboard 2¼ inches above the curved edge of the umbrella. Use the red marker to trace around the rectangle. Continue tracing the rectangle shape at evenly spaced intervals around the umbrella, keeping the bottom of the cardboard parallel with the bottom of the umbrella. Use small brush to paint the area inside the traced rectangles with red and let dry.

Use paint pen to draw parallel track lines on top of the red railroad ties. The tracks should be approximately ½ inch from ends of each tie; dry.

Position pockets on tracks as desired; glue in place with all-purpose cement and dry. Stack a ½-inch button on the top of a 1½-inch button. Sew button pairs to bottom of each pocket for wheels. Cement decorative buttons, appliqués, and acrylic jewels to pockets and umbrella as desired. Cut 7x7-inch squares from scraps of bandanna fabric and tuck into the pockets. Place toys in pockets.

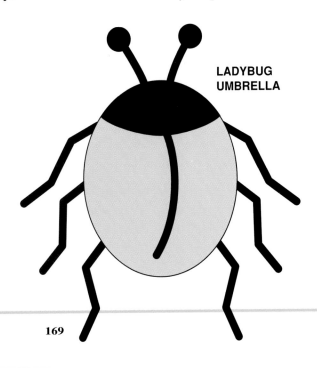

LADYBUG UMBRELLA

169

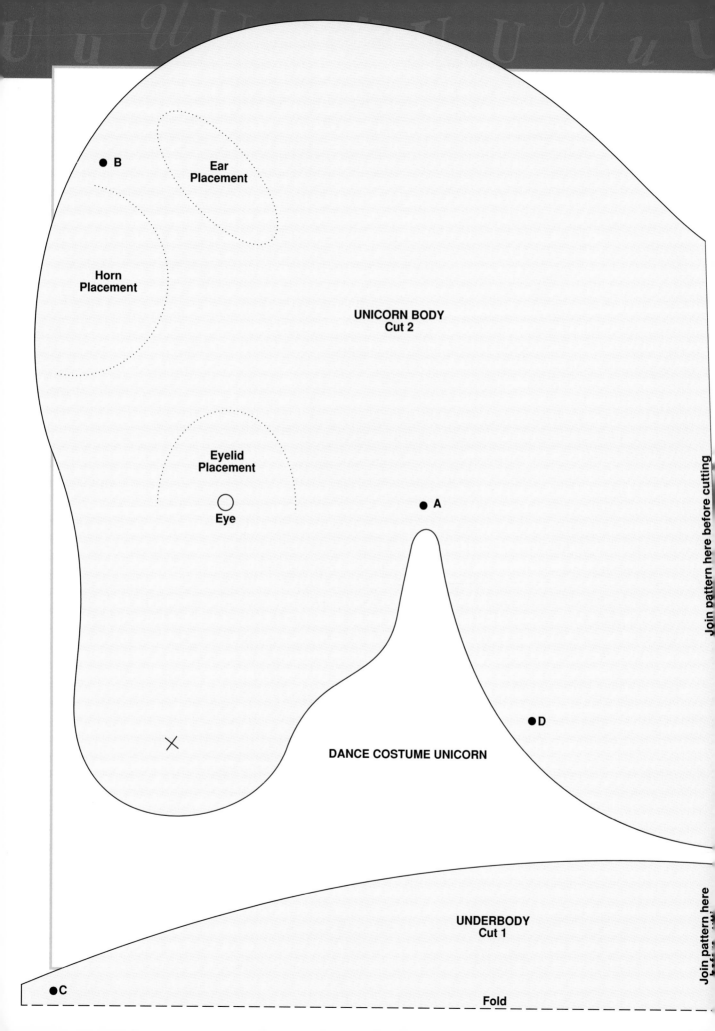

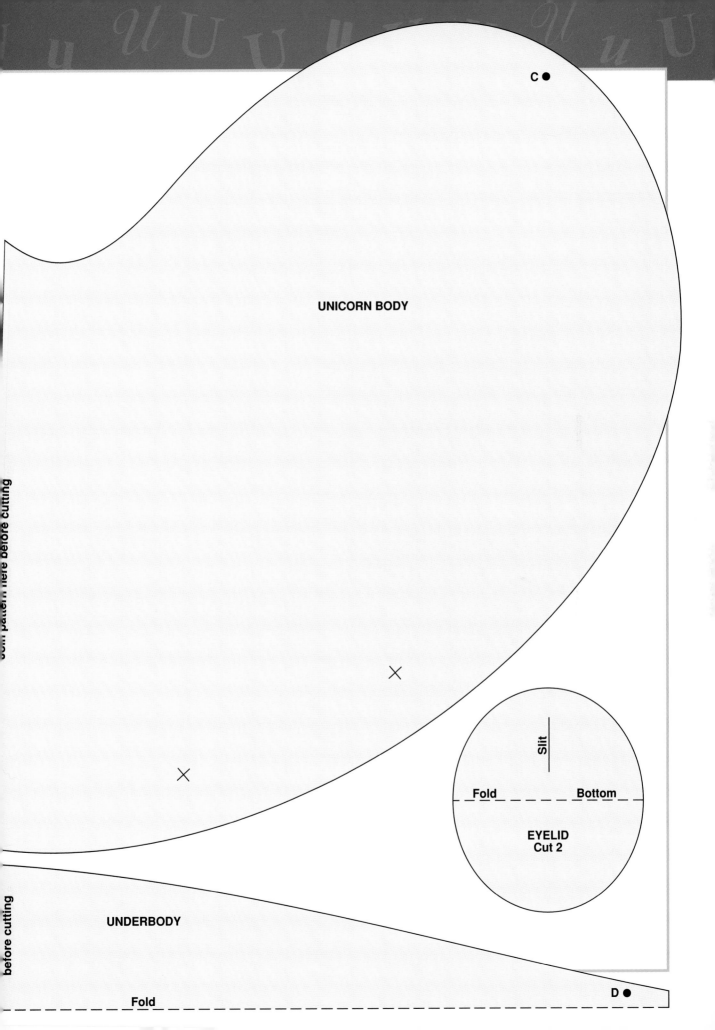

C ●

UNICORN BODY

✕

✕

Slit

Fold --- --- --- Bottom

EYELID
Cut 2

UNDERBODY

D ●

Fold

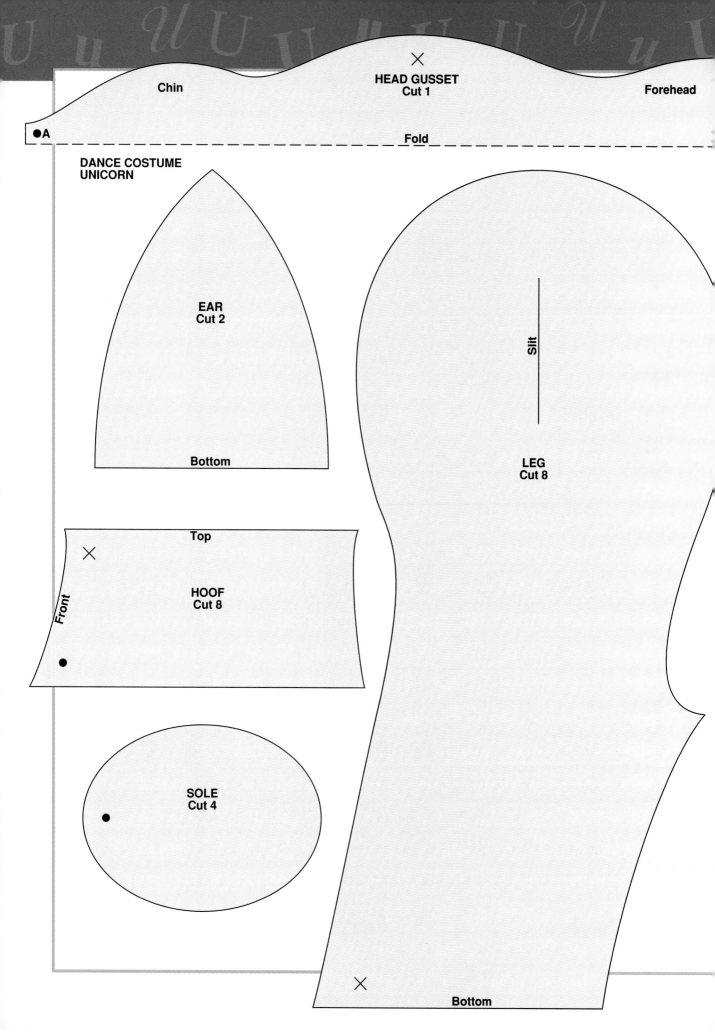

Chin

HEAD GUSSET
Cut 1

Forehead

●A

Fold

DANCE COSTUME
UNICORN

EAR
Cut 2

Slit

Bottom

LEG
Cut 8

Top

✕

HOOF
Cut 8

Front

●

SOLE
Cut 4

●

✕

Bottom

Join pattern here before cutting
Forehead
HEAD GUSSET
Fold
B

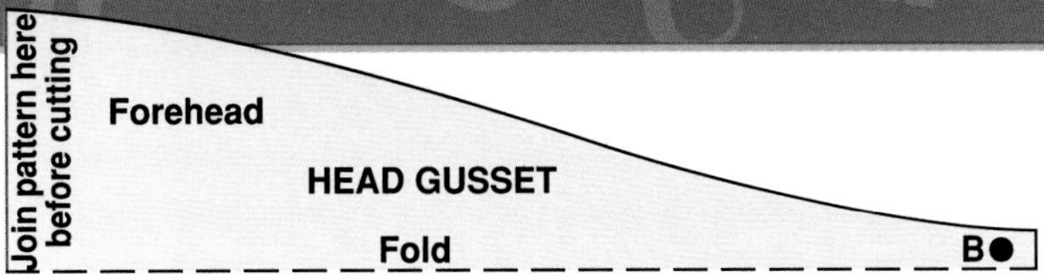

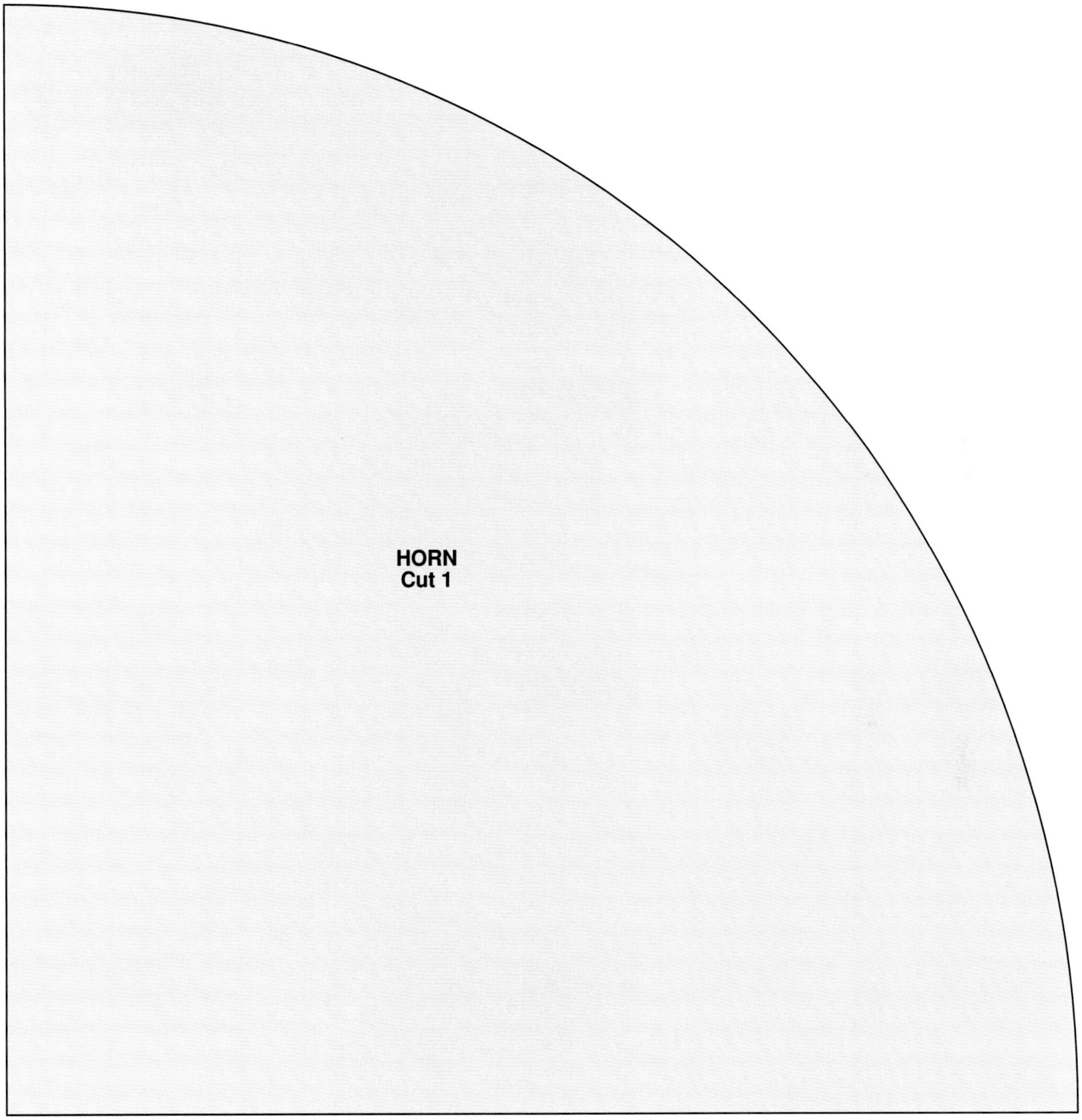

HORN
Cut 1

V is for *Vivid Vests*

Denim and Crocheted Vest

Crocheted with scraps of yarn and embellished with granny squares and denim jeans pockets, our country vest is easy to make and fun to wear. Granny squares worked in rose and denim-colored yarns are sewn around the neck and down the sides of this clever vest. Instructions are on page 177.

DESIGNER: ANN SMITH ● PHOTOGRAPHER: SCOTT LITTLE

Wool and Copper Vest

An unusual blend of materials make this vest one-of-a-kind. The unfinished wool and tweed strips are woven together to produce a primitive country look and the copper star motifs add seasonal charm. Instructions for the vest are on page 179 and full-size patterns are on page 178.

DESIGNER: SUSAN CAGE-KNOCH ● PHOTOGRAPHER: HOPKINS ASSOCIATES

Fancy Patches Vest

Fancy fabrics and sparkling trims make this bright and shining vest a festive favorite. The scrap shapes are stitched on the vest using a buttonhole stitch and the vest is trimmed with colorful buttons, charms, beads, and jewels. Complete instructions are on page 179.

Complete instructions are on page 179.

DESIGNER: BARBARA BARTON SMITH ● PHOTOGRAPHER: HOPKINS ASSOCIATES

DENIM AND CROCHETED VEST

As shown on page 174, directions are for size small. Changes for size large follow in parentheses. Finished chest measurement, buttoned, is 43 (49) inches. Crochet abbreviations are on page 17.

MATERIALS

SUPPLIES

4-ounce skeins (190 yards each) of worsted weight yarn: five (seven) skeins of dark blue; one skein *each* of rose and tan
Size H aluminum crochet hook or size to obtain gauge
Yarn needle
Six ¾-inch-diameter buttons
Two denim jean pockets
Sewing needle; matching thread

GAUGE

Double crochet pattern: 8 sts = 3 inches; each granny square is 3x3 inches

INSTRUCTIONS

For body, with blue, ch 113 (129). **Row 1:** Dc in fourth ch from hook and in each ch across 111 (127) sts; ch 3, turn.

Row 2: For dc pattern stitch, dc between dc's across working last st between last dc and turning dc; ch 3, turn—111 (127) sts counting turning ch as st. Repeat Row 2 for total of 26 rows.

For armhole and neck shaping (right front), work established pattern on first 21 (28) sts, ch 3 turn. Dec 1 st at armhole every other row 3 times, *at the same time,* shape neck. For size small, dec 1 st at neck edge every other row 8 times; for size large, dc 1 st every row 15 times. End off. Total of 42 rows.

For back, with right side facing, skip 6 spaces to the left of right front for underarm. Join with sl st between next 2 sts, ch 3 for first dc. Work across next 56 (58) sts in dc pattern.

For armhole shaping, dec 1 st each edge every other row 3 times—51 sts. Work even to 37 rows from beginning.

For back neck shaping, work 14 sts (counting turning st at neck edge), dec 1 at neck edge; turn. Rep dec each row 3 times more. Work even 1 row. End off. Skip center 23 (25) sts, join yarn between the next 2 sts; ch 3, work remaining stitches. Work second side as for first, reversing shaping.

For armhole and neck shaping (left front), with the right side facing, skip 6 spaces to left of back for underarm. Join with sl st between next 2 st and ch 3 for first dc. Work remaining stitches as for right front reversing neck and armhole shaping.

Join shoulder seams. With right side facing, sc evenly around armholes; join with sl st in first sc; ch 1, turn. Sl st in each sc around; join in first sl st. End off.

For border, Rnd 1: With right side facing and with blue, draw lp at center back neck, ch 1. Sc in same st as join and in each st to corner of back neck, hdc in corner; sc evenly to shoulder seam, hdc at shoulder seam; sc around, working 3 sc at each outer corner and hdc in next shoulder seam and at corner of back neck.

Rnd 2: Sc to last sc before hdc at back neck corner, sc dec over next 2 sts; sc around, working 3 sc at each outer corner, and working dec over next hdc and following sc at back neck.

Rnds 3 and 4: Rep Rnd 2, working dec over dec at back neck.

Rnd 5: Work Rnd 2 to end of lower right front corner; sc in next 2 sc, * ch 3, skip 3 sc, sc in next 7 sc; rep from * 5 times more for six buttonholes; sc to end of rnd.

Rnd 6: Sc in each st around, working 3 sc in each ch-3 loop.

Rnds 7–9: Rep Rnd 2. Sl st in each st around. End off. Sew buttons opposite buttonholes.

For granny squares, with blue, ch 6; join with sl st to form ring.

Rnd 1: Ch 3, 2 dc in ring, * ch 3, 3 dc in ring; rep from * twice, ch 3, sl st in top of beg ch-3. End off.

Rnd 2: With right side facing, join rose with sl st in first dc to left of a ch-3 corner sp, ch 3. * In next corner sp, 2 dc, ch 3, 2 dc, dc in next 3 dc. Rep from * twice. In next corner sp, 2 dc, ch 3, 2 dc, dc in next 2 dc. Sl st to first ch-3. End off. Make 18.

Pin granny squares around neck along front edges of vest with points of squares approximately 2 inches from vest edge with points ⅛-inch apart. Use a double strand of blue to join squares; attach to vest by sewing in ch-3 corners of squares. Sew pockets in place with needle and thread.

For embroidery, beginning at center back, use Chart 1 to work

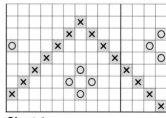

Chart 1

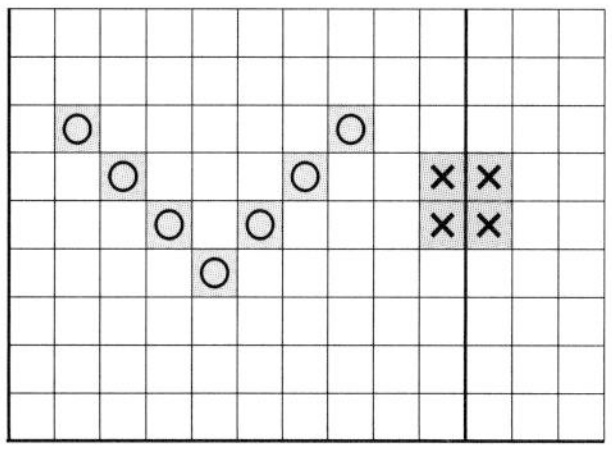

Chart 2
KEY
⊠ Rose   ⊡ Tan
DENIM AND CROCHETED VEST

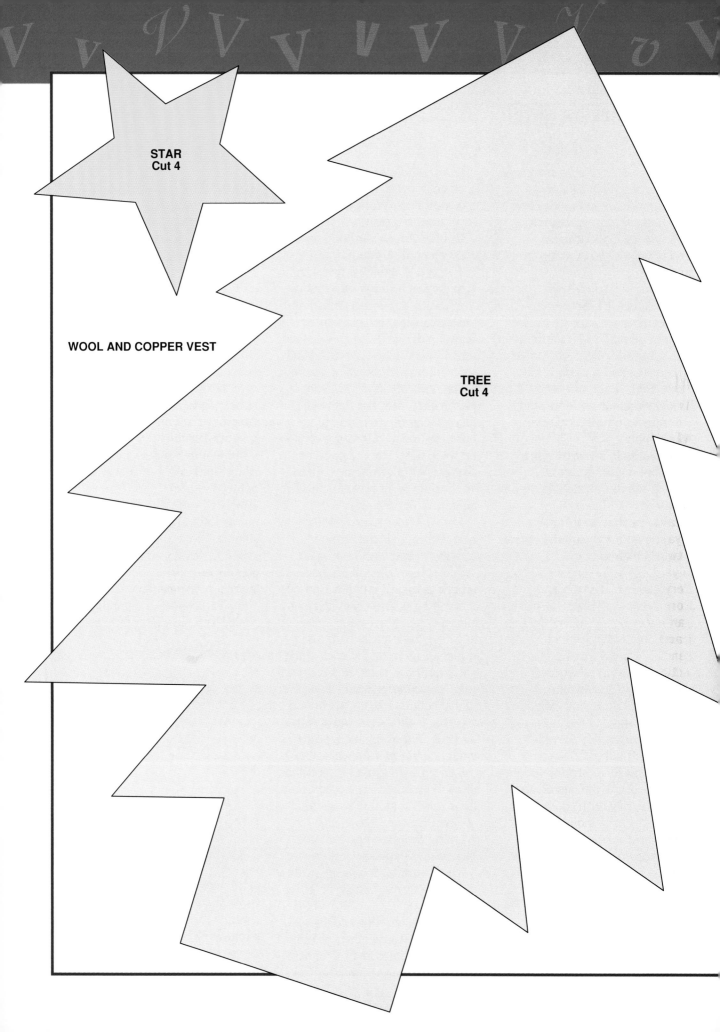

STAR
Cut 4

WOOL AND COPPER VEST

TREE
Cut 4

a cross-stitch over one sc along bottom border, repeating to front corner on each side. Work Chart 2 beginning at 5th stitch above the top buttonhole on the right front and working around the border to the top button on the left front. Beginning at fourth stitch above top buttonhole, work tan cross-stitch in every fourth stitch, ⅜ inch from vest edge to bottom of border. Work a 4-stitch rose block evenly-spaced between each set of buttonholes.

WOOL AND COPPER VEST

As shown on page 175.

MATERIALS

Purchased simple vest pattern without darts
1 yard of ivory cotton fabric
¾ yard of navy wool fabric
1 yard of ivory wool fabric
1 yard of brown and white tweed wool fabric
¼ yard of gold wool tweed fabric
Ivory sewing thread
Ivory #5 pearl cotton
Darning needle
Tracing paper
Pencil
8x16-inch piece of 36-gauge copper tooling foil
Tin snips
Awl

INSTRUCTIONS

Cut out two vest front pieces and one vest back from cotton fabric, *except* cut the seam allowances to ¼ inch. Cut wool fabrics into 1½-inch-wide strips.

Lay one vest front piece on tabletop. Position a strip of navy wool on front edge of vest with short end of strip even with the bottom edge of vest. Trim the excess strip at top even with top of vest; pin the ends of the strip

in place. Continue to pin vertical wool strips, alternating navy and ivory strips, until vest front is covered. Repeat this process with vest back piece and remaining vest front piece. Baste along top and bottom edges of the vest pieces to secure strip ends.

Weave tweed strips across the vest pieces in horizontal rows, working the strips over and under vertical ivory and navy strips. Trim ends of strips and baste along sides of vest pieces to secure ends of the strips.

Thread a darning needle with pearl cotton. Work vertical and horizontal running stitches through all layers of fabric at center of each woven strip.

Trace tree and star patterns, *opposite,* onto tracing paper; cut out. Cut four trees from gold wool. Center a tree on vest front with bottom of trunk 3 inches from bottom edge. Work pearl cotton running stitches around tree ¼ inch from the edge of the fabric. Repeat for remaining vest front. Position the remaining two trees on vest back with bottom of trunks 3 inches from the vest bottom and inside edges of the trunks 6½ inches apart.

To cut stars, position pattern on tooling foil. Use a pencil to trace around four star shapes; cut out using tin snips. Use awl to pierce a hole ⅛ inch from end of each point of each star. Use a doubled length of pearl cotton to sew a star atop each tree.

Sew the vest front pieces to the vest back at shoulder and side seams; press. Sew the narrow ends of the remaining ivory strips together to make one long binding strip. Sew the binding around the edges of vest, right side of binding facing lining, raw edges even, and using ¼-inch seams. Clip curves. Fold the binding to the

front of the vest. Easing the fabric at curves and corners, work pearl cotton running stitches ⅛ inch from the cut edge of the binding.

FANCY PATCHES VEST

As shown on page 176.

MATERIALS

Purchased lined vest pattern without darts
Black fine-wale corduroy in amount specified on pattern envelope
Lining fabric in amount specified on pattern envelope
Twenty 3x3-inch squares of assorted fancy fabrics
Gold metallic embroidery thread
Embroidery needle
Sewing needle
Sewing thread
Notions as specified on pattern envelope
Assorted buttons, charms, beads, ribbon roses, and acrylic stones
Crafts glue (optional)

INSTRUCTIONS

Cut out vest pieces following the pattern instructions. Turn the edges of 3-inch squares under ¼ inch along each side of squares and baste; press.

Baste the squares to the vest front pieces randomly, grouping and overlapping squares as desired, and taking care to avoid the seam allowances. Sew the squares in place using the metallic gold thread and buttonhole stitches (diagram, *page 185*).

Sew the vest together following the pattern instructions. Work the buttonholes and sew on the fastening buttons.

Hand-sew or glue charms, buttons, and assorted trims to the vest as desired.

W is for Wonderful Wearables

Folk Art Jacket

Rich jewel-tone fabrics are strip-pieced together to make this stunning jacket. The appliquéd shapes are accented with beads, buttonhole stitches, and chain stitches. Instructions and patterns begin on page 183.

DESIGNER: MARGARET SINDELAR ● PHOTOGRAPHER: SCOTT LITTLE

Needlepoint Belt

Scraps of colorful yarns transform ordinary canvas mesh into an extraordinary fashion accessory. A purchased decorative buckle and metallic ribbon provide extra sparkle. Complete instructions and chart are on page 186.

DESIGNER: MARGARET SINDELAR ● PHOTOGRAPHER: SCOTT LITTLE

Apple Sweat Suit

Apple shapes are stamped onto a sweatshirt and sweatpants for a fun-to-wear outfit. This project is so easy and quick to make, the entire family will want to join in. Complete instructions are on page 186.

DESIGNER: CAROL DAHLSTROM ● PHOTOGRAPHER: HOPKINS ASSOCIATES

FOLK ART JACKET

As shown on page 180.

MATERIALS

Purchased shawl-collared or
  collarless unlined jacket
  pattern
Black cotton print fabric in
  amount specified on pattern
  envelope
White tailor's chalk
Yardstick
½ yard *each* of 45-inch-wide
  dark green, red, rust, mustard,
  and yellow cotton print fabrics
⅓ yard *each* of 45-inch-wide
  gold solid and periwinkle solid
  cotton fabrics
⅓ yard of 45-inch-wide dark pink
  cotton print fabric
¼ yard *each* of 45-inch-wide
  red solid, purple solid,
  turquoise solid, and dark green
  solid cotton fabrics
¼ yard *each* of 45-inch-wide
  purple, periwinkle, dark blue,
  hot pink, light maroon, dark
  maroon, yellow-green, teal,
  and dark green cotton print
  fabrics
⅛ yard *each* of 45-inch-wide
  bright blue and orange cotton
  print fabrics
Tracing paper
Paper-backed iron-on fusible
  adhesive
Medium gray and transparent
  nylon sewing threads
Green, gold, black, orange,
  lavender, and turquoise cotton
  embroidery floss
Large-eyed embroidery needle
Quilt batting
Sixteen 4-millimeter round black
  beads
5 yards of ⅜-inch-wide black
  piping

INSTRUCTIONS

Sew all seams with right sides
of fabric facing unless otherwise
indicated. Use ¼-inch seam
allowances for patchwork and
strip piecing. Construct jacket
using seam allowances specified
in pattern instructions.

Trim the sleeve pattern piece
⅝ inch below the line indicating
finished sleeve length. Cut all
jacket pattern pieces from black
print fabric.

For jacket body, sew the jacket
fronts to the back at side seams;
press. Lay the joined jacket body
on table, wrong side up. Lay the
sleeves, parallel to the jacket
fronts, wrong side up.

Use tailor's chalk and yardstick
to draw the jacket strip pattern
plan on the jacket body and the
sleeves, making straight lines
parallel to the bottom edges.
Draw each appliqué and patchwork strip to the finished height
given below. Vary the heights of
the *plain* strips to accommodate
different jacket sizes, if necessary.
The jacket shown on page 180
includes, *from bottom to top*:

Red solid plain strip, as shown,
1½ inches (may vary).

*Green print and dark green
solid checkerboard patchwork
strip*, 3 inches.

Purple solid plain strip, as
shown, 1 inch (may vary).

*Gold solid appliqué flower
strip*, 4½ inches.

Turquoise solid plain strip, as
shown, ⅝ inch (may vary).

*Purple, rust, and black print
diagonal block patchwork strip*,
3⅛ inches.

Mustard print plain strip, as
shown, ½ inch (may vary).

Dark pink print appliqué strip,
4 inches.

Yellow-green print plain strip,
as shown, 1 inch (may vary).

*Mustard and red print diagonal
patchwork strip*, 2⅛ inches.

Teal print plain strip, as shown,
¾ inch (may vary).

Periwinkle solid appliqué strip,
3½ inches.

Dark maroon print plain strip,
as shown, 1¼ inches (may vary).

*Dark green and yellow print
checkerboard patchwork strip*
will vary in height depending on
the distance from the last strip to
the top of the shoulder, sleeves,
and collar on specific pattern.
*Prepare all of the strips before
beginning strip piecing.*

For plain strips, measure red
solid, purple solid, turquoise
solid, mustard print, yellow-green
print, teal print, and maroon print
markings. Add ½ inch to each
measurement for seam
allowances. Cut each strip long
enough to cover width of jacket
body and both sleeves, piecing
short ends of fabric as necessary.
Set aside. Cut the gold solid, dark
pink print, and periwinkle solid
background strips for appliqué in
the same manner. Set aside.

For green checkerboard strip,
cut three 1½x45-inch strips *each*
from the dark green print and
dark green solid fabrics. Make
one strip by sewing one solid strip
to each long edge of a print strip.
Make another strip by sewing a
print strip to each long edge of a
solid strip. Press all seams in one
direction. Lay seamed strips
wrong side up. Cut across pieced
strips, at a right angle to the
seams, every 2 inches. Sew the
solid-print-solid pieces between
the print-solid-print pieces to
form strips the width of the jacket
body and sleeves. Set aside.

For flower appliqué strip, trace
flower pattern, *page 184.* Cut out
circle and leaves separately. Draw
around each 20 times on paper
side of iron-on adhesive; cut out.
Fuse the circles to the wrong side
of the red print fabric; cut out.
Fuse leaves to wrong side of the
yellow-green print fabric; cut out.

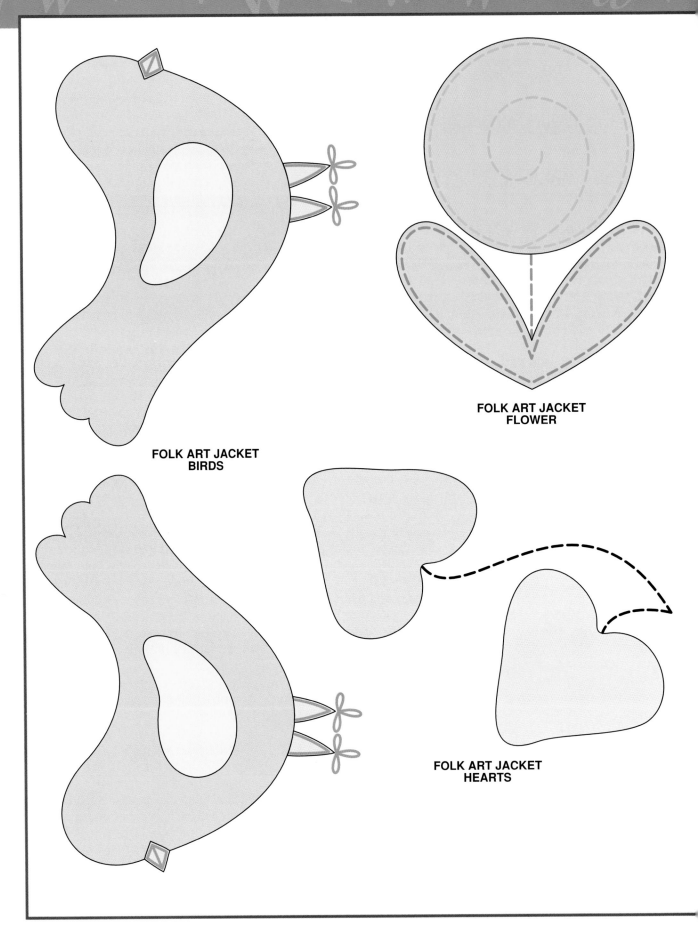

**FOLK ART JACKET
FLOWER**

**FOLK ART JACKET
BIRDS**

**FOLK ART JACKET
HEARTS**

Using the pattern as a guide, position evenly-spaced flowers along the center of the gold solid strip of fabric; fuse following manufacturer's instructions. Use three plies of gold floss to work chain stitches (diagram, *below)* around the flower as indicated on pattern by yellow dashed lines. Work chain-stitch stems and chain stitches around leaves using three plies of green floss. Set aside.

For purple, rust, and black print strip, cut 2½x45-inch strips from purple print, rust print, and black print fabrics. Sew a purple strip to the top long edge of each rust strip and a black strip to the bottom long edge. Cut the piece crosswise on a 30° angle into 2-inch-wide pieces. Sew pieces together matching bottom of purple to top of rust and bottom of rust to top of black in a tri-color diagonal block pattern to form strips the width of the jacket body and sleeves. Trim the long edges of the strips to measure 3¾-inches wide. Set aside.

For bird appliqué strip, trace the patterns, *opposite.* Trace outline of eight right-facing bird and eight left-facing birds on paper side of iron-on adhesive; cut out. Also trace enough wings, beaks,

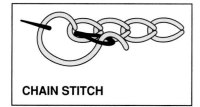

CHAIN STITCH

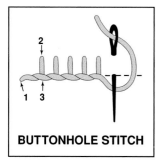

BUTTONHOLE STITCH

and legs for the 16 birds; cut out. Fuse the birds to periwinkle print fabric, wings to bright blue print fabric, and beaks and legs to orange print fabric following manufacturer's instructions; cut out. Starting at the center back, position ten birds evenly-spaced along the center of the dark pink strip of fabric, facing the birds toward the center front of the jacket and staying within the seam allowance; fuse. Arrange and fuse three birds to each sleeve. Position the wings, beaks, and legs in place; fuse. Work buttonhole stitches (diagram, *below left)* around bird using three plies of lavender floss and around wings using three plies of turquoise floss. Using three plies of orange floss, work straight stitches around beaks and legs as shown on pattern. Work lazy daisy stitches for feet, using three plies of orange floss. Sew black bead eyes in place using three plies of black floss. Set aside.

For mustard and red print strip, cut six *each* of 1½x45-inch mustard print and red print fabric strips. Join long edges, alternating fabrics. Cut the joined piece into 2⅝-inch-wide diagonal strips. Join the cut pieces to make strips the width of the jacket body and sleeves. Set aside.

For heart appliqué strip, trace the heart pattern, *opposite,* cut out. Draw around one heart 32 times on paper side of iron-on adhesive; cut out. Fuse hearts to blue print fabric, light maroon print fabric, and hot pink print fabric as desired following manufacturer's instructions; cut out. Position hearts in pairs on periwinkle strip using pattern as a guide. Use three plies of black floss to work the buttonhole stitches around the edges of the hearts and to work the chain stitches connecting the hearts together. Set aside.

For yellow and green checkerboard strip, cut three 1½x45-inch strips *each* from green print fabric and yellow print fabric. Make one long strip by sewing one yellow strip to each long edge of a green strip. Make another long strip by sewing a green strip to each long edge of a yellow strip. Press all seams in one direction. Lay the seamed strips wrong side up. Cut across the pieced strips at a right angle to seams, every 1½ inches. Sew the yellow-green-yellow pieces between the green-yellow-green pieces to form strips. Sew strips together as necessary to make strips tall enough to cover shoulder area, top of sleeves, and collar. Set aside.

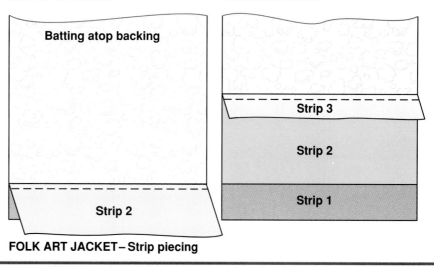

Batting atop backing

Strip 2

Strip 3

Strip 2

Strip 1

FOLK ART JACKET–Strip piecing

Baste quilt batting to wrong side of jacket body and sleeves, with batting extending at least 2 inches beyond pattern outlines.

To strip-piece jacket, position bottom edge of red solid plain strip slightly beyond actual pattern outline. Lay green checkerboard patchwork strip atop red strip, referring to diagram, *page 183*, with right sides facing and top edges aligned. Sew through all layers ¼ inch from top edge.

Press green patchwork strip right side up and away from red plain strip, covering seam. Sew purple strip to the top edge of green patchwork strip and press in same manner. Continue sewing strips to jacket body in order designated on page 183 until jacket body is covered. Strip-piece sleeves in same manner and order.

Baste around the perimeter of all of three jacket pieces along the seam lines to hold the edges of the strips in place. Trim away the excess batting from the pieces along the pattern cutting lines.

Sew the center back seam of shawl collar following pattern instructions. Stitch black piping around the jacket opening, collar, jacket bottom, and sleeve bottom edges. Sew facings and any remaining seams following the pattern instructions.

Turn under any remaining raw edges so piping is along outer edge. Topstitch around jacket and sleeve edges using transparent nylon sewing thread.

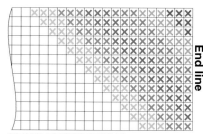

NEEDLEPOINT BELT

NEEDLEPOINT BELT

Directions below are for the narrower belt shown on page 181. Adjust the measurements and diagonal design as desired.

MATERIALS
FABRIC
3½x36-inch strip of 10-count interlock needlepoint canvas
THREADS
Assorted colors of three-ply Persian yarn for a total of approximately 80 to 85 yards, depending on length of the belt
⅛-inch-wide metallic gold embroidery ribbon (optional)
SUPPLIES
Tape measure; needle
1 yard of 1-inch-wide grosgrain ribbon in desired color
Sewing thread to match ribbon
Purchased two-piece belt buckle

INSTRUCTIONS
Measure waist, adding one or two inches for ease. Measure closed buckle between fabric attachment points. Subtract the buckle measurement from the waist measurement and add three inches. Cut canvas to that length.

Tape the edges of the canvas to prevent fraying. Mark a line across each end of the canvas 1½ inches from end.

Select first yarn color and thread two plies into the needle. Count ten threads from the top edge of the canvas along the marked line at the right edge of the canvas. Begin working first basket-weave or continental stitch there. Work two more diagonal rows of stitches in the area shown in blue on the chart, *left*.

Change yarn color and work the area shown in pink. Continue stitching the diagonal rows across the length of the canvas as shown

on the chart. Square the opposite end of the belt by working partial rows in the same manner as the beginning.

Trim each end of belt ½ inch from stitched area. Trim the long edges of the belt ¼ inch from the stitching; finger press the canvas to back.

Slide the unstitched end of the belt through the loop on one end of buckle. Fold belt to the back and whipstitch in place. Repeat for the opposite end of the belt. Whipstitch the long edges of the belt using one strand of yarn or gold embroidery ribbon. Cut the grosgrain ribbon to fit the inside of belt and whipstitch in place.

APPLE SWEAT SUIT

As shown on page 182.

MATERIALS
Purchased sweatshirt and sweatpants
Waxed paper
Apples with stems
Plastic plate; red acrylic paint
Green leaf-shaped acrylic jewel (optional)
Fabric glue (optional)

INSTRUCTIONS
Lay sweatshirt and sweatpants on a flat surface with waxed paper between the fabric.

Cut an apple in half with the stem at the top. Spread paint out evenly on the plastic plate.

Dip apple with stem into paint and press onto shirt. Press the stem against fabric with fingers, if necessary. Continue stamping the apple shapes in a random fashion onto fabric until the desired number of prints are established.

Glue a green jeweled leaf onto top of each apple to resemble leaf, if desired.

X is for
X-tra Special X-stitch

Cross-stitch Labels

*Proudly display your talents with these handmade labels using cross-stitches
and buttonhole stitches. Simply study the design suggestions, then use the alphabets
and motifs in the chart to lend a personal touch to all needlework.
Complete instructions and chart begin on page 188.*

PHOTOGRAPHER: HOPKINS ASSOCIATES

Even-weave Shirt Trims

Shirt cuffs and blouse pockets can be decorated and personalized using a variety of motifs and lettering. These work up easily using scraps of even-weave cross-stitch fabrics, such as Lugana and Jobelan, as a grid for cross-stitches instead of waste canvas. The chart is below and the instructions and how-to photograph are opposite.

DESIGNER: EVE MAHR
PHOTOGRAPHER: SCOTT LITTLE

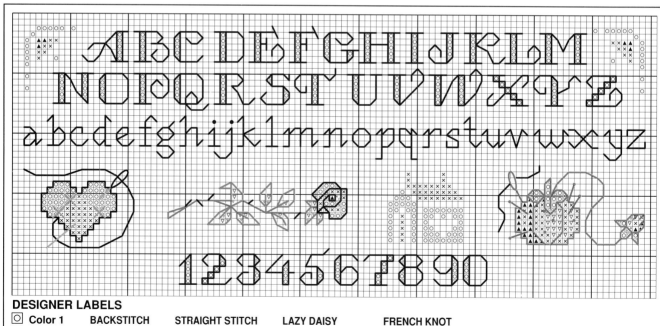

DESIGNER LABELS

○ Color 1	**BACKSTITCH**		**STRAIGHT STITCH**	**LAZY DAISY**	**FRENCH KNOT**	
⊠ Color 2	/ Color A		/ Color A	/ Color A	● Color A (2X)	
▲ Color 3	/ Color B		/ Color B	/ Color A (2X)	● Color B (2X)	
▽ Color 4	/ Color C		/ Color B (2X)			

CROSS-STITCH LABELS

As shown on page 187.

MATERIALS

For each label

FABRICS

Small scraps of Aida cloth, linen, or even-weave cross-stitch fabric

Lightweight fusible interfacing

FLOSS

Cotton embroidery floss in assorted colors

SUPPLIES

10-squares-per-inch graph paper

Needle

INSTRUCTIONS

Chart the desired motifs and lettering, *opposite,* onto the 10-squares-per-inch graph paper. Draw a border that goes four squares beyond the outermost stitches of the motif.

To calculate finished size of label, count the number of the squares on the chart horizontally and vertically. Divide each of the numbers by the stitches-per-inch count of the fabric to produce the height and the width of the label in inches.

For a single label, cut the fabric three inches larger than the dimensions of the label. When creating multiple labels on one piece of fabric, allow three inches between each of the labels that are stitched. Tape or zigzag the edges of the fabric to prevent them from fraying.

Work all cross-stitches using three plies of floss for 11-count fabric, two plies of floss for 14- or 18-count fabric, and one ply of floss for higher counts of fabric. Stitch over one square when using Aida cloth or two threads when using linen or even-weave fabrics.

Fuse the lightweight interfacing to the back side of the stitched design area, following the manufacturer's instructions.

Finish edges of each label using two or three plies of floss and buttonhole stitches (diagram, *page 185*) worked over two squares of Aida or four threads of linen. Position first buttonhole stitch by inserting needle from back of fabric 6 squares or 12 threads from bottom of motif. Weave ends of cotton embroidery floss under stitches on back side of fabric. Trim away excess fabric close to the buttonhole stitches.

EVEN-WEAVE SHIRT TRIMS

As shown on page 188.

MATERIALS

FABRICS *for shirt cuff*

1½x3-inch scrap of 25-count Lugana

Purchased man's shirt

FABRICS *for rose pocket*

2x5½-inch scrap of 16-count Jobelan

Purchased woman's blouse with pocket

FLOSS

Cotton embroidery floss in assorted colors

SUPPLIES

10-squares-per-inch graph paper (optional)

Needle

INSTRUCTIONS

Wash and dry the shirt or blouse before starting to stitch.

For shirt cuff, chart the letters, if desired, separating each with two squares. Zigzag the edges of the 25-count Lugana fabric to prevent them from fraying.

Baste the Lugana to the cuff of the left sleeve with one 3-inch edge aligned to the bottom of the cuff. Find the center of the desired middle initial on the chart and measure 1½ inches to the left of the buttonhole and ½ inch above the bottom of the cuff; begin stitching there.

Work cross-stitches using two plies of embroidery floss over two threads of fabric. Work all of the backstitches using one ply.

For rose pocket, zigzag the edges of the 16-count Jobelan to prevent fraying. Baste the fabric to the top edge of the pocket.

Find the center of the rose motif on the chart, *opposite.* Find the vertical center of the pocket. Measure ¾ inches from the top of the pocket; begin stitching there.

Work all of the cross-stitches using four plies of embroidery floss over two threads of fabric. Work all of the backstitches using two plies of floss.

For shirt or blouse, cut away zigzagged edges and gently pull Lugana or Jobelan fabric threads from under the cross-stitches. Press on the wrong side.

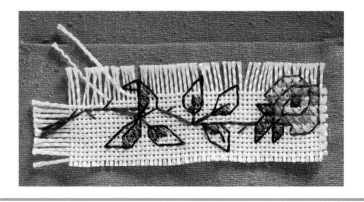

Y is for *Yesterday's Yo-yos*

Harvest Apple Place Mat Set

Crunchy red apples inspired this brimming quilted basket place mat and napkin. The apples are oversized yo-yos trimmed with bright red buttons. Yo-yos are fun and easy to make using our step-by-step photos on page 195. Instructions and patterns begin on page 192.

DESIGNER: MARGARET SINDELAR ● PHOTOGRAPHER: HOPKINS ASSOCIATES

Calico Yo-yo Dolly Quilt

Treat your favorite dolly to a cozy blanket of spring yo-yo flowers.
Personalize the quilt by choosing leftover fabric scraps from your favorite little
girl's home-sewn dresses. Instructions and patterns begin on page 192.

DESIGNER: BETTY AUTH ● PHOTOGRAPHER: SCOTT LITTLE

HARVEST APPLE PLACE MAT SET

As shown on page 190, place mat measures 14½x16 inches.

MATERIALS

For each place mat

Graph paper; template plastic
½ yard of 45-inch-wide red calico
15x18-inch piece of lightweight fleece
11x16-inch piece *each* of light and dark brown calico
Paper-backed iron-on adhesive
6x6-inch scraps of assorted red solid and print fabrics
Small scraps of assorted green calicos
Matching sewing threads
Red and green shank buttons in assorted sizes

For each napkin

16x16-inch piece of green and white checked fabric

INSTRUCTIONS

Enlarge pattern, *right,* using graph paper; cut out. Trace the three circular templates and leaf pattern, *opposite,* onto template plastic; cut out. Patterns include ¼-inch seam allowances.

Cut two place mat shapes from red calico and one from fleece. Cut pattern along top of basket. Draw around basket on paper side of iron-on adhesive. Fuse to dark brown calico following manufacturer's instructions; cut out. Cut out each light brown shape on pattern. Draw around shapes on iron-on adhesive; cut out. Fuse to light brown calico; cut out.

For yo-yos, cut two large, eight medium, and two small circles using patterns, *opposite,* from red fabrics. Cut five pairs of leaves from green calicos.

Position dark brown basket on one red place mat shape with bottom and side edges even; fuse. Position the light brown shapes on basket as indicated on pattern and fuse.

Baste fleece to back of fused place mat. Using matching thread, machine satin-stitch along sides of light brown rectangles and across top of dark brown basket. Work a parallel line of machine satin-stitches across place mat at top of light brown rectangles.

Sew place mat shapes together with right sides facing, leaving an opening at bottom. Clip curves and turn. Sew opening closed; press. Sew leaf shapes together in pairs, leaving straight edge open; turn and press. Set aside.

Fold raw edges under ¼ inch around outside edge of circles. Work gathering thread through both layers of the fabric as shown in the second photograph on page 195. Pull to tighten; secure the thread ends.

Arrange yo-yos on red fabric at top of place mat as desired. Secure in place by sewing buttons in centers of yo-yos. Make a small tuck at open end of each leaf. Sew leaves into centers or behind red yo-yos as desired.

For napkin, topstitch ½ inch from all edges of fabric. Remove threads between edges and machine stitches for fringe. Attach a medium yo-yo in one corner with a button.

CALICO YO-YO DOLLY QUILT

As shown on page 191, finished size is 18x18 inches.

MATERIALS

Template plastic
½ yard *each* of 45-inch-wide pale blue and dark green calico
Scraps of blue, rose, and yellow calico
18x18-inch piece *each* of pale yellow calico and unbleached muslin
18x18-inch piece of batting
Quilting thread; quilting needle
Matching sewing threads

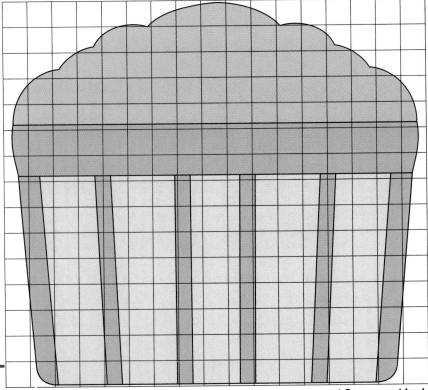

HARVEST APPLE PLACE MAT **1 Square = 1 Inch**

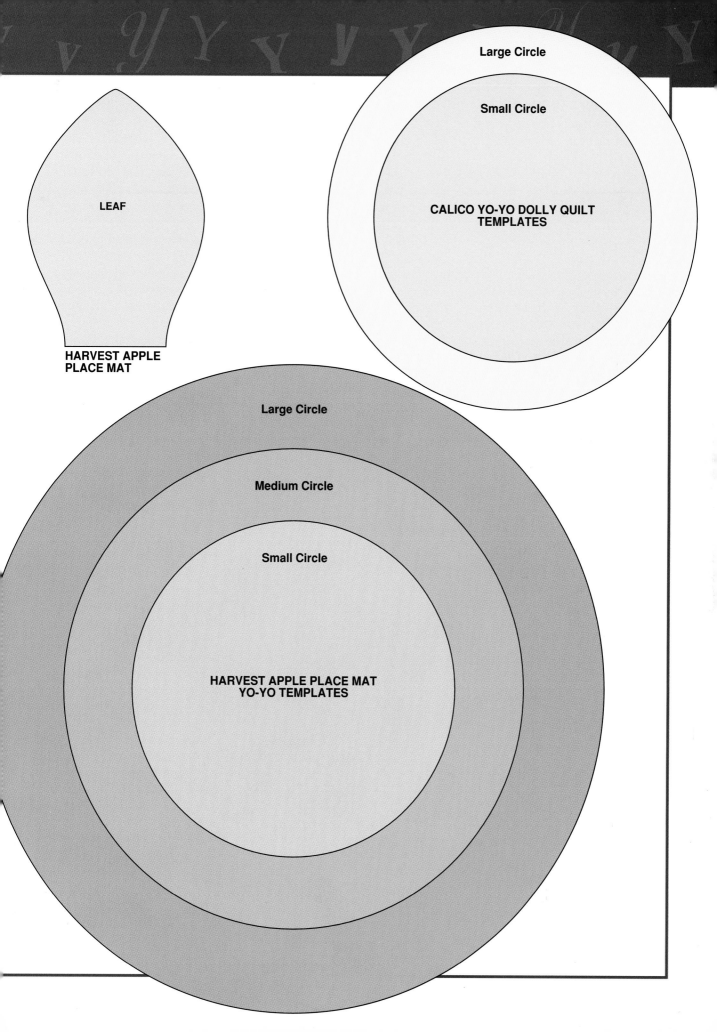

LEAF

HARVEST APPLE
PLACE MAT

Large Circle

Small Circle

CALICO YO-YO DOLLY QUILT
TEMPLATES

Large Circle

Medium Circle

Small Circle

HARVEST APPLE PLACE MAT
YO-YO TEMPLATES

INSTRUCTIONS

Trace the two circular templates, *page 193,* and the leaf patterns, *below,* onto the template plastic. Cut out. All the templates are drawn on the wrong side of the fabrics. All measurements and templates include a ¼-inch seam allowance.

Cut 2½ yards of 2-inch-wide bias strips for the binding and two small yo-yo circles from the pale blue calico. From green calico, cut the following bias stem strips: four ¾x17-inch-long pieces, two ¾x12-inch-long pieces, and two ¾x9-inch-long pieces. Also from green calico, cut nine large and eight small leaves. From the blue, rose, and yellow calico scraps, cut fourteen small yo-yo circles and eight large yo-yo circles.

To prepare quilt, sandwich the batting between the pale yellow fabric and the unbleached muslin. Baste layers together diagonally and horizontally. Baste quilt ½ inch from raw edges.

To make yo-yos, refer to photographs and instructions, *opposite.* Turn raw edges of all leaves under ⅛ inch; steam press. Press under ¼ inch on one short end of each stem strip, then press strips in half lengthwise with wrong sides facing.

To appliqué quilt, referring to the diagram, *below,* lightly sketch positions for curved stem lines onto the pale yellow calico, from the ½-inch basted line along bottom edge to where large yo-yo flowers are indicated on diagram.

Pin the stems in place with finished stem ends on basted bottom line and raw stem edges along pencil lines. Hand-sew each stem with a running stitch through all layers, ⅛ inch from the raw edges. Fold the stem over the running stitches and appliqué along the other edge, sewing through all layers of the quilt.

Pin large yo-yos on the quilt, referring to diagram, *below,* for placement, making sure each stem top is covered with a yo-yo. Using the quilting thread, hand-appliqué yo-yos to quilt, sewing through all layers.

Arrange small yo-yos above and below the large yo-yos. Hand-appliqué, stitching through all of the layers.

Pin the large leaves along the bottom of the stems and the small leaves above. Hand-appliqué through all layers of the quilt.

To finish quilt, round off the quilt corners by drawing around the large yo-yo template at each corner and cut away excess fabric.

Quilt flowing lines in between the stems, following the curves, from the top edge of each large leaf, in between the yo-yos, to the top edge of the quilt. Following the same flowing-line pattern, quilt from the top of each large yo-yo to the top edge of the quilt.

To make binding, join short ends of bias strips to make one long piece; fold in half lengthwise with wrong sides together. Pin binding to right side of quilt top, both raw edges even with quilt edge and sew. Turn folded edge of binding to wrong side of the quilt and hand-stitch to the quilt back. Remove basting threads.

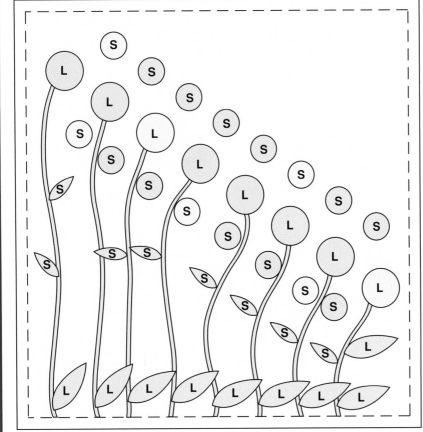

CALICO YO-YO DOLLY QUILT

SMALL LEAF
Cut 8

LARGE LEAF
Cut 9

Step-by-Step Yo-yos

Yo-yo quilting projects are wonderfully portable—a pile of cut circles, needle, thread, and scissors are all you need.

1. Trace circle pattern onto quilting template plastic; cut out. Draw around template on fabric. To speed cutting, "glue" several layers of fabric together with a mist of spray starch.

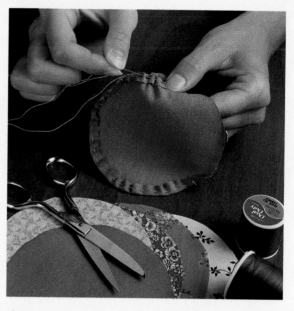

2. Fold ¼ inch of a section of outer edge to wrong side. Use a doubled thread to work running stitches through both layers. Continue folding and stitching all the way around.

3. Pull thread to gather outside edge and draw it to center of circle. Pull tightly and secure thread. Flatten completed yo-yo, but do not press.

4. For a traditional yo-yo quilt, completed circles are sewn together in rows. They can also be secured with buttons in center or they can be appliquéd in place.

Z is for *Zany Zebras and Zippers*

Zebra Pull Toy

This charming striped friend makes a great pull toy or whimsical accent on any shelf. The zebra is crafted from a 5x6-inch scrap of 1-inch pine with wheels made from wooden checkers that are stenciled with a tiny moon and star design. Complete instructions and pattern are on page 200.

DESIGNER: SUSAN CAGE-KNOCH ● PHOTOGRAPHER: SCOTT LITTLE

Zebra Puppet

Here's a fun fellow that will be enjoyed by kids of all ages. Encouraging young imaginations, this perky puppet is made from scraps of fabric, yarn, and paint. Instructions begin on page 200, pattern is on pages 202–203.

DESIGNER: JIM WILLIAMS ● PHOTOGRAPHER: SCOTT LITTLE

Zipper Jacket

A clever project for all those leftover zippers that seem to accumulate over the years, this colorful jacket will get rave reviews any time of the year. To achieve this striking effect, zippers are topstitched randomly to the jacket body and sleeves. We've shown rich earth tones, but you can choose your own personal favorites.
Complete instructions are on page 201.

DESIGNER: MARGARET SINDELAR ● PHOTOGRAPHER: SCOTT LITTLE

Zipper Vest And Hat

Bright-colored zippers and big plastic buttons add lots of pizzazz to a plain hat and matching vest. When using purchased garments, this special occasion outfit is so easy to make, all you need is a couple of hours before the party! Instructions are on page 201.

DESIGNER: MARGARET SINDELAR ● PHOTOGRAPHER: SCOTT LITTLE

ZEBRA PULL TOY

As shown on page 196, toy measures 4¹/₄x5 inches.

MATERIALS

Black ultra-fine point permanent
   marker
Stencil acetate
Crafts knife with small blade
Tracing paper
Graphite paper
5x6-inch piece of 1-inch pine
Scroll or band saw
Medium grit sandpaper
Drill
¹/₈- and ³/₁₆-inch drill bits
White, black, dark blue-green,
   and yellow acrylic paints
4 small wood checkers
Artists' brushes
Tiny stencil brush
Tea bag
Clear polyurethane spray
Three 14-inch-long strands of
   raffia
½-inch-diameter wood bead
Two 1½-inch-long pieces of
   ³/₁₆-inch-diameter dowel
Wood glue

INSTRUCTIONS

Trace wheel stencil pattern, *right*, onto the stencil acetate using the marker. Using the crafts knife, carefully cut out the star and the moon shapes. Set the wheel stencil aside.

Trace the zebra pattern, *right*, onto the tracing paper. Layer the graphite paper between the tracing and the pine and transfer the pattern outlines.

Cut out zebra using a scroll or band saw. Round edges of zebra with sandpaper for a worn look.

Place graphite paper and pattern over wood again and mark holes, mane, tail, and hooves. Drill ³/₁₆-inch-diameter holes through the zebra's legs and neck as indicated by the dots on the pattern. Drill a ¹/₈-inch-diameter hole ¼-inch deep in the center of the ridged side of each checker.

Paint the zebra white and let dry. Paint the mane, hooves, and tail black; let dry. Using pattern as a guide, paint freehand stripes on the body and dot the nostril and eye black. Paint the checker wheels, the bead, and the dowels dark blue-green.

Stencil the moon yellow and the stars white on the smooth side of each wheel. When all of the paint is dry, lightly sand the edges of the zebra and wheels.

Steep the tea bag in ½ cup *hot water* to make a strong tea solution. Paint the zebra and wheels with tea. Allow tea solution to dry thoroughly. Spray all pieces with clear polyurethane.

Tie one end of the raffia strands through hole in the zebra's neck. Slide bead onto the opposite end and knot. Slide dowels through the leg holes and glue a wheel to each end.

ZEBRA PULL TOY

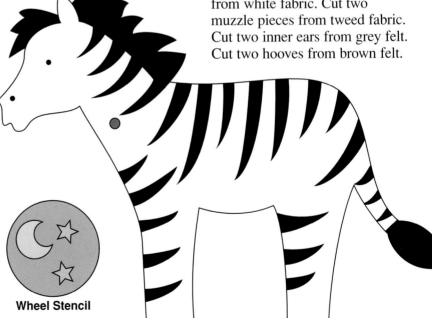

Wheel Stencil

ZEBRA PUPPET

As shown on page 197, puppet measures 16½ inches high.

MATERIALS

Tracing paper
½ yard of 45-inch-wide white
   fabric
Scraps of gray tweed fabric
Scraps of gray and brown felt
Black fabric paint
½-inch-wide flat paint brush
Polyester fiberfill
Paper towel tube
Hot glue
Hot glue gun
Scraps of white and black yarn
   to equal 12 yards
Two ½-inch-diameter buttons

INSTRUCTIONS

Trace patterns, *pages 202–203;* cut out. Patterns and measurements include a ¼-inch seam allowance. Sew seams right sides facing unless otherwise specified.

Cut head pieces, body pieces, and two ear pieces from white fabric. Also cut a 1x6-inch strip from white fabric. Cut two muzzle pieces from tweed fabric. Cut two inner ears from grey felt. Cut two hooves from brown felt.

Use black fabric paint to paint stripes on front and back body pieces and both sides of head, referring to photograph on page 197. When paint is completely dry, heat-set it by ironing on wrong side.

Sew the muzzle pieces to the head pieces and press. Align the muzzle seams and stitch around the head, leaving the neck open. Clip the curves and turn. Stuff with fiberfill to within 1 inch of neck edge.

For ears, stitch felt inner ears to white outer ears. Clip curve, turn, and press. Fold raw edges under, fold in half at bottom, and hand-stitch to head.

Cut paper tube to a length of 3½ inches. Insert 2½ inches of tube into head and hot glue in place. Set aside.

For body, pin felt hooves in place at end of puppet arms. Stitch front to back. Clip curves, turn, and press. Fold raw edge at bottom under twice and machine-hem. Fold raw edges of neck under ½ inch and insert end of cardboard tube into neck to cover about 1 inch of raw edges of zebra neck. Hot glue in place.

For mane, paint stripes on 1x6-inch strip of white fabric. Cut seventy 6-inch lengths of desired yarn. Center yarn strips on right side of fabric strip, side-by-side and alternating colors, to form a 6x6-inch square. Machine-stitch yarn to fabric strip along centers of each. Fold yarns to one side and press. Topstitch through two rows of yarn, close to the fabric strip. Topstitch again ¼ inch beyond first stitching. Trim yarn evenly 1½ inches from fabric strip. Fold under raw edges of strip and blind-stitch to head along seam beginning ½ inch in front of ears. Sew button eyes on each side of head.

ZIPPER JACKET

As shown on page 198.

MATERIALS

Purchased unlined jacket or pattern for unlined jacket and fabric and notions as called for on pattern envelope
Transparent nylon sewing thread
15 to 20 zippers of various lengths, colors, and types
10 to 15 charms from old jewelry

INSTRUCTIONS

If using a purchased jacket, topstitch the zippers to the jacket at random using transparent thread. Refer to the photograph on page 198 as a guide. Hand-stitch the zippers to the sleeves if machine stitching becomes too difficult.

If constructing a jacket, follow the pattern instructions for the assembly *except* sew the zippers to the sleeves before stitching the underarm seams. Sew remaining zippers to the jacket randomly after the jacket is completed.

Stitch charms to zipper pulls as desired. Tack or pin a brooch to the jacket front.

ZIPPER VEST AND HAT

As shown on page 199.

MATERIALS

Transparent nylon sewing thread
25 zippers of various colors, lengths, and types
For vest
Purchased unlined vest or pattern for unlined vest and fabric and notions (except buttons) as specified on pattern envelope
Plastic buttons in desired colors and sizes

For hat
Purchased floppy brim hat or pattern for floppy brim hat and notions as specified on pattern envelope
Three 1¼-inch-diameter plastic buttons in desired colors

INSTRUCTIONS

If using a purchased vest and hat, topstitch the zippers to the garments as for the jacket. Refer to the photograph on page 199 as a guide for the zipper placement. Hand-stitch the zippers if machine stitching becomes too difficult. For the vest, remove buttons and replace with the colored plastic buttons. For the hat, turn up the front of the brim and sew three 1¼-inch-diameter plastic buttons to the hat brim, securing it to the crown with the stitches. Refer to the photograph on page 199 for the approximate placement of the plastic buttons.

If constructing the vest, follow the basic pattern instructions *except* eliminate all of the facings when cutting. Sew a zipper into each side sem. Turn the armhole, neck, front opening, and bottom seam allowances to the inside and topstitch. Sew zippers to the completed vest at random using the transparent nylon sewing thread, taking care not to cover an area that is marked for buttonholes. Make the oversized buttonholes and sew on the plastic buttons.

If constructing the hat, follow the basic pattern instructions. Randomly sew five or six of the zippers to the hat using transparent nylon thread. Turn up the brim and sew the plastic buttons in place as described above for the purchased hat.

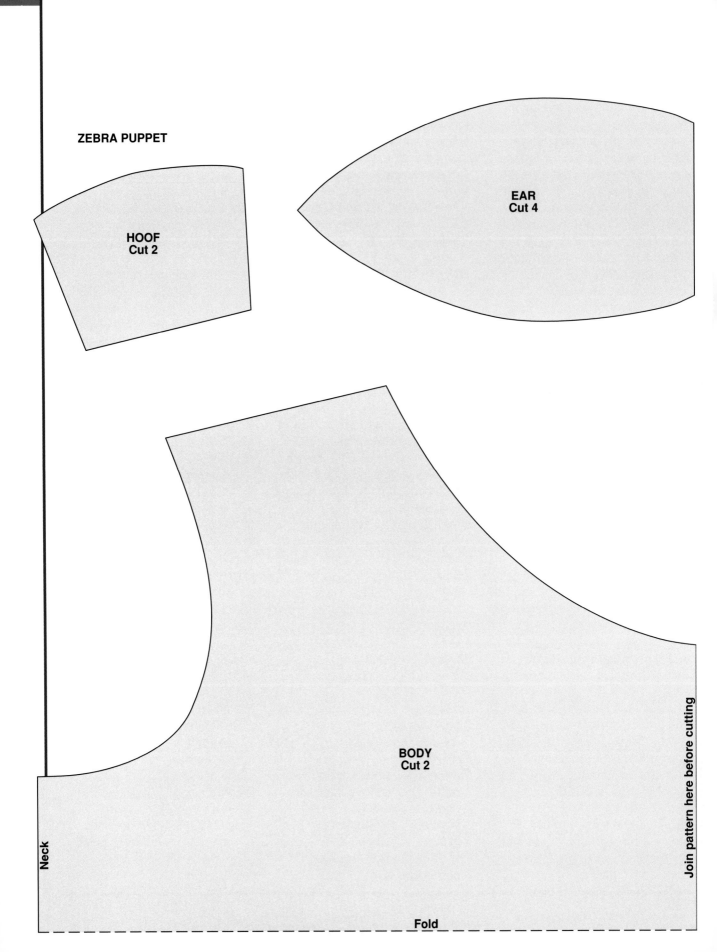

ZEBRA PUPPET

HOOF
Cut 2

EAR
Cut 4

BODY
Cut 2

Neck

Join pattern here before cutting

Fold

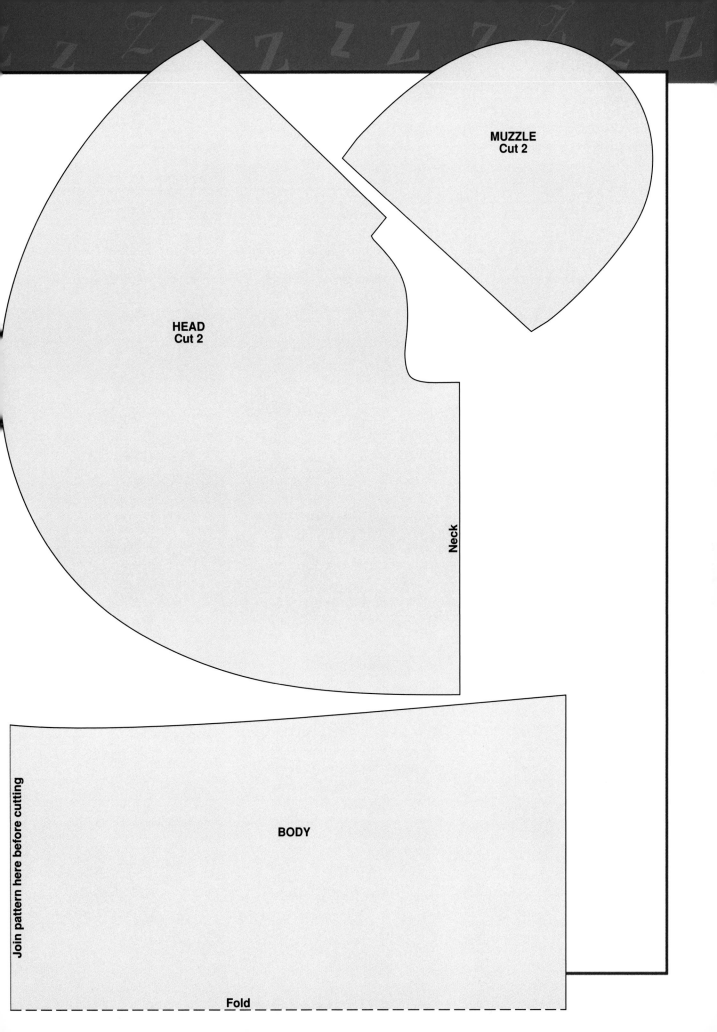

MUZZLE
Cut 2

HEAD
Cut 2

Neck

Join pattern here before cutting

BODY

Fold

STITCH GUIDE

A wide variety of stitches are used to complete the projects in this book. Refer to the following diagrams and instruction if stitching help is needed.

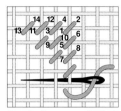

Basket-weave Stitch

Basket-weave Stitch

This needlepoint tent stitch is distinguished by its diagonal working order. When properly executed, the needle will travel vertically under two mesh threads in one row and horizontally in the next, forming a woven pattern on the back of the canvas. This alternating horizontal-vertical pattern helps keeps the canvas square.

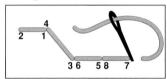

Backstitch

Backstitch

To outline and define shapes in any design, backstitches provide a simple, straight line that flows around corners and curves easily. Individual stitches may be equal to each other or of varying lengths.

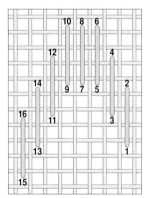

Bargello Stitch

Bargello Stitch

This is a specialized form of satin stitch used in needlepoint. Repeating rows of zigzagging stitches quickly cover the canvas.

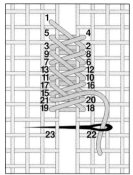

Binding Stitch

Binding Stitch

This needlepoint stitch can be used to join two edges of many fabrics besides canvas. Its overlapping x-shaped stitches form a braided appearance at the seam line.

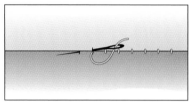

Blind Stitch

Blind Stitch

This stitch works well for hand-finishing the edges of crazy quilt pieces. The needle usually travels through to the back layer.

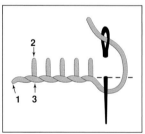

Buttonhole Stitch

Buttonhole Stitch

Use this embroidery stitch to finish edges of projects including crazy quilt patches, appliqué, and hems.

Chain Stitch

Chain Stitch

The looped appearance of chain stitch adds decorative interest to crazy quilt and appliqué projects.

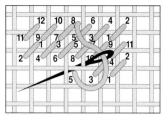

Continental Stitch

Continental Stitch

Best known of all needlepoint stitches, continental stitch is worked in an overlapping manner that helps to keep the canvas square. If desired, turn the canvas upside down after the first row and work the second row in exactly the same manner as the first.

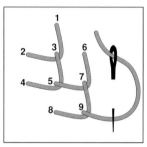

Feather Stitch

Feather Stitch

The most common use for this lacy stitch is crazy quilt embellishment. It's easy to create a different look by varying the length and angle of the stitches.

French Knot

French Knot

There are two secrets to making smooth French knots, whether the project is embroidery, needlepoint, or cross-stitch. Wrap the loose thread around the needle two full turns. After reinserting the needle into the fabric, pull it smoothly and evenly, but firmly to make a knot that lies on the fabric surface.

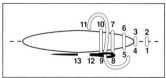

Ladder Stitch

Ladder Stitch

This stitch provides a very secure way to close a seam in a firmly stuffed animal or doll. Use the tiniest stitches the fabric will allow.

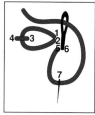

Lazy Daisy Stitch

Lazy Daisy Stitch

Use this pretty stitch to embellish with almost any kind of thread or yarn, on almost any fabric. It's a favorite for forming simple embroidered flowers and leaves.

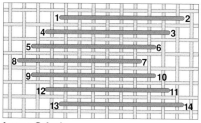

Long Stitch

Long Stitch

Often used in needlepoint to save yarn, long stitch looks similar to satin stitch, but the needle does not pass under the length of the stitch on the back of the canvas.

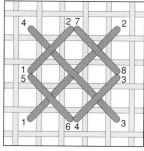

Rice Stitch

Rice Stitch

This large crossed stitch is used in many kinds of counted thread work including needlepoint and cross-stitch. It consists of a large cross usually worked with one color thread. A second color thread is then used to cross each leg with a stitch placed perpendicularly to the leg.

Running Stitch

Running Stitch

For decorative purposes, running stitches work up fast. Although they are usually equal in length, uneven stitches give an attractive novelty effect.

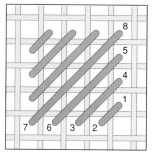

Scotch Stitch

Scotch Stitch

Worked in blocks, this diagonal stitch looks like satin stitch, but the thread is not carried under the canvas from one end of the stitch to the other. The entire block can be worked with one color or two colors as shown.

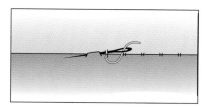

Slip Stitch

Slip Stitch

For joining two pieces of fabric or for hemming, slip stitch makes an almost invisible seam. Turn the seam allowance of one fabric under the appropriate amount and overlap it onto the second piece. (Usually the fold goes at the seam line.) Secure the tail of a threaded needle and take the tiniest stitch possible in the second fabric. Slide the needle under the fold, taking a stitch $1/4$- to $3/4$-inch long. These two components of the stitch can be worked separately or in one motion.

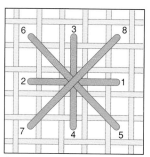

Smyrna Cross Stitch

Smyrna Cross Stitch

This double cross-stitch consists of an upright cross-stitch and an x-shaped stitch. The two shapes may be worked in separate colors. It is frequently used in needlepoint and cross-stitch.

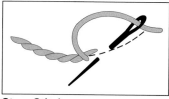

Stem Stitch

Stem Stitch

Also referred to as outline stitch, it fits well around curves. The spiral-like appearance of stem stitch has many uses in embroidery.

Straight Stitch

Straight Stitch

This stitch is often used to create special elements such as sun rays and animal whiskers, in embroidery, cross-stitch, and needlepoint.

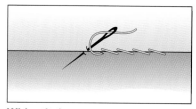

Whipstitch

Whipstitch

Use this stitch to securely close seams in stuffed animals and dolls quickly. It will be more visible than other stitches, so use thread that matches the fabric.

INDEX